From Honolulu to Brooklyn

Running the American Empire's Base Paths with Buck Lai and the Travelers from Hawai'i

JOEL S. FRANKS

Rutgers University Press

New Brunswick, Camden, Newark, New Jersey, and London

Library of Congress Cataloging-in-Publication Data

Names: Franks, Joel S., author.
Title: From Honolulu to Brooklyn : running the American empire's base paths with Buck Lai and the Travelers from Hawaii / Joel S. Franks.
Description: New Brunswick : Rutgers University Press, [2022] | Includes bibliographical references and index.
Identifiers: LCCN 2021057000 | ISBN 9781978829251 (Paperback : alk. paper) | ISBN 9781978829268 (Cloth : alk. paper) | ISBN 9781978829275 (ePub) | ISBN 9781978829282 (PDF)
Subjects: LCSH: Hawaiian Travelers (Baseball team)—History. | Asian Americans—Sports—History. | Pacific Islander Americans—Sports—History. | Baseball—United States—History. | Racism—Hawaii—History.
Classification: LCC GV875.H39 F75 2022 | DDC 796.357/64096931—dc23/eng/20220509
LC record available at https://lccn.loc.gov/2021057000

A British Cataloging-in-Publication record for this book is available from the British Library.

∞ The paper used in this publication meets the requirements of the American National Standard for Information Sciences—Permanence of Paper for Printed Library Materials, ANSI Z39.48-1992.

www.rutgersuniversitypress.org

Manufactured in the United States of America

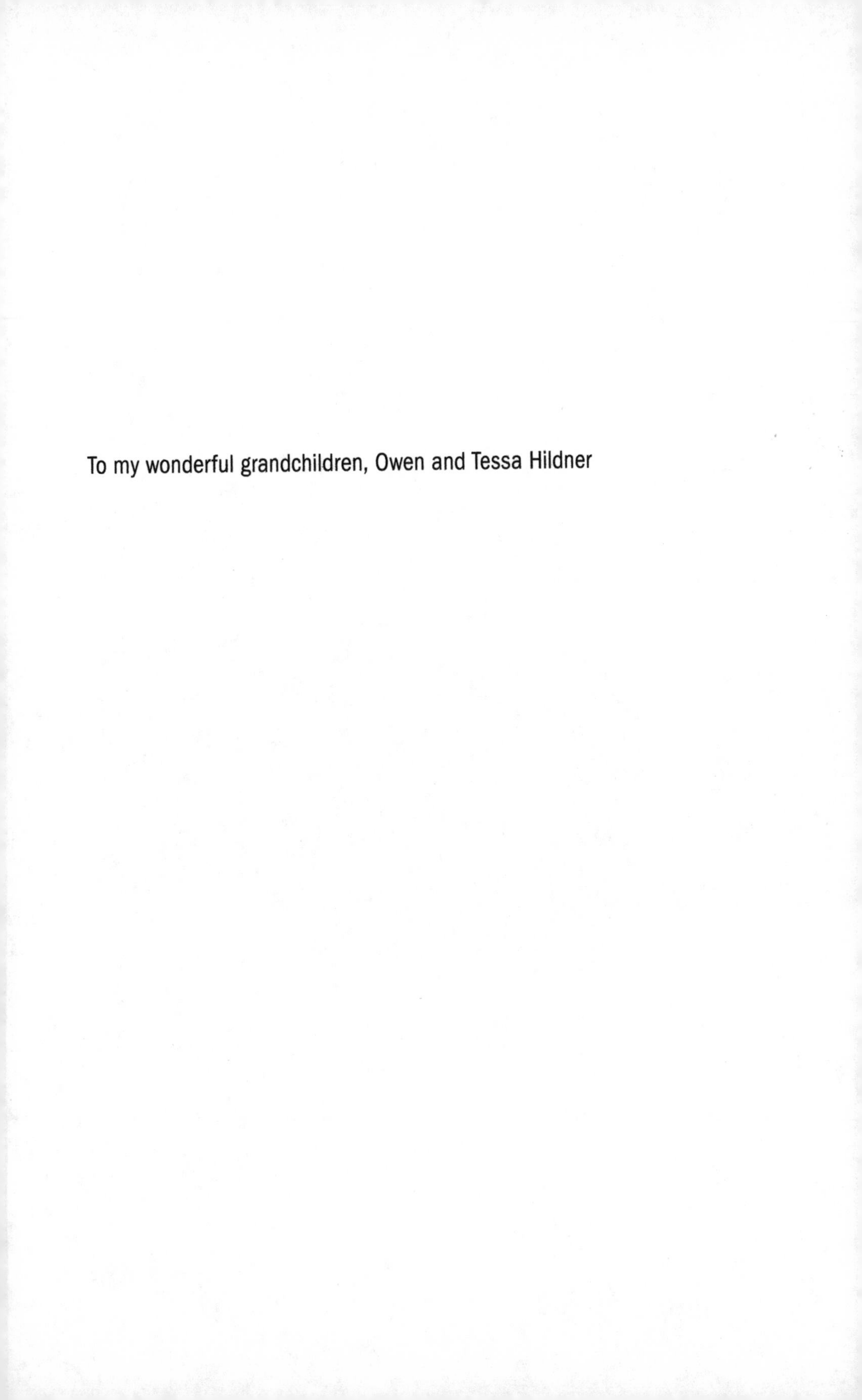

To my wonderful grandchildren, Owen and Tessa Hildner

Contents

From Honolulu to Brooklyn

Introduction

During the 1990s, I was not only teaching Asian American studies but also trying to research the history of Asian American athletic experiences. As Hawai'i had been colonized by the United States in the late 1890s, a team of island ballplayers of presumably Chinese descent barnstorming the mainland in the 1910s piqued my interest. Earlier, Steven Riess's fine book on professional baseball in the Progressive Era drew my attention to a couple of Hawai'i Chinese ballplayers recruited by elite professional franchises—one by the Portland Beavers of the Pacific Coast League and the other by the major league Chicago White Sox. As it turned out, these two ballplayers—Lang Akana and Lai Tin—played on the barnstorming team from Hawai'i.[1]

Inspired by the possibility of researching what seemed an intriguing and overlooked aspect of not only baseball but American and Asian American history, I decided to focus more of my energy on a team I eventually called the Hawaiian Travelers. The result was the 2012 publication of a book concentrating on the journeys of the Travelers as they traversed geographical as well as racial and ethnic borders throughout the U.S. mainland from 1912 to 1916. I hoped that the book would at least make the case that the Travelers pioneered hazardous cultural borderlands constructed and maintained across the early twentieth-century American empire. And while I wanted the book to be considered a work of analysis rather than celebration, I also hoped readers would seize on the remarkable journeys of those ballplayers.[2]

Given their racial and ethnic backgrounds, the Travelers accomplished much in baseball and American sport in general. In the process, the Travelers very likely crossed the foul lines of more ball fields in the American empire than any ballplayers of their era, while crossing hazardous borders separating colonizers from the colonized and whites from nonwhites. Displaying speed, dexterity, aggressiveness, and baseball "smarts," the Travelers often dominated the white teams that opposed them. Some Travelers provoked interest from elite professional franchises. In 1917, two former Travelers, Vernon Ayau and Andrew Yamashiro, became the first Asian Americans to play organized baseball in the United States. The next year, Lai Tin, better known on the mainland as Buck Lai, became the first Asian American to join the spring training camp roster of a major league baseball team—the Philadelphia Phillies. Unfortunately, the Phillies dispatched Lai to the minors before he got a chance to become the first Asian American major leaguer.

Indeed, Buck Lai, around whom much of this book is assembled, was able to do things in the first half of the twentieth century that few Chinese Americans were allowed to match. While Yamashiro's and Ayau's stints in organized baseball were brief, Lai competed in relatively top-level minor league baseball for four years, from 1918 to 1921. In 1928, he got another chance to play major league baseball—this time with the celebrated New York Giants. And while he played a few exhibition games with the Giants, Lai was once against sent down to the minors. Meanwhile, and for some years after his tryout with the Giants, Lai earned a reputation as one of the better independent or semiprofessional ballplayers on the East Coast, adeptly performing with and against some of the best diamond artists outside of organized baseball, including prominent Black ballplayers racially barred from the big leagues. A versatile athlete whose speed and jumping ability prompted one publication to declare he might make it to the 1912 Summer Olympics, Lai also displayed talent in basketball. Starring in the early 1920s on a team of Chinese hoopsters competing on the East Coast, he probably ranks among the first Asian American professional basketball players.[3]

In the 1930s, Lai turned to coaching and sports entrepreneurship. In Hawai'i, coaches and sports entrepreneurs possessing Asian or Hawaiian ancestry were fairly common by the mid-twentieth century. On the U.S. mainland, they were almost nonexistent. To be sure, Chinese Americans coached Chinese Americans, but Lai headed teams largely made up of white athletes when he led barnstorming basketball squads during the decade. In the mid-1930s, moreover, he fronted Asian and Pacific Islander barnstorming baseball teams from Hawai'i.[4]

As Lai grew older, his baseball career still reigned as unique for someone of his race and ethnicity. Major league teams hired the resident of New Jersey's Camden County as a scout. He served as an umpire of semiprofessional games in the Philadelphia area—games in which white and Black ballplayers would have to respect his calls. From the late 1930s through at least the 1950s, he coached not only white semiprofessional ballplayers but also youth ballplayers, few of whom, it seems safe to say, were coached by Asian Americans on the mid-twentieth-century mainland. Vernon Ayau, who also lived on the New Jersey side of the Delaware River, had many of the same baseball experiences as Lai, but on a smaller, less publicized scale.

The athletic career of the biracial Buck Lai Jr. quietly contested racial boundaries in mid-twentieth-century America. A son of a Hawai'i Chinese father and a white mother, he excelled in academics and athletics, playing basketball and baseball at, as well as graduating from, Long Island University (LIU). After serving as a naval flier during World War II, Lai Jr. returned to his alma mater as an assistant basketball coach and head baseball coach at a time when only one other American of Asian ancestry coached an intercollegiate athletic team on the U.S. mainland—Japanese American Bill Kajikawa. In the 1950s, Lai added the duties of LIU's athletic director and head basketball coach after a scandal rocked the university's hoops program. Blurring the lines between amateur and professional sports, Lai Jr. was also employed by the Brooklyn Dodgers as a baseball scout and instructor. He even wrote and illustrated two popular instructional books—one teaching the fundamentals of baseball and the other, basketball.[5]

In Hawai'i, Andrew Yamashiro had made history before World War II. After becoming the first Japanese American to play organized baseball, Yamashiro returned to the islands, where he eventually engaged in electoral politics. In 1930, he was elected to the territorial legislature, making him and another Japanese American the first of their ethnicity to fill any elected office in the U.S. empire. Two years later, Yamashiro became the first Japanese American picked as a delegate to a major party convention in which he represented Hawai'i's Democrats in their nomination of Franklin Delano Roosevelt. The *Nikkei*, people of Japanese ancestry living in Hawai'i and elsewhere, were regarded with racialized suspicion not only by *haoles*, a term used by Hawaiians to describe people of European ancestry. But also members of other ethnic groups worried about the Nikkei as economic and political threats. Thus, a Hawai'i Japanese such as Yamashiro needed some courage, but not just because of the racism and xenophobia they encountered. Influential Nikkei on the islands urged political quiescence and stressed that if Japanese in Hawai'i participated in territorial politics, they should do so as Republicans, the political party favored by the islands' political and economic elite.

Other Travelers apparently lived worthy, respectable, and sometimes controversial lives while remaining passionate about baseball even as they got too old to play the game well. A handful, like Buck Lai and Vernon Ayau, decided to stay on the East Coast in the late 1910s to play baseball for pay and advance their educations, although they all returned to Hawai'i later. Among these were Chinese Alfred Yap and Hawaiian Fred Markham. One Traveler did not get to choose whether to stay on the mainland or go back to Hawai'i. Pitcher Apau Kau, while still in his early twenties, left his new home and job in Philadelphia to perish on the killing fields of Europe during World War I. His story, as well as those of other Travelers who fought during the war, should puncture our racialized visons of American doughboys.

Hopefully, readers will recognize the accomplishments, baseball and otherwise, of these young, generally Asian and Hawaiian, men, whether in colonized

Honolulu or Philadelphia. Yet we should be mindful of the backdrop for the Travelers as they journeyed from baseball field to baseball field from Honolulu to Brooklyn and lived their post-Traveler lives not only in Hawai'i but also thousands of miles away in New Jersey. Weaving together this backdrop were strands of American colonialism, racialized nativism, and the labor and cultural demands of expanding capitalism. Many of the Travelers were children of workers brought to Hawai'i to provide exploitable labor for sugar plantations that inhabited land taken from Hawaiians. Other Travelers possessed indigenous ancestry; that is, they descended from people deemed racially and culturally unfit for self-government and economic autonomy despite Hawai'i enduring as an independent nation for much of the nineteenth century.

The creation of the Travelers constituted an ambiguous response to all this. Young men possessing Chinese ancestry filled the roster spots on the first Traveler trek to the mainland. When the sugar plantations needed labor, they gazed westward to China and thus thousands of Chinese were imported largely as contract laborers to the islands in the latter decades of the nineteenth century. A Chinese community composed of former plantation laborers seeking economic independence and business owners and professionals accompanying the Chinese diaspora to Hawai'i developed in Honolulu. By the second decade of the twentieth century, this community could boast of some prosperity and keen self-awareness. It sought to combat anti-Chinese racism, which was more dominant on the mainland but quite persistent on the islands. In the process, leaders of the Honolulu Chinese community protested the Chinese Exclusion Act (1882), which had not only prevailed for thirty years but also experienced considerable bolstering by the U.S. government. By sponsoring an all-Chinese baseball team's tour of the U.S. mainland, they hoped to undercut the argument that Chinese were incapable of thriving as good Americans. After all, was not baseball America's national pastime?

Hawai'i's haole elite expressed support for dispatching the all-Chinese nine to the mainland. Hoping to perpetuate capitalism's and haole dominance on the islands, they sought more mainland investment and tourism, as well as white residents of Hawai'i. To do so meant emphasizing Hawai'i as both exotic and familiar. A sufficient number of skillful haole or haole ballplayers lived on the islands. These ballplayers could barnstorm the mainland, but what would be the point? All-white baseball teams were hardly news on the mainland. An all-Chinese nine, however, would demonstrate Hawai'i's distinctiveness—that the people who made up the islands' population were different from those who lived in Kansas or central Pennsylvania. At the same time, a competent all-Chinese nine would demonstrate how American Hawai'i had become despite its relatively recent colonization and separation by thousands of miles from the mainland. And just to be sure that the ballplayers would boost Hawai'i as both exotic and a site where modern Americans and American capitalism could feel comfortable, they were outfitted with promotional literature and pineapples and urged to play and sing putative Hawaiian songs for curious mainlanders.

The individuals who managed the Travelers' journeys, as well as those who booked and advertised their games, felt compelled to tell all sorts of stories about the Travelers and why they tore around the base paths of dozens of ball fields throughout the mainland. These stories were not always consistent with one another, and they often, as in the case of the Travelers representing a fictional Chinese University of Hawaii, strayed far from the truth. Indeed, mischievous players took it upon themselves to offer their own narratives such as providing specific details about the nonexistent university. Thus, one of the intriguing aspects of following the Travelers' journeys throughout the mainland is not just how the press reproduced and undermined racial hierarchy through its accounts of the ballplayers from Hawai'i but also how the largely nonwhite Travelers manipulated that press. Accordingly, the Travelers' journeys expose the shifting identities imposed on them as well as those they seemed willing to assume.

Organization

This book is organized chronologically and thematically. The first two chapters explore the historical context of the Travelers' journeys. Chapter 1 stresses the experiences of Asians and Hawaiians on the islands, as well as the early experiences of Asian Americans and Asian Americans playing baseball on the mainland. Focusing more on the Travelers, chapter 2 relates their experiences with the development of baseball as well as its interactions with American culture and capitalism. Chapter 3 provides a chronological narrative of the Travelers' journeys to the American mainland from 1912 to 1916. In 1917 and 1918, a contingent of former Travelers, including Buck Lai, sought to settle into mainland life and baseball, crossing perilous racial borderlands. Chapter 4 examines these experiences. Chapter 5 focuses on Buck Lai's career careening around professional and semiprofessional baseball diamonds from 1919 to 1934, while casting an eye on the attempts of other former Travelers to earn money at America's national pastime during this time period. Most Travelers either stayed in Hawai'i after 1916 or returned to the islands after a taste of mainland life. Chapter 6 examines their lives between World War I and World War II within the context of what was happening on the islands during this tumultuous era. Chapter 6 helps set the stage for chapter 7 as the latter narrates the ambiguous experiences of Buck Lai fronting barnstorming teams from Hawai'i in 1935 and 1936 and putatively from Hawai'i in 1937. Chapter 8, aptly titled "Playing in the Twilight," covers the experiences of the Travelers living in Hawai'i or on the mainland from World War II to the end of their lives. In the process, it deals with key social and economic changes throughout much of the American empire while attending particularly to Buck Lai and his son, Buck Lai Jr. The conclusion ties all the book's strands up as neatly as possible, while making the case that the Travelers' experiences, though burdened by racism, xenophobia, and colonialism, significantly represent the democratic possibilities of sport at a time when, in many ways, sport was demonstratively undemocratic in the American empire.

Names and Terminology

Buck Lai was known by different names during his life. In the U.S. census manuscripts of 1900, he is referred to as Gum Lai Tin. By the time he gained notice in the Honolulu press as a ballplayer, Lai was referred to as Ah Lai or Lai Tin, although I did encounter a Honolulu newspaper reference to "Buck Tin" in October 1912. Even before he permanently settled on the East Coast, he referred to himself as William Tin Lai or William T. Lai. Accordingly, when Lai joined the Bridgeport Americans of the Eastern League in 1918, the press often referred to him as Bill Lai. Apparently, he had earned the nickname of Buck while on the islands, probably because of his foot speed. One unverified story proclaimed he was called Buck because he worked as a cowboy on the islands. In any event, by the early 1920s he was called Buck Lai on the East Coast. Interestingly, when he returned to the islands in the mid-1930s, the press called him Buck Lai Tin. When writing about his time in Hawai'i as a youth, I refer to him as Lai Tin, and as Buck Lai after he settled on the East Coast of the United States.

Traditional Chinese names have proved difficult for me. Lai Tin's surname was clearly Lai since family members, in the process of anglicizing their names, kept Lai as their surname. However, in the case of Apau Kau, the fine Traveler pitcher and a tragic reminder of how deadly war can be, his family members used the surname of Kau. I hope I got things right, but I am sure I have made mistakes.

I have also tried to rectify my unfortunate choice of calling the then famous barnstorming team from Hawai'i the Hawaiian Travelers. Instead, I will refer to them simply as the Travelers. I have done so out of respect for the indigenous people of Hawai'i who refer to themselves, regardless of whether they possess some European ancestry, as Hawaiians. For people from other ethnic groups on Hawai'i, I use terms like Japanese or Chinese, on the one hand, or Hawai'i Japanese or Hawai'i Chinese, on the other.

1

Defying Assumptions

Baseball, Asians, and Hawai'i

Buck Lai was not a typical Chinese American. Born and raised in Hawai'i, he, unlike the immigrants who largely inhabited the mainland's Chinatowns, could claim American citizenship. He could further look about him as he walked the streets of early twentieth-century Honolulu or attended classes at the city's only public secondary school, McKinley High School, and see racially and ethnically diverse people, many of whom, like him, possessed Asian ancestry. Yet in his early twenties, Lai Tin chose to live and work among white people on the East Coast of the American mainland. In the process, he did what few Chinese American males could do on the mainland in the early twentieth century: marry a white woman with whom he raised a small family in New Jersey. But what decidedly set Lai apart from most Chinese Americans, indeed from most Americans, is that he was an outstanding and, at that time, relatively famous athlete and sports' entrepreneur. Arguably, outside of movie actress Anna May Wong, he was the most famous Chinese American of the first half of the twentieth century. To be sure, his fame faded considerably over time and, even then, did not approach that of his far more illustrious contemporary, Babe Ruth. Still, American sports fans, especially followers of the national pastime of baseball on the East Coast between World War I and World War II, knew Buck Lai as a skilled and colorful baseball player. He never played in the big leagues, but in a baseball netherworld encompassing semiprofessional, independent, and Negro League baseball, Buck Lai was still royalty. And when he became too old to spear line drives and steal bases, his biracial son and namesake,

Buck Lai Jr., gained distinction as a college basketball and baseball coach and educator.

Lai Tin first attracted attention in early twentieth-century, ragtime America as a member of a traveling baseball team from colonized Hawai'i. From 1912 through 1916, this team crossed the Pacific to contest a variety of college, town, semiprofessional, and professional nines on the U.S. mainland. It even managed a brief excursion into Canada and a much longer journey to Cuba. On the team's maiden trek to the United States in 1912, its roster was composed entirely of young men of Chinese ancestry. Over time, some of the initial team members dropped out or were shoved aside because they were not good enough. Their places were filled by Hawai'i-born Nikkei and Hawaiians as well as a couple of haole ballplayers.

Lai Tin's story confounds those of us who prefer our tales about race and ethnicity neatly packaged. Many Americans exclude Asians from discussions of race even as they concede that African Americans, Latino/as, and American Indians have suffered significantly from racism and continue to do so. But supposedly Asians have made it and can bypass racism and such trivialities as sports in favor of collecting academic honors at Harvard or MIT. Lai Tin's story, moreover, does not readily fit the dominant narrative about the relationship between race, ethnicity, and sport. At its best, this Atlantic-centric narrative focuses on people of European and African ancestry. It can tell us much of value regarding the arduous struggles of Black and even white ethnic groups to use sport to maintain a sense of community, build cultural bridges to other groups, and, in some cases, attain significant prestige and wealth as athletes and sports entrepreneurs. At the same time, it too frequently marginalizes or ignores the interactions of race, ethnicity, and sport among people of Mexican, American Indian, Asian, and Pacific Islander ancestries living in the Far West of the American mainland, as well as Hawai'i and other Pacific islands. Borrowing the insights of historians such as Patricia Nelson Limerick and Richard White, we should note that while traditional U.S. history textbooks take readers from the East to the West in a roughly linear fashion, Lai's life, like those of many Americans of Asian Pacific ancestry, was marked by journeys from the West to the East.[1]

Among those of us who acknowledge racism's centrality to American life and its relevance for Asians in America, Lai Tin's story appears doubly confusing. Racism, we often believe, has littered American history with victims from day one. Lai Tin was no victim. He apparently encountered white people who were not overtly racist or at least nurtured a civility sufficient to trump their bigotry. Moreover, he asserted a sense of agency in relatively unique ways for people of Asian ancestry in the United States in the first half of the twentieth century. He accomplished what few non–Asian Americans thought someone like him could do—play baseball and, for that matter, basketball very well, along with setting Hawai'i records as a track and field performer. And while it was riskier to do so on the anti-Asian West Coast than on the East Coast, Lai demonstrated courage by marrying the woman he loved, regardless of her race—a courage that was shared by his wife, Isabelle.

But this book is not just about Buck Lai. Some of his Traveler teammates also wound up living and playing baseball in the urban mid-Atlantic region. They made up a racially and ethnically mixed group of temporary and permanent island expatriates. Pitchers Apau Kau and Luck Yee Lau, as well as infielders Vernon Ayau and Alfred Yap, were, like Lai, Chinese Americans. Outfielder Andy Yamashiro was a second-generation Japanese American or *Nisei*. And catcher Fred Markham was a Hawaiian. Accordingly, Lai Tin and some of his Traveler teammates exposed both the possibilities and the limitations of sport as a democratic project by attempting to expand the racial and ethnic frontiers of America's national pastime. Accordingly, their lives tell intriguing tales of a changing twentieth-century American culture, significantly obsessed with baseball and other sports.

Other Travelers seemed perfectly content with returning to Hawai'i for good after the final 1916 tour. Their Hawai'i was not an island paradise, as it confronted colonization, combined with tensions revolving around race, ethnicity, and class. Over the years, some more than others would get caught up in those tensions, responding to them in various ways, while often remaining active in island baseball as participants, coaches, and franchise owners.[2]

Baseball, Race, and Colonization

During the first few decades of the twentieth century, baseball influenced the disparate experiences of all sorts of people living in the United States and its colonial possessions such as Hawai'i. How else can we explain Lai Tin, a child of Chinese immigrants, taking up the game in Honolulu in the early 1900s? Being an American, especially an American male, correlated in too many minds with a capacity to like the game and, even better, play it with some passion and skill. Baseball, consequently, buttressed what the late historian Robert Wiebe called the "raised hierarchies" of race, ethnicity, gender, class, sex orientation, and colonialism, because American identity in the 1910s substantially entailed accepting, if not actively reinforcing, those hierarchies.[3]

However, early twentieth-century baseball and other popular American sports could undermine those raised hierarchies. They could sustain what sociologist Elijah Anderson has called a "cosmopolitan canopy" in which people of diverse social and cultural backgrounds meet, perhaps not as political and social equals but at least as more willing to respectfully interact with one another. Cosmopolitan canopies afford marginalized peoples with fleeting expressions of cultural citizenship and spatial entitlement—to connect to a larger American culture without surrendering their identities or distinctive social spaces. In other words, a sport like baseball certainly failed to eliminate racial and other social barriers in early twentieth-century America. But it could destabilize them.[4]

Buck Lai witnessed twentieth-century American sport at its best and worst. Lai played over twenty-five years of semiprofessional and professional baseball, making some money, earning some recognition, and seemingly having a very good time. Yet as fast as Buck Lai was, and there were probably few ballplayers of his time at any level who were faster, he could not always outrun what literary scholar Elaine Kim has called "racism's traveling eye." For Buck Lai, possessing Chinese ancestry carried weighty disadvantages in early twentieth-century America. U.S. naturalization laws barred Chinese and other Asians from citizenship. The Chinese Exclusion Act, originally enacted by the U.S. Congress in 1882, banned all Chinese immigrants to America and its colonial possessions save those arrivals who could prove they were students, diplomats, professionals, and businesspeople. Congress and the court system combined, moreover, to bar Chinese immigrants, regardless of class and status, from U.S. citizenship rights. In states such as California, Chinese immigrants could not own or lease farmland. And in many of the same states, even American-born citizens of Chinese ancestry could not marry white people. Further, during the late nineteenth and early twentieth centuries, as scholar Jean Pfaelzer writes, anti-Chinese legislation often encompassed the least of the worries facing Chinese in the United States. They were often victimized by mob violence and threatened by Sundown Laws enacted throughout the West—laws imperiling their safety if they appeared in town after sundown. As for Nikkei like Andy Yamashiro, Japanese ancestry offered little, if any, advantage in the United States. By 1910, Japanese immigrant laborers were kept from U.S. ports. Those who had made their homes in Hawai'i and California were denied U.S. citizenship. Moreover, like Chinese immigrants, Japanese immigrants lost access to farm ownership in states such as California in the 1910s, nor could those of Japanese ancestry legally marry whites in the Golden State.[5]

In Hawai'i, where relatively large populations of Hawai'i Chinese and Japanese were first recruited for plantation work, race worked ominously but differently than on the mainland. While lower-class status stigmatized them and racialized nativism inflicted grave pain, Hawai'i Chinese and Japanese faced less overtly onerous racially based legal barriers in Hawai'i than in the States. For example, antimiscegenation laws did not exist on the islands, in order to permit economically and politically advantaged haole males to marry into more privileged Hawaiian families and, uncoincidentally, access more land. Thus, although interracial marriage remained socially problematic on the islands, the lack of an antimiscegenation law opened doors to all sorts of cross-cultural, interracial unions.[6]

Through sport some Asians edged toward transcending social and cultural barriers on the islands. In Hawai'i, people of varied racial and ethnic backgrounds had been playing baseball for several years before the inaugural trip of Lai Tin and the entirely Chinese Travelers' nine to the U.S. mainland in 1912. Additionally, ballplayers of Chinese ancestry were not nearly as unusual as many mainlanders seemed to believe. Perhaps as early as the 1870s, young Chinese male scholars played America's national pastime at various East Coast educational institutions, according to Joseph A. Reaves's fine book, *Taking in a Game*. In 1872, a group of thirty young men was dispatched by the Chinese government to the United States. The ruling Qing dynasty expected these young men to concentrate on their studies in America and transport to China knowledge of what apparently made America a growing power in the world. However, the young men involved in the Chinese Educational Mission were not obsessed with academic achievement. Arriving in the United States wearing the silk gowns and queues demanded by the Qing dynasty, they were sensitive to the ridicule of Americans who rarely failed to taunt them over the "plaited cues" and long gowns that made them "look like girls." Indeed, the students' desire to rid themselves of their "traditional" attire and play baseball intertwined. They observed that American young men took up baseball, and many of the Chinese students wanted to join the fun. But playing baseball in silk gowns and queues was not going to work. Accordingly, at least some students braved the ire of their government by cutting off their queues and dressing like American students. Perhaps overstating the lure of assimilation, Reaves writes, "Baseball quickly became for some members of the Chinese Educational Mission what it would become for successive generations of immigrants during the next century and a half—a badge of validation, a stripe of social acceptance, a slice of the American Pie."[7]

Chinese immigrants picked up bats and balls on the American mainland during the late nineteenth and early twentieth centuries, although much of the press coverage treated the matter lightly and perhaps exaggerated the extent of such involvement to better ridicule Chinese residents of the United States. In 1887, the *San Francisco Chronicle* published a flippant description of a supposedly real game of baseball in the city's Chinatown, claiming that on "any Sunday afternoon on Stockton Street one may see a team of rising Mongolians wrestling with the technicalities of the Great American game, while different pawnbrokers, pork butchers, and influential high binders and their wives beam down approvingly from the rickety balconies."[8]

In Chicago, the *Chicago Tribune* reported that a team called the Hip Lungs competed in the city's First Ward League in 1908. The Hip Lungs presumably commanded the dangers of big-city street baseball. Team captain Henry Moy told the press, "It takes nerve combined with rare skill to chase a hot one under rapidly moving street car and that's where the China boys have the beat of it."[9]

In late June 1908, a derisive *San Francisco Call* reported "the Chinese baseball club of San Francisco" had just been beaten by the Japanese "Banzai team of Alameda." Alluding to the region's powerful anti-Asian movement and that movement's most powerful organization at the time, the Asian Exclusion League, the *Call* dubbed the game the first played by the "Asian Inclusion League." Loading up on ethnic and national clichés, the writer remarked that "the Mandarins" did well enough for six innings, except for handling their bats "like chopsticks." Their pitcher, a "valuable attaché in a local laundry," held the opposition down until, referencing a key battle in the recent Russo-Japan War, the "besiegers of Port Arthur" started to hit him. To make matters worse, his left fielder allowed three runs because "he confused a tuft of grass with chop suey." The game ended in a 17–9 victory for the Nikkei.[10]

Hawai'i Chinese

The Chinese who came to Hawai'i were more varied than the sons of the elite who composed the Chinese Educational Mission. More than likely, they journeyed to Hawai'i in the second half of the 1800s to work on sugar plantations then pervading the islands. Plantation owners hoped that the Chinese would furnish them with inexpensive, plentiful, and controllable labor. They knew that some Chinese had already acquired a familiarity with Hawaiian sugar during the early 1800s. A paper read before the Royal Hawaiian Agricultural Society in 1852 claimed the first sugar manufacturer on the islands was "a Chinaman, on the island of Lanai, who [in 1802] came here in one of the vessels trading for sandalwood, bringing with him a stone mill and boilers."[11]

Sugar plantation owners believed that Chinese laborers would prove more productive than Hawaiian laborers, who had shown themselves reluctant wage-workers. After all, Hawaiians had survived quite nicely on the islands for centuries without working ten to twelve hours a day, six days a week on some plantation for haole agricultural capitalists, and preferred not to start now. Further, Hawaiians were too rapidly succumbing to the diseases transported to the islands by whites and reinforced by the poverty many of them experienced through their displacement by large-scale agrarian capitalism. Accordingly, Hawaiians were neither sufficiently plentiful, nor controllable, nor healthy. The Chinese worker, however, entered Hawai'i burdened with the reputation of servility. Plantation owners expected that workers would perform menial, arduous work with few or no complaints. And if they were unhappy, the labor contract they signed to come to Hawai'i would mute their discontent.[12]

Chinese workers typically arrived on the Hawaiian Islands in the nineteenth century as contract laborers from the southeastern provinces of China and speaking the Cantonese dialect. Pressured by the ravages of the Opium Wars, civil strife, natural disasters, and an oppressive state, they agreed to labor on Hawaiian plantations for a specified period. In the process, they found themselves frequently stigmatized with the label of coolies as a way of linking their fates with those of enslaved Black laborers—that is, supposedly racially inferior, servile working machines. Meanwhile, Chinese merchants and professionals accompanied the movement of Chinese laborers to the islands. The former had been undermined financially by European imperialism through the notorious Opium Wars, while disrespected by the Confucian tendencies of Chinese culture for their focus on making money. In any event, approximately 50,000 Chinese migrated to Hawai'i between 1852 and 1900, inspiring Mark Twain to declare that the secret to the success of the Hawaiian sugar industry in the late 1800s was "cheap Chinese labor."[13]

By the 1880s, plantation operators clearly suspected that the Chinese would not resolve their labor problems. That is, Chinese immigrants refused to supply the expected trouble-free labor force. They were not as servile as plantation owners had hoped, often resenting the long hours and poor pay. They organized strikes aimed at both white employers and Chinese labor contractors. More typically, they refused to stay with plantation work after the term of their contracts ended or even absconded before their contracts terminated. Many headed to Honolulu and tried their hand as peddlers and shopkeepers. Others took up small-scale rice farming as either independent owners or tenant farmers.[14]

An anti-Chinese movement appearing in the late 1800s on the Hawaiian Islands diminished plantation operators' enthusiasm for Chinese laborers. It was not as vociferous as its mainland counterpart, but planters had second thoughts about depending on Chinese workers. Hawaiian nationalists and haole allies accused Chinese immigrants of bringing terrible diseases such as leprosy and smallpox to the islands, while claiming that Chinese also endangered the Hawaiian population with a presumed propensity for opium, gambling, and prostitution. The issue of interracial marriage also loomed over Hawai'i's debate over Chinese immigration. Scholar Sucheng Chan writes that Hawaiians and haole allies hoped that whatever Asian group planters chose to import would help replenish the indigenous population by intermarrying with Hawaiians. Chinese immigrants married or cohabited with Hawaiians. But on the islands, critics of the Chinese complained that they would not do. As a "race," Chinese were inadequately "cognate" to the Hawaiian people. The Hawaiian government, accordingly, issued regulations in the 1880s to restrict Chinese immigration.[15]

Those haoles initially supporting Chinese immigration also very likely craved the eventual U.S. takeover of the islands. By 1882, however, the United States had substantially restricted Chinese immigration. In Hawai'i, Chinese immigrant workers initially came into a situation where labor competition was minimal. Hawaiians, as mentioned earlier, did not really want to do what Chinese were recruited to do, and a white working class did not exist much beyond the docks. In the United States, a white working class, buffeted by the vicissitudes of capitalism, not only existed but substantially opposed nonwhite immigrant competition. Still, anti-Chinese sentiments crossed class lines on the mainland. Chinese immigrants represented cheap labor for employers and potential trade partners for American commercial interests. Yet they also represented a race and culture branded as inferior by all but a minority of Americans, regardless of class. Thus, the Chinese Exclusion Act, passed by Congress in 1882, achieved widespread support. It, indeed, contained a class bias. Chinese immigrants identified as laborers would not be allowed to enter the United States. Chinese business owners, scholars, professionals, and students could enter American ports, but since these people were deemed a small slice of the Chinese immigrant population and were seen as potentially beneficial to U.S. global ambitions, we should hold our admiration for Congress's generosity in check. Moreover, all Chinese immigrants, regardless of class, suffered a denial of naturalization rights. Finally, Congress rendered the Chinese Exclusion Act renewable every ten years.[16]

Over the following years, Chinese exclusion was strengthened. For example, Chinese claiming Hawai'i as their point of departure to the United States were for a while eligible for entry. Congress put an end to that. The United States sought to deny entry to even U.S.-born Chinese. However, in the underappreciated U.S. Supreme Court case of *Wong Kim Ark v. U.S.*, the U.S. Supreme Court claimed in the late 1890s that Wong Kim Ark, born in San Francisco, was a U.S. citizen based on the 14th Amendment to the U.S. Constitution and therefore not subject to the Chinese Exclusion Act. Further, even exempt groups faced harassment and delays by U.S. immigration authorities, and much of the good done by the *Wong Kim Ark* case was undone by the U.S. Supreme Court in its *U.S. v. Ju Toy* verdict (1905), which barred American-born Chinese from using the courts to assert their right to re-enter the United States. Meanwhile, Congress, happy with the act's intent and effectiveness, renewed the law in 1892 and then again in 1902. Wondering why it had bothered renewing Chinese exclusion every ten years, Congress, in 1904, made the restriction of Chinese immigration to the United States and the denial of citizenship rights to Chinese immigrants indefinite. Accordingly, Chinese exclusion remained on the books until 1943, when it struck the U.S. government as unseemly given China's alliance during World War II.[17]

Aware of the anti-Chinese politics on the mainland, Hawai'i's planters realized in the 1880s and 1890s their need to cease dependency on Chinese immigrants. They, accordingly, sought Japanese labor to replace the Chinese during the 1880s, hoping that the Japanese would furnish the uncontroversial, inexpensive, plentiful, and controllable labor they had long desired. Subsequently, agricultural capitalists would turn to Korean and Filipino laborers to perform the more onerous tasks of field labor.[18]

By the end of the nineteenth century, Chinese in Hawai'i fostered robust community ties, and those residing in Honolulu had established a durable, albeit sometimes controversial, Chinatown. Writing about Honolulu's Chinatown in the late 1880s, Yunte Huang proclaims, "Evolving from just a few waterfront stores in the mid-1850s, it eventually occupied thirty-seven acres, with claptrap restaurants, grocery stores, laundries, bakeries, pharmacies, slaughterhouses, warehouses, whorehouses, gambling parlors, and opium dens." Thus, Honolulu's Chinatown mocked the desires of Hawai'i's haole elite to control the islands' nonwhite residents. Its population was largely composed of former plantation workers who thought they could, and very often did, do better economically in the islands' biggest city. Indeed, Hawai'i's legislature had sought to bar Chinese from certain nonagricultural jobs. But Honolulu's Chinatown endured even when catastrophe struck it in the late 1890s. One of the biggest complaints that the anti-Chinese movement lodged against Chinese immigrants was that they harbored dreaded contagious diseases. In 1894 the bubonic plague appeared in Canton and Hong Kong, and in 1899 two cases of bubonic plague flared in Honolulu's Chinatown. Several thousand of its residents were evacuated and their homes burned, but the city's Chinese community survived.[19]

Honolulu's Chinatown nurtured a keen interest in Chinese politics. Yunte Huang writes, "Honolulu's Chinatown in particular played a crucial role in the birth of modern China. It was here that Sun Yat-Sen, founding father of the Republic of China, came of age and struck the first spark of revolution, which put an end to four thousand years of monarchical rule in China." While pro-dynasty forces resided in Honolulu's Chinatown, many of its residents openly advocated an end to monarchical rule in China and its replacement by a representative form of government or, at the very least, significant political reform in the land of their births. More than occasionally ideological tensions in Chinatown provoked violent confrontations between monarchists and republicans.[20]

Supported by anti-dynasty forces in Honolulu, Hawai'i Chinese entered the relatively small but dynamic world of island sports by the early 1900s. Hoisted on the backs of military, political, commercial, and spiritual representatives of European, U.S., and Japanese imperialism, modern sports such as baseball entered societies far from their places of origin. Colonizers taught the "natives" to engage in such sports in part, no doubt, because they truly believed that they were enjoyable, but if the British could inculcate in Indians a love of cricket and Americans could inculcate in Filipinos a love of baseball, perhaps that would help them establish cultural hegemony over the colonized. Moreover, the globalization of modern sports expanded the market for European, U.S., and Japanese firms engaged in the production and merchandising of athletic apparel and equipment.[21]

Colonizing Hawai'i

In Hawai'i, American empire building moved slowly but insidiously during the nineteenth century. Located as close to the middle of the Pacific as any chunk of landmass, the Hawaiian Islands attracted considerable interest from outsiders. In the late 1770s, English sailors commanded by the ill-fated Captain James Cook opened the islands for the curious, ambitious, spiritual, and profit-minded from Europe and North America. During the 1790s, the English navy helped Kamehameha, the ruler of the island of Hawai'i, to consolidate the islands under his command, eventually setting up his capital in Honolulu. Great Britain's influence on the islands was later superseded by that of the United States. For example, the American whaling industry was enticed to the waters off Maui. And many New England–based missionaries found the idea of thousands of

Hawaiians, unadorned with pants or dresses and seemingly content in their ignorance of hell or heaven, too much to resist. As it turned out, these missionaries, often self-righteous and bigoted but also well meaning, composed the spear point of American imperialism in Hawai'i.[22]

Just as Europeans transported dreaded diseases to the Americas a couple of centuries earlier, haoles carried pathogens to the islands that were deadly to the native people. American missionaries brought not only their desire to convert the Hawaiians but also an ability to stem, if not halt, the "Great Dying" in the islands. The *ali'i*, Hawaiian nobles, were impressed and perceived a connection between Christianity and the ability of the missionaries to treat the diseases plaguing Hawaiians. Accordingly, ali'i proved amenable to converting to Christianity and extended political and economic influence to missionaries and their offspring. The common Hawaiian people, known as *maka'āinana*, were not so impressed and often contested the growing power of the haoles.[23]

Through political influence and intermarriage with Hawaiians, American missionary children accumulated Hawaiian land and used their sway to guarantee that the common access to land enjoyed by Hawaiians for centuries was transcended by the new rules of capitalist agriculture. The imposition of capitalist agriculture and the corresponding emergence of a legal system abetting that imposition constituted a form of neo-imperialism. Hawaiians still constituted an independent people, claiming an independent government. But their economic and legal system experienced considerable encroachment from non-Hawaiians, mainly Americans or children of Americans.[24]

While not true of all haoles, many often fretted over Hawai'i's independence. The plantation system developed under haole hegemony in the mid-nineteenth century depended on sugar cultivation and export. Not only was a large labor force needed, but requisite markets as well. The United States figured as an important market, but planters in Hawai'i worried about the United States raising tariffs on foreign sugar to protect domestic cultivators. A sound way to put aside such a worry would be for Hawai'i to join the United States. Interacting with economic concerns was the belief entertained by many haoles that Hawaiians were racially and culturally incapable of self-government. Although an admirer of Anglo-American culture, King David Kalakaua, reigning from 1874 to 1891, struck powerful haoles as irresponsible and much too inclined toward Hawaiian nationalism. Indeed, Kalakaua sought to revive Hawaiian traditions frowned on by missionaries and their offspring, such as the hula and surfing. More seriously, Kalakaua troubled many haoles and the U.S. government by fostering good relations between Hawai'i and America's emerging rival in the Pacific region, Japan.[25]

Looking to expand its presence in the Pacific, the United States pursued a military base on the islands. Hawai'i, in turn, sought to avoid onerous tariffs on its sugar headed for American markets. In order to accomplish this, Kalakaua and the Hawaiian government in the late 1880s agreed to the installation of a

U.S. naval base at Pearl Harbor, about eleven miles from Honolulu and the king's Iolani Palace. Emboldened by the nearby existence of American military personnel, a contingent of powerful haoles opposed to Hawaiian nationalism forced the king to agree to what many Hawaiians have bitterly called the "bayonet constitution." Ostensibly in the name of representative government, this constitution would significantly limit the power of the monarch. Yet democracy was not really that much of a motivating factor behind the new constitution in that suffrage rights for common Hawaiians were limited as well.[26]

Kalakaua died in 1891, and because he and his wife sired no children, Kalakaua's sister, Liliuokalani, assumed the throne. Admired for her poetry and musicianship, Liliuokalani proved even more of a Hawaiian nationalist than her brother, and she was determined to revoke the "bayonet constitution." Liliuokalani's haole opposition responded with a coup, aided by U.S. authorities and military personnel on the islands. Liliuokalani was ultimately placed under house arrest, the Republic of Hawaii was proclaimed, and its leaders awaited U.S. colonization.[27]

The coup leaders would have to wait longer than they expected. In 1893, when the coup took place, Democrat Grover Cleveland was president. For good and bad reasons, Democrats expressed more caution about colonization than their GOP opposition. Many Democrats sincerely believed that for America to possess colonies betrayed the origins of the United States, that if Hawaiians wanted self-government, as they clearly did, they should be afforded their independence. Many Democrats, just as sincerely, expressed certainty that tucking several thousand nonwhite people under U.S. sovereignty was not a clever idea. However, Cleveland, while denouncing the overthrow, did nothing to return the islands to the sovereignty of the Hawaiian people.[28]

When Republicans returned to power in the late 1890s, they honored a more aggressive approach to colonialism. While not all were as exuberant imperialists as Teddy Roosevelt, Republicans happily sought to colonize Hawai'i. Meanwhile, significant protests erupted over the prospect of a U.S. takeover; protests included sending a petition to Congress signed by 39,000 Hawaiians. A treaty endorsed by the United States and representatives of the republic had been submitted to Congress. This treaty intended to make Hawai'i an American colony. However, thanks in part to the objections of the Hawaiian people, it failed to muster the requisite two-thirds majority. Going to war with Spain in 1898 empowered the pro-annexation argument as Hawai'i's strategic location in the Pacific became more apparent. Pro-annexation forces in Congress pushed for a joint resolution calling for Hawaiian annexation. As opposed to a treaty, a joint resolution required only a majority. It passed and was signed by President McKinley in 1898. Consequently, Hawai'i was declared a territory of the United States. Significantly, anyone born in Hawai'i was accorded U.S. citizenship. While no doubt done in recognition of the islands' haole leadership, it left open the possibility that nonwhites such as Hawaiians and the children of

Asian immigrants could also aspire to U.S. citizenship, but not necessarily equal citizenship rights.[29]

America's National Pastime in Hawai'i

Even before annexation, American cultural imperialism had planted itself on the islands through popular American sports, which meant baseball leagues formed by the 1890s. Outfitted with baseball equipment manufactured on the mainland, baseball clubs generally were composed of haoles and Hawaiians. Young men attending Kamehameha, a private school designed to educate youths of Hawaiian descent, organized a competitive baseball team in the 1890s. The more prominent newspapers in Honolulu covered baseball regularly as well as other sports and athletic activities associated with Europe and North America, such as cricket and the various versions of football.[30]

During the early twentieth century, Chinese created a dynamic presence in island sports. The Chinese Athletic Club was formed in Honolulu. Moreover, secondary school coaches could hardly put together a decent lineup, let alone a roster, if they ignored Chinese recruits. Among the Chinese to emerge in the early 1900s as one of Hawai'i's most superb athletes was En Sue Pung, born in 1888 in Pahala, an area in the southeastern part of the island of Hawai'i. According to descendant Chris Pung, En Sue Pung's parents and two older siblings came from Canton, settling on the Big Island in 1881. The family initially did plantation work but eventually moved to Honolulu, where the father established himself as a merchant and where En Sue Pung and his nine siblings grew up.[31]

A 1906 article in the *New York Tribune* was accompanied by a photograph of a Hawai'i Chinese baseball team with En Sue Pung among the players. The article claimed that Chinese in Hawai'i had largely avoided the antipathy manifested for people of Chinese descent on the American mainland. One reason was that they had intermarried among Hawaiians. Another was their participation in sports. The Chinese Athletic Club (CAC) had been organized in 1906, and community leaders were "distinctly animated by race pride and an ambition to demonstrate race capabilities and to foster athletic spirit among the Chinese and develop athletic ability among them." According to the *Tribune*, the CAC had assembled a competitive baseball team and would soon launch cricket and football squads, while staging a very successful track and field meet in Honolulu.[32]

Islanders of Chinese as well as Japanese ancestry demonstrated a fervent dedication to the American national pastime at an early age. A pioneer of Hawai'i Japanese baseball, Methodist minister C. P. Goto recalled "many a bloody battle" between Japanese and Chinese boys in the Nuuanu River district of Honolulu during the early 1900s. Among those playing for the Chinese was a young Buck Lai, whom Goto called Ah Tin. Goto remembered that Ah Tin did not wear a catcher's mask while performing catching duties for his team and that the gloves of players on both sides were torn—if they had gloves at all. The two teams would play all day until one side was decisively beaten.[33]

Clearly, baseball came to significantly represent Honolulu's Chinese community. In November 1907, the *Hawaiian Gazette* announced that a game between the CAC nine and the multiethnic Palamas would occur on Thanksgiving as a preliminary to a contest involving visiting pros from the Pacific Coast League. The *Gazette* speculated that the game should entice the Coast League professionals as a novelty, while boasting that only in Honolulu could one find an all-Chinese nine. Writing as a member of the Chinese Students Alliance (CSA), Tom Ahoy told the Honolulu press that he looked forward to a game between the CSA and CAC nines early in 1908. Regardless of which team won, Ahoy insisted, the ballplayers would reinforce interest in baseball in Chinatown and enjoy a "wholesome Chinese dinner" after the game. Apparently, rivalries between Chinese nines could get serious. In March 1908 the *Pacific Commercial Advertiser* complained, "The Chinese Alohas and Chinese Athletics are scrapping over baseball talent. Such a naughtiness!" Several months later, Tony Phong, described as a former Honolulu merchant who had moved to New York City, donated a cup to the winner of a CSA/CAC game. The daily declared, "The cup is a beauty and well worth striving for." After a Chinese New Year game in 1910, the *Honolulu Evening Bulletin* praised the crowd that watched the CAC handily defeat the CSA thanks in part to "Ah Tin"'s homer and En Sue Pung's feats in the outfield. A big crowd watched, including many Chinese merchants. A *Honolulu Evening Bulletin* expressed amazement that the "Sons of China" could play baseball so well and that scorekeeper Sam Hop knew the game so well. The next year, the CAC nine edged the CSA, 5–4. The *Advertiser* cheered the game as good, despite it taking place early in the season. The daily noted that both teams were rivals and that their supporters displayed their partisan enthusiasm by "[keeping] up a string of remarks."[34]

Meanwhile, the *Pacific Commercial Advertiser* announced that the first "Chinese Baseball League" of its kind had been formed in Honolulu in 1909. In a story headlined "To Keep the Devil Away," the *Advertiser* reported that the league's opening game was slated for an empty lot behind the Oahu Railroad Depot. Hoping to exoticize the event, it added, "As usual for such occasions, the opening ceremonies will be unique. There will be plenty of chop sticks and fireworks." Reportedly, a prosperous merchant named Lee Mun Chun offered much of the financial backing for the league.[35]

The names of Chinese young men appeared in many interethnic lineups in the early twentieth century. Similar to the Boy Scouts, Honolulu's Boys Brigade engaged in a variety of sports in the early twentieth century. In a Boys Brigade indoor baseball game in the fall of 1905, the Kauluwelas beat the Palamas with future Chinese Travelers on display in that F. L. Akana played for the victors, while Albert Akana, who captained the Travelers in 1912, played for the losers. Performing for the Honolulu Athletic Club in the early 1900s was not only "Ensue" but the talented Hawai'i Chinese Henry Kuali. In April 1908, Sam Hop, a prominent and versatile Chinese athlete, played right field for the Aala Athletic Club nine against the Japanese Asahi aggregation. Playing with Hop was a skilled Hawai'i Chinese named Alex Asam. Nonetheless, by 1911 baseball supporters among Honolulu's Chinese expressed disenchantment with Hawai'i Chinese ballplayers teaming up with members of other ethnic groups. In April 1911, the *Hawaiian Star* reported that Honolulu Chinese merchants pressured Chinese ballplayers to leave interethnic teams and exert their energies and skill on behalf of an all-Chinese nine.[36]

Based in Honolulu, the Oahu League materialized as the top organization in Hawai'i baseball in the early twentieth century. While it suffered through a variety of controversies, it seemingly rode high in the baseball public's mind in the summer of 1909. The *Hawaiian Star* praised the league and voiced admiration for one of its strongest teams—the nine representing the CAC. The *Star* also commended the Japanese Athletic Club (JAC) nine, but while Nikkei investors backed the JAC, the team generally did not field Nikkei ballplayers. As far as the *Star* was concerned, the CAC and JAC teams formed the nucleus of the league, which sponsored a junior league for younger players. With Sam Hop serving as treasurer, the junior league included a nine representing the CAC, as well as the Nikkei Asahis, and a team formed by the Mohawk Athletic Club, more commonly known as the Muhocks.[37]

Hawai'i Chinese athletic achievements outside of baseball began to gain notice, and in 1908 the interethnic Kauluwela Boys Club organized a track meet. Competing in that meet were Lang Akana, Vernon Ayau, and "Ah Tin." A "Chinese Field Day" occurred annually during the early 1900s. Many of Honolulu's finest athletes were present, such as En Sue Pung and Lang Akana with Sam Hop on the track committee. Ah Tin shone as one of the track meet's biggest stars. "Chinese Americans," according to the *Pacific Commercial Advertiser*, commemorated New Year's with athletic competition in baseball as well as track and field. Many future Travelers performed, such as Lai Tin, who won the 115-yard hurdles and shot put in 1911.[38]

In 1910, the *Pacific Commercial Advertiser* published an article attempting to explain the athletic ability of Chinese in Hawai'i, as well as other ethnic groups. The article was written by Dr. E. H. Hand, director of the YMCA in Honolulu. He purported to have physically examined 271 persons of all ethnic backgrounds in Hawai'i save Nikkei, while observing all of Hawai'i's ethnic groups performing athletically. Hand's observations stemmed from American racial science or, more accurately, pseudoscience, which insisted that racial differences could be objectively measured. For Chinese, Hand offered lukewarm praise, conceding that the Chinese athlete "is a plucky little contestant but only under certain conditions," adding "that if he goes up against better men, he is easily 'buffaloed' from the start and will not put up a good showing." As physical specimens, according to Hand, Chinese possessed a mixture of attributes. Hand argued that the Chinese possessed the strongest backs but weak arms, which was interesting given their growing dominance in Hawai'i baseball. They were, in addition, "thin but strong" as well as "wiry and tough." Japanese, Hand observed, "can be strong but don't know how to use their strength."[39]

The first U.S.-born Nikkei to play professionally in the United States and one of the first to get elected to public office in the U.S. empire, Andrew Yamashiro represented Hawai'i's largest ethnic group by the 1920s, as did two other Travelers—Jimmy and Clem Moriyama. In the late 1860s, the Meiji dynasty assumed the emperorship of Japan, sponsoring, in the process, efforts to modernize Japan along European and American lines in response to the United States forcing its way into Japanese markets. Consequently, Japan became accessible to outside labor recruiters. Hawai'i's sugar plantation owners, hoping to supplement their Chinese labor forces, sought to import labor from Japan; thus, well over one hundred Japanese were brought to Hawai'i in 1868. They were scattered among different plantations on O'ahu, Maui, Kaua'i, and Lanai to perform contract labor. But the experiment in Japanese labor recruitment failed at the time. Many of those recruited complained about the foul food and even fouler treatment. Planters, figuring that the Japanese workers were not worth the effort, temporarily discarded plans to recruit from Japan. Yet thousands of Nikkei would journey to the islands by the turn of the century. For this to happen, not only did commercial interactions between Japan and other nations need to stabilize, but Japan had to become a harder place in which to live. Taxation falling inequitably on rural people and a military draft made the Japanese diaspora to places like Hawai'i more attractive.[40]

In Hawai'i, plantation operators anticipated the Japanese immigrants, or the *Issei*, would both replace Chinese laborers and spur on those Chinese and Hawaiian workers remaining in their employ. As it turned out, Issei proved more difficult to manage than the Chinese. Against their bosses' wishes, they ceased working to celebrate the emperor's birthday. If they had options, Issei fled the plantations for employment elsewhere—even the U.S. mainland, where racist nativism may have been harsher, but the wages were higher. Moreover, Issei understood the importance of their labor to the sugar industry and the increasingly important pineapple industry and understood the need as well for labor militancy as the early twentieth century witnessed several Issei-inspired strikes.[41]

Hawai'i Japanese forged substantial community ties around work, family and kin, spirituality, politics, and play. Japanese immigrants, unlike many other immigrants to the United States regardless of origins, were familiar with baseball. However, the sport brought to Japan by American educators, military personnel, and businesspeople was largely adopted by the more economically privileged Japanese to expose themselves to Western modernity. Accordingly, an Issei professional—a Christian preacher named Takie Okumura—proved instrumental in spreading baseball among Hawai'i's working-class Nikkei. As progressive modernizers did among immigrant working-class communities on the

U.S. mainland, Okumura used baseball to "uplift" impoverished Nikkei youth. In the late 1890s, Okumura formed a baseball team called the Excelsiors out of the young men boarding in a home he supervised. The Excelsiors constituted the first Japanese American baseball team, but as historian Samuel Regalado has pointed out, it clearly would not be the last.[42]

During the first decade of the twentieth century, the Asahi baseball club was formed in Honolulu. Reverend C. P. Goto maintained in the 1930s that the Honolulu Asahis derived from the desire of youthful Nikkei ballplayers to pick the very best from their numbers to meet the challenge of local Chinese. A teenager, Steere Noda, led the team, which included Goto and future Traveler Jimmy Moriyama. Andrew Yamashiro was initially the team mascot. By selling newspapers, team members earned enough money to purchase uniforms at $1.50 each. In 1908, the Asahi nine beat a team called the Oukwas to emerge as the representative Nikkei team in Honolulu. By the advent of the 1910s, the Asahis were deemed good enough to take on the talented nines playing in the Oahu Baseball League. Considered adept at all facets of the game except for hitting, the Asahis held their own against Chinese, Portuguese, Hawaiian, and haole competition, as well as the top-notch 25th regiment team, an all-Black aggregation serving in Honolulu. Eventually, they were able to not just hold their own but win championships. In the process, the Asahis produced some of the finest ballplayers on the islands.[43]

Baseball and Hawai'i's Emerging Local Culture

Lang Akana and Fred Markham as well as other Travelers of mixed, indigenous descent, of course, represented a vital Hawaiian experience. Akana's father was Chinese and his mother was Hawaiian. Markham's father was white, and his mother possessed Hawaiian ancestry. When Europeans initially encountered Hawai'i in 1776, approximately 500,000 to 1 million people lived on the islands. Descendants of Southeast Asian people who over centuries migrated by boat to various Pacific islands, Hawaiians engaged in a variety of economic activities and pursued a variety of political agendas. Like premodern people around the globe, they were highly spiritual and devoted to a collectivist culture that saw the individual not so much as autonomous but as a product of interactions with larger social units—the family, kin, and village. Private productive property is central to capitalism. It was not, however, central to the way Hawaiians ran their economy. Land, therefore, belonged to the group—not to any individual or family. To be sure, Hawaiian political systems were hardly democratic. Inherited political power afforded the ali'i more access to land and the wealth that land produced, but not ownership, for the land was perceived as too sacred for humans to own.[44]

Because interracial marriage was legally accepted and, in some cases, encouraged on the islands, bi- and multiracial and ethnic people pervaded Hawai'i as nowhere else on the mainland in the early twentieth century. In part, this was because the nation and, after U.S. annexation, the territory of Hawai'i allowed interracial marriages. Another factor is that plantation employers sought labor and encouraged single workers to marry to tie them to the islands, curb militancy, and produce more plantation hands. That workers might find spouses possessing different racial and ethnic backgrounds failed to disturb Hawai'i's haole elite hungry for large workforces.[45]

The hard-and-fast racial borders existing on the mainland were tougher to police in Hawai'i, where laborers from not only East Asia but also the Philippines, the Iberian Peninsula, and Puerto Rico were largely recruited to work by the 1910s. Haole supremacy thrived along with frequently severe tensions between various island ethnic groups, but an emergent local culture, based significantly on class and neighborhood, somewhat diffused racism and nativism on the islands. Promoted by Hawaiian Creole, better known as Hawaiian Pidgin English, the local culture crossed racial and ethnic lines by facilitating communication between ethnic groups. At the same time, the local culture helped transform Hawai'i's baseball fields into cosmopolitan canopies.[46]

Racialized colonialism complicated baseball on the islands. While baseball in Hawai'i acted as an extension of American colonialism and reinforced ethnic communities, it also nurtured a racially and ethnically hybrid local culture. Thus, Chinese in Hawai'i carved out a prominent ethnic niche in local baseball just as many of their ballplayers performed with non-Chinese on various nines. After the CAC nine won a league championship in 1906, the *Honolulu Evening Bulletin* observed, "Well the only Chinese baseball team known is this one and they can now swell up as champions of the Riverside League." The *Pacific Commercial Advertiser* claimed that "the game was witnessed by a large and enthusiastic Chinese delegation, sporting flags, colors, brooms, ribbons, and horns. They seem to have a hunch that their representatives would win, and the hunch made good." Over a year later, the CAC nine won the Kalanianole League title, prompting a big luau at the home of a local Chinese, and celebrants brought "nearly all the firecrackers of Chinatown for the occasion."[47]

That Chinese in Hawai'i were highly skilled at baseball gained coverage in the mainland press. Mainlanders favoring American assumption of the "white man's burden"—the highly racialized ideology justifying U.S. colonialism—seemed heartened. In 1904 the *Hartford Courant* published an article on a haole Hawaiian missionary, Doremus Scudder, who lectured a Congregationalist church audience. Reprinted in the *Pacific Commercial Advertiser*, this article purported that Scudder showed two photos to his receptive audience. One was of a Chinese baseball team, presumably based in Honolulu, and the other of the Nikkei Excelsiors. Scudder's point was that a "real American spirit" had conquered the islands. The *Oakland Tribune*'s T. P. Magellan informed readers in 1907 that a group of "pig-tails" from Hawai'i had beaten a team of American military personnel. To Magellan, the victory of the Chinese demonstrated the effectiveness of American missionary work at spreading the gospel of baseball. However, some in the mainland press appeared distressed by such intelligence, evoking the fear of Asian global empowerment. Although perhaps in jest, the *Newark News* opined that "the yellow peril seems to be more real than some of us had thought" when informing readers of the success of Chinese ballplayers in Hawai'i.[48]

Conclusion

Chinese baseball teams shared ball fields with players of ethnic groups. By the 1910s, Honolulu's elite Oahu Baseball League had teams representing Chinese, Japanese, Hawaiians, Portuguese, and whites. During the 1910s, Filipinos and Koreans as well as the all-Black 25th regiment nine would be added to the mix. Indeed, there seemed a consensus among Oahu League management that exploiting racial and ethnic rivalries through baseball was good for business. In this, the league echoed efforts to reinforce racial and ethnic differences on the plantations. Yet, beginning as all-Chinese and then evolving into a racially and ethnically mixed team, the Travelers would send a shock wave through the racialized hierarchy pervading the American empire.[49]

2

The Travelers from Hawai'i

Culture, Capitalism, and Baseball

The Travelers' experiences on the American mainland interwove with the development of a comparatively casual pastime for the mid-nineteenth century, engaged in by European American white-collar workers eager to divert themselves from their sedentary jobs to a business and a way of life that was deeply entrenched in American culture by the early twentieth century. Disrupting white male ownership of America's national pastime, the Travelers appeared in small towns, big cities, and college campuses throughout much of the continental United States. They came with their bats and gloves, ready to take on local nines with a skill that between the years of 1912 and 1916 transformed them into perhaps the most famous non–major league baseball team in America. However, their talents alone did not entice thousands to baseball parks from California to Massachusetts. Rather, they were promoted and largely viewed as a team of exotics—ostensibly darker skinned young men raised in a land that seemed strange to most of the people they encountered on the mainland. To those who watched and reported on them, it was not always clear what that land was. Was it Hawai'i? After all, they were often advertised as a baseball team representing the Chinese University of Hawaii. Or since promoters depicted them as Chinese, perhaps they were weaned in Shanghai or in the shadow of the Great Wall. The details frequently failed to matter to those boosting their upcoming games. What did matter was that these "foreigners"—hardly a precise way of describing American citizens born in the U.S. territory of Hawai'i—frequently beat American (that is, white) men in America's game.[1]

Two reasons stand out as to why they came to the mainland. First, Chinese in Honolulu wanted to demonstrate to the United States the injustice of restricting immigration from China. A class bias infiltrated these concerns. The team's Chinese sponsors and spokespersons seemed determined to show white Americans that not all the country's Chinese residents were lower-class, socially ostracized "coolie" laundry operators or workers. Rather, they wanted white Americans to know that Chinese could exhibit civility in terms of formal education and acculturation to middle-class American ways. Angered by the extension of the Chinese Exclusion Act in the early 1900s, members of Honolulu's Chinese community had participated in the failed project of a global boycott of U.S. goods by the Chinese diaspora. If confronting the United States over its racialized and corrupt immigration policy would not work, perhaps deploying baseball to prop up a cultural bridge to white mainlanders might. In any event, considerable money was raised in Honolulu's Chinatown's to finance the team's first trip to the U.S. mainland in 1912. Second, the largely haole business community in Hawai'i supported the Travelers, because that community hoped the ballplayers would cultivate mainland markets for island-grown sugar and pineapple, as well as lure mainland tourism, capital, and permanent white residents to the islands by demonstrating that nonwhites in Hawai'i may be exotic but welcoming, and not the savages and what the poet Bret Harte famously denigrated as "heathen Chinee" troubling mainlanders.[2]

These journeys to mainland baseball diamonds tended to inspire more wonder than resentment from mainlanders, despite the institutionalized and personal racism facing people of Chinese and Asian ancestry in general throughout the United States. The Travelers did not constitute baseball's equivalent of the contemporary prize fighter Jack Johnson, the masterful African American heavyweight champion who doomed "Great White Hopes" with brains, finesse, and power. They were not Black, and they did not win a prestigious championship. Thus, it was possible for the white sports world to perceive them as curiosities rather than threats, although the idea of Chinese or Asians in general donning baseball uniforms and competing with whites on a regular and relatively equitable basis appeared unsettling for at least some mainlanders.[3]

That the Travelers came from an American colonial possession may have ameliorated some of the hostility to their success in baseball. After all, the notion of the white man's burden frequently served to explain and rationalize American imperial ventures among the nonwhite denizens of the Pacific and the Caribbean. Very purposefully, American imperialists could claim baseball as a force for progress in the Philippines. Toothbrushes and baseballs would, American imperialists insisted, help transport Filipinos from savagery toward at least the outskirts of civilization. In the case of Hawai'i, colonial uplift could assume a more generous tone, evoking the possibility that nonwhites on the islands might gain access to an American melting pot. In 1911 the *Honolulu Evening Bulletin* cited a mainland visitor who happily proclaimed that baseball powered assimilation in Hawai'i.[4]

Acknowledging the Travelers' efficient mopping up of several mainland college and semipro nines, the mainland press argued that "Uncle Sam's Old Tricks" transformed these young men from Hawai'i into good ballplayers. Therefore, white mainlanders need not feel threatened by their local nines losing to the Travelers. The ability of Asians and Hawaiians to steal bases and stop line drives illuminated the wise beneficence behind white Americans shouldering the responsibilities of empire. At the same time, the Travelers were often viewed as a perhaps less worrisome version of the "Yellow Peril," a termed coined by Kaiser Wilhelm to encapsulate his anxieties about the potential of Asian nations surpassing the West in global dominance. European and American expansion into the Asian Pacific region encountered resistance. While the military and commercial expansionism of Japan seemingly represented the Yellow Peril at its worst to many Americans by the early 1900s, they could not help but notice that Chinese nationalists engaged in the Boxer Rebellion and Filipino guerrilla fighters fiercely contested the white man's burden. Asian defiance was too easily translated in the minds of white Americans and Europeans into Asian quests for supremacy over them. An English writer named Sax Rohmer expressed this in a series of melodramatic novels revolving around a diabolical villain bent on world conquest, Fu Man Chu. Not very coincidentally, the Travelers were often described in the mainland press as invading "yellow perils."[5]

In a country where Asian immigrants were denied citizenship rights and generally found it hard to enter in the first place, a complicated racial ideology coalesced over the years to justify inequitable treatment of people of Asian ancestry. This racial ideology was not always hell-bent on insulting American residents of Asian ancestry. But it insisted on the truth of Kipling's line "East is East, and West is West, and never the twain shall meet." That is, Asians were irrevocably distinct from "Westerners." God or nature drew lines in the sand that could not be crossed by "Orientals" or "Occidentals." To the more generous, Asians may appear fine in their own way and in their own countries, but they posed an "unassimilable" problem in American society.[6]

The Chinese male, for example, was widely perceived by white America as courteous to the point of servility, kind, clever, and, if Confucian, wise. Yet he was also seen as lustful, depraved, and treacherous. Meanwhile, many white Americans wondered, Why do so many Chinese men wear "pigtails," appear so small, and lack even the appearance of facial hair? Why do so many Chinese men labor as cooks or work in laundries? The answer affirmed the widespread belief that Chinese men lacked the requisite characteristics of manliness, which emerged as an important element and, for many, a selling point of sport in America. In baseball, as in prize fighting and football, American males supposedly tested their masculinity. The game required, it was widely asserted, all the salient characteristics of manliness—courage, strength, intelligence, patience, and maturity. However, some of the more successful baseball players relied on stealth to succeed and fell into displays of ill temperament and addictive behaviors even though the game's more naive promoters ignored the shadows chasing hardly wholesome exemplars of the game, while proudly proclaiming baseball as the national pastime.[7]

Western observers, meanwhile, complained that the Chinese avoided physical exercise and competition. Writing in *Outing* at the turn of the last century, a publication extolling the blessing of physical exercise, Price Collier noted that the Chinese hated physicality so much that they "can scarcely be driven to fight, even for their own country, and their pulpy condition of dependence are now all too manifest." Casper Whitney, famed for his reverence for the benefits of physical conditioning, piled on, asserting that the Chinese were notably "not athletic."[8]

Thus, thousands of American baseball fans were probably befuddled when the Travelers, largely perceived as Chinese, regularly defeated many of the country's best amateur and semiprofessionals teams, even though the ball club was never the home team and often endured draining travel schedules. The Travelers won by conforming to the dictates of baseball's "dead ball" era—an era roughly concurrent with the pre-Ruthian first two decades of the twentieth century. During this time, home runs were rare, and teams such as the 1908 Chicago Cubs could win pennants without much in the way of consistent hitting as long as they played smart and aggressive baseball.[9]

Victories during the "dead ball" era began even more emphatically then than now with pitching and defense. The Travelers could always count on pitcher Apau Kau. Like the census takers and many others outside of Chinese communities who found it difficult to deal with Chinese family names coming before given names, I have found it difficult to trace the social and occupational backgrounds of Hawai'i Chinese. Nevertheless, the 1910 U.S. Census Manuscript schedules tell us that a nineteen-year-old individual named Pau T. Kau lived with a Chinese-born mother and worked in a Honolulu grocery store run by her. Capable of a commanding fast ball, Apau Kau relied on an assortment of deceptive pitches, including the "spitter," which the *Honolulu Star-Bulletin* claimed he picked up from Ed Walsh, the Chicago White Sox' Hall of Fame pitcher, during the 1912 journey. Moreover, once an opponent got on base against the Chinese hurler, he had better remain alert since Apau Kau harbored a deceiving pickoff move, which some claimed more than bordered on a balk. In 1915, he threw a perfect game of twenty strikeouts at the Baylor University nine in Texas. Throughout the Travelers' journeys, minor league clubs reportedly sought Apau Kau's services.[10]

Pitching for the Travelers in 1913 and 1914, Foster Robinson was probably Apau Kau's equal if not his superior on the slab. And like Apau Kau, Robinson attracted attention from minor league franchises. Because of his name and the concerted effort to promote the Travelers as exotic Chinese, he was occasionally publicized as possessing a variation of his mother's surname, Ah Heong or A Heong, in order to promote him as more Chinese when he toured with the barnstormers. Born in 1894, he was the son of a Chinese immigrant mother and a father possessing English and "Polynesian" descent. Living on Maui in 1900, Foster's father labored as a carpenter. Robinson was hailed on the mainland as "the Matty of the East" in reference to the remarkable New York Giants pitcher Christy Mathewson. Similar to Apau Kau, Robinson counted on an assortment of pitches. Robinson's brother, Alvin, joined the Travelers in 1915 as a utility man. Because of his mixed racial ancestry, Foster Robinson's appearance on the presumably all-Chinese Travelers confused some mainlanders. In 1913, the *Pacific Commercial Advertiser* informed readers that mainland baseball fans concluded that Robinson was a "Chinaman" masquerading as white. In 1935, Buck Lai recalled Foster Robinson as a diligent, versatile ballplayer, capable of handling many positions as well as a bat.[11]

In addition to Apau Kau and Foster Robinson, the Travelers effectively used other skilled hurlers. Buck Lai recalled that Luck Yee Lau, who pitched regularly for the Travelers in 1912 and 1913, displayed considerable skill as a pitcher but tended to "groove" the ball too much and get himself and the team in trouble. Luck Yee Lau came from relatively privileged economic circumstances. According to 1900 census data, his Chinese immigrant father managed a rice plantation in Wailua on Oahu's north shore and his family possessed a live-in servant. Hawaiian Luther Kekoa, known in the mainland press as "Aki" or "Ako," hurled for the Travelers from 1914 to 1916. Hailing from Hilo, his father was a lawyer. While with the Travelers, Kekoa learned to master the emery ball, a nasty, later illegal pitch he learned from watching former major leaguer George Mullin use it to tie up Traveler batters for a semipro nine in Kokomo, Indiana. Promoted as "Bo" on the mainland, Hawaiian George Bush toed the rubber for the Travelers during the 1915 and 1916 seasons. Fred Swan, advertised as "Suan" on the mainland, was the ace of the 1916 squad, while Clement Moriyama and haole Bill Inman also pitched.[12]

Mainland commentators were often stunned by the athleticism displayed by the Travelers' fielding. The two men who did the bulk of the catching attracted curiosity from minor league teams on the mainland. A son of Chinese immigrants, Kan Yen Chun performed much of the backstop work for the Travelers from 1912 through 1914. Perhaps small in stature for a catcher even at that time, he had a whip for an arm and was hailed for his sagacity. Hawaiian Fred "Denny" Markham joined the Travelers in 1913 as an infielder. According to the manuscript census schedules, his father, John, claimed German as well as Hawaiian descent. His mother, Annie, was the daughter of a prominent Maui plantation owner, haole August Drier. In addition, John Markham was a political activist. In 1902, he stood with the Home Rule Party, which accepted U.S. colonization as a given but claimed to seek equal rights for Hawaiians within the empire.

When the party collapsed, Markham became a Democratic Party activist in Honolulu. During the 1910s, he served on Honolulu's Board of Supervisors and later the territorial Board of Health and Honolulu's Civil Service Commission. After Kan Yen Chun decided to remain on the islands rather than venture eastward in 1915 and 1916, Markham, who was often advertised as a Chinese surnamed "Mark," soundly assumed most of the catching duties.[13]

In the infield, individual Travelers performed spectacularly. For all five years of Traveler treks to the mainland, Vernon Ayau stirred comparisons to some of the best shortstops in professional baseball. Small and acrobatic, Ayau displayed an arm strength that often surprised mainland baseball players and fans. According to the U.S. census data, he was nineteen years old in 1910 and worked as a railroad depot agent while living in Maui. His father was born in China; his mother, Hawai'i. In 1900, Ayau's father was described in the census manuscripts as a "salesman."[14]

Ayau's Traveler mates at second base varied over the years. But probably Nisei Chinito Moriyama was the best as he seemingly matched Ayau's athleticism. Born on Kaua'i in 1893 and 1895, respectively, Chinito and his brother Tsuneo joined the Travelers in 1915. Later in their lives, Chinito would be called James or Jimmy, and Tsuneo would be called Clement or Clem. Both Moriyama brothers played for the legendary Japanese Asahi nine and would continue to play for the Asahis after their Traveler run ended. During the winters, between sojourns with the Travelers, the brothers played for other Nikkei nines. Meanwhile, Chinito was identified as an employee of the Palama Settlement House in 1912, which was established to help the multicultural youths of the largely working-class Honolulu neighborhood of Palama, while Tsuneo, called a "clever player" by the *Star-Bulletin*, earned a reputation as a "tough pitcher" to hit.[15]

Most years, excluding 1914, Lai Tin anchored third base for the Travelers. He could make dazzling plays of hot smashes, line drives, and bunts sent his way even though he occasionally muffed easy grounders and made inaccurate throws. Lai Tin's father, according to was a merchant and his mother a temple priestess. Indeed, she served in that capacity until the 1930s, heading the How Wong Miu Temple on Old School Street in the largely Chinese "Tin Can Alley" section of Honolulu, a neighborhood often denigrated by privileged haoles.[16]

An examination of U.S. census manuscripts clarifies matters regarding Lai's background, but only a bit. In 1900, a census taker found Say Lai, a shopkeeper, and his wife, Lum See Lai, in Honolulu. The latter, by the way, will be accorded different spellings of her name in the local press. Census data reveals that Say Lai was born in 1852 in China and came to Hawai'i in 1871. Lum See Lai was forty-three at the time of the census, and she arrived in Hawai'i from China in 1885. The two had been married since 1874 and had a daughter, Ah Chan, who was born in China. One of Say Lai and Lum See's sons, Gum Tin, is probably Buck Lai, recorded to have been born in 1893. The family lived on Dorsey Lane in the Nuuanu neighborhood of Honolulu. The 1910 U.S. census manuscripts reveal a sixteen-year-old Lai Tin, living with siblings, in-laws, and a mother on Beretania Street in Honolulu. His father was deceased by this time. Confusing matters, both his parents were described as Hawaiian born as were both of his maternal grandparents. Lai Tin and his siblings were also reported as racially Chinese. Two of his older brothers, Pui Lai and Hook Lai, were identified as clerks, with Pui Lai listed as the head of household. The rest of the siblings were too young to work apparently. The 1920 U.S. census manuscripts show William Lai, who was then residing in Philadelphia, as racially Chinese but the son of Hawaiian-born parents. Ten years later, the census manuscripts repeat this claim while Lai and his family lived in Audubon, New Jersey. Interestingly, the 1930 census reports that his sister Jessie was a child of Chinese immigrants, which is more accurate than the census data likely derived perhaps from Buck Lai's recollection of his parents' origins in 1920.[17]

Stories about Buck Lai's parents appeared in Honolulu newspapers in the 1890s and early 1900s. In the late 1890s Say Lai was involved in various legal disputes over property ownership. Called Joss Houses at the time, Chinese temples provoked exoticism wherever they were erected in the American empire. At the time of his death, Say Lai owned the Joss House in which his wife served as priestess. A 1901 report in the *Honolulu Star* maintained he made $750 a year from it. Say Lai died in 1904. He entrusted his estate to his wife, naming her as "executrix." The estate consisted of $2,400 in real estate and $100 in furnishings. "Lone Observer," a correspondent for the *Pacific Commercial Advertiser*, visited Lum Shee Lai 's temple in 1909. Patronizingly the correspondent revealed that the priestess served him "abominable tea with the surest hospitality." In 1910, Lum Shee Lai evinced a political side by attending a Chinese Women's Reform Association meeting in Honolulu. Disputing the patriarchalism of dynastic China, she told other attendees that before he died, Say Lai made her promise not to sell any of their daughters. A couple of years later, she sold three parcels of land acquired by Say Lai in the 1890s.[18]

Relatively privileged economically, Buck Lai's family were willing to let him attend McKinley High School, a public secondary school situated in downtown Honolulu. Originally known as the Fort Street English Day School, it was established in 1865. Later in the nineteenth century, the school's name was changed to Honolulu High School and then again, in 1907, to honor the recently assassinated President McKinley. At McKinley, Lai displayed his all-around athletic skills. He played end on the football team and starred on the track team as a sprinter and long jumper. Lai even did some shot putting. At a track and field meet staged by Honolulu Chinese, he competed for the Chinese Athletic Union, which surfaced as a rival to the Chinese Athletic Club. Lai's performances in track and field challenged those of En Sue Pung, who earlier in the decade was often hailed as the swiftest of island athletes. Lai reportedly ran the 100-yard dash in a notable 9.5 seconds and set an island long jump mark of 23 feet 8½ inches.[19]

As 1912 dawned Lai Tin continued to demonstrate his athletic versatility while Hawai'i's sports world was following the exploits of its remarkable aqua athlete

Duke Kahanamoku. The Hawaiian had caught the world's attention when he broke a sprint record in swimming a few years earlier. Because tales of Kahanamoku's speed originated in far-off Hawai'i, some mainland followers of competitive swimming scoffed as did, more importantly, American Athletic Union (AAU) officials. Determined to quiet the critics and place Kahanamoku on the U.S. Olympic team, his island supporters sent him to the mainland. Thus, it was at a benefit track and field meet intended to help defray Duke Kahanamoku's expenses as he tried out for the 1912 Olympic team that Lai Tin won the 100-yard dash. On that same day, he played baseball for an all-Hawaii team that beat a sailor contingent from the USS *West Virginia*. In late February, Lai Tin competed for the Chinese Athletic Union in a track meet sponsored by Honolulu's Chinese community. He won the 100- and 200-yard dash and placed third in shot put. A week later, Lai Tin performed at an AAU meet in Honolulu. Lai took second in the 100-yard dash and won the 50-yard sprint. The teenager's track and field achievements garnered him publicity on the mainland. The Peoria, Illinois–based *Day Book* published a photograph of "Lai Ting" winning a 100-yard dash event in Honolulu in April 1912. The accompanying text declared, "Fast Chinaman Olympic candidate." Proclaimed a possible member of the U.S. Olympic team in 1912, Lai was further identified as a "Chinaman but a native one."[20]

In 1912, Albert Akana captained the Traveler squad in addition to handling first base. Apparently not related to outfielder Lang Akana, Albert, like Lang, was a powerful hitter and possessed both Chinese and Hawaiian ancestry. Albert's father, John, was born in Hawai'i and served as president of the sport-oriented Chinese Aloha Club. According to the 1910 census data, the twenty-two-year-old Albert clerked for the territorial government. Joining Lai, Ayau, and Chinito Moriyama in the Traveler infield in 1915 was first sacker Alfred Yap, who played for the Travelers only during the spring and summer. While his sojourn with the Travelers was relatively brief, he proved a good hitter and a useful chronicler of the team's 1915 journeys for the *Honolulu Star-Bulletin*. Both of Yap's parents were Chinese born. In 1910, his father, William Kwai Fong Yap, worked as a bank clerk. Indeed, William Kwai Fong Yap is credited as the first Hawai'i Chinese to work in a predominantly white financial institution in Hawai'i and years later with inspiring the name change of College of Hawai'i to the University of Hawai'i.[21]

In the outfield, the Travelers summoned young men who covered a great deal of ground to end the lives of extra base hits before they began. The mainland press found much to praise in the work of Hawai'i Chinese such as En Sue Pung and Lang Akana, as well as Nikkei Andrew Yamashiro. Other outfielders included Mon Yin Chung, En Sue's brother Ping Kong Pung, Tan Lo, Jimmy Aylett, Sing Hung Hoe, and Henry Kuali. Aylett would often play as "Ah Let" or "Let," and Kuali would perform as "Ah Lee." Both Aylett and Kuali ranked among the hardest hitters on the Travelers.[22]

If a ball got through the left side of the infield, Lang Akana was in left field to pick it up during the 1912 and 1913 tours. Akana's father was a Chinese-born physician and his mother was Hawaiian, according to the 1910 U.S. Census. Called Fong Lan in the census, Lang Akana was then a twenty-two-year-old bookkeeper, employed by the California Feed Company, for which he had been working since 1908. Dr. C. T. Akana was a leader of Honolulu's Chinese community in the late nineteenth and early twentieth centuries. We can find him in 1900 addressing a Chinese Reform Association meeting in Honolulu, supporting the ultimately failed efforts of youthful emperor Guangxu to render the dynastic rule less oppressive. According to sportswriter Bill Pacheco, Lang Akana got his baseball start in Honolulu by playing in the Boys' Brigade League. He recalled for Hawai'i Chinese sportswriter Loui Leong Hop that as a youth he walked to the Makiki district of Honolulu to play sandlot baseball with En Sue Pung and his brothers, as well as other notable Honolulu-based ballplayers in the process of learning the game. An accomplished singer, Akana skipped baseball to tour Australia with a Hawaiian choir in 1911. Akana was celebrated as both a swift outfielder and a strong left-handed hitter who got more than a glance from mainland professional franchises. Buck Lai recalled in 1935 that Akana brought along his guitar on his journeys to the mainland, strumming and singing wherever the Travelers went. He even organized a concert the Travelers gave at New York City's Waldorf-Astoria in 1912.[23]

En Sue Pung usually held down the center field spot in 1913 and 1914. According to family historian Chris Pung, the outfielder's parents and older siblings performed plantation labor until they were able to move in 1881 to Honolulu, where they operated a store. The 1910 census data tells us that En Sue Pung was working in a hardware store in Honolulu, living with his Chinese-born mother, Det Yin, and Hawai'i-born siblings. His father, Wing Ming Pung, had returned to China the previous year. The fifty-year-old Wing Ming Pung was described as a grocer on the departing ship's manifest. However, in the 1907 Honolulu City Directory, he was designated as a laborer and hailed as one of the "leading Chinese merchants in Honolulu" when he died in 1920. Meanwhile, En Sue Pung surfaced as one of Hawai'i's most formidable athletes, particularly in track and baseball.[24]

Pung's fame intrigued organized baseball on the mainland. In the fall of 1906, the press in San Francisco reported that En Sue Pung and Hawaiian southpaw Barney Joy would be offered a chance to try out with the San Francisco Seals of the relatively prestigious Pacific Coast League (PCL). Indeed, by the end of the year the *Washington Post* proclaimed that the Seals' offer had been accepted by both Joy and Pung. However, while Joy showed up at the Seals' training camp, Pung did not. Perhaps Pung's failure to appear on the mainland in the spring of 1907 was voluntary. He may have preferred to stay in Hawai'i—and given the Bay Area's historical anti-Chinese political culture and a losing fight with Mother Nature due to the devastating earthquake in April 1906, who could blame him?

However, inspired by the racialized xenophobia prevalent in the Bay Area, the Seals may well have changed their mind and asked Pung not to report to spring training. Still, interest in Pung as a mainland professional continued. In 1908, Frank Chance, a Hall of Fame first sacker and manager of the Chicago Cubs, returned from a trek to the islands claiming he would like to bring "a Chinese boy named En Sue" to the Cubs training facility. Other mainland pros who had visited Hawai'i with Chance also expressed admiration for En Sue Pung. Around the same time, the mainland press noted Pung's track performances. Readers of the *Washington Post* learned that he had broken the American record in the 50-yard dash with a time of 5.2 seconds. Pung was unsurprisingly then hailed by the Honolulu press for his baserunning skills. The *Pacific Commercial Advertiser* quipped after one game in 1912, "He should have been arrested a number of times, but the police claim they are powerless to arrest him as the laws of the country do not cover base stealing."[25]

Nisei Masayoshi "Andy" Yamashiro was another speed burner in the outfield. Because he was a Nikkei on a team advertised as Chinese, Yamashiro played under the surname of "Yim." Yamashiro's father was a prominent Japanese community leader and owner of a hotel which became a gathering place for striking Nikkei agricultural workers in the region during the 1900s and 1910s. Further, the elder Yamashiro served as treasurer of a Nikkei labor organization known as the Higher Wages Association and was indicted but not tried as a co-conspirator in the attempted murder of an antistrike Japanese language newspaper editor. Andrew Yamashiro was born in Spreckelsville on the island of Maui, which suggests his parents were part of the large contingent of Japanese laborers recruited by Claus Spreckels to work on his sugar plantation. As a Traveler, he formed an enduring friendship with the Chinese Buck Lai, who later insisted that the outfielder was fine with his pseudonym of "Yim."[26]

Counting on their speed and defense, the Travelers generally managed themselves when it came to baseball. There was, therefore, no Traveler counterpart to John McGraw or Connie Mack to guide them to baseball nirvana. They had learned baseball on the islands and refined their education by playing on the mainland. One of the ballplayers, either Albert Akana, Lang Akana, Apau Kau, Vernon Ayau, Kan Yen Chun, or Lai Tin, served as captain or field manager. And while some mainland observers noted signs of baseball ignorance during the 1912 maiden trek to the mainland, later years saw less evidence of mental mistakes. In other words, the Travelers could be beaten, but they rarely beat themselves.[27]

The Consumer Culture and Baseball

The Travelers not only were an accomplished team, capable of defeating nearly all amateur and many play-for-pay nines on the mainland. They were also entertaining and fit well into an age of vaudeville, silent films, and ragtime music—an age in which popular culture as well as the Travelers traversed cultural borders.

This all seemed to correspond to a budding American consumer culture about which many formidable cultural historians have written extensively.

This consumer culture expected Americans to seek and pay for enjoyment. Doing so would not only make them feel better but hopefully shield them somewhat from the vicissitudes of capitalism by narrowing the gap between production and consumption. Of course, cultural conservative and left-wing ideologues at the time railed against the time people spent at silent movies or ballparks when they should be home reading the Bible or *The Communist Manifesto*, but dominant American culture largely proposed that it was fine for people to have fun, especially if they did not overdo it and, of course, paid for their enjoyment.[28]

Commercialized spectator sports in America proved vital in fostering and justifying the development of the consumer culture. They inspired Americans to spend money on tickets to ballparks and other sports venues, where they would also pay for programs and refreshments. Urban transit systems rationalized operating outside of commuter hours because they could depend on passengers seeking transportation to the ball game. An assortment of businesses merchandising more food and drink clustered around sporting venues. As the popularity of spectator sports grew, the manufacturing and retail of athletic equipment burgeoned. Organized sports teams required athletic equipment, and regular folks who just wanted to play ball at picnics coveted gloves, bats, and balls. Through spectator sports, businesses could promote themselves by running ads in programs and placing ads on outfield fences of baseball parks. Newspapers and other forms of print media hoped to profit from aiding the marketing of spectator sports by boosting sporting events and sports celebrities. And celebrity athletes were merchandised as vaudeville and movie performers, as well as magazine and book authors, who took the money for whatever appeared in print under their names but rarely did the actual writing.[29]

Barnstorming baseball teams such as the Travelers interwove with all this. The popularity of organized baseball composed of locally based professional teams, structured in a hierarchical pattern from class D minor leagues to the major leagues, might well have dimmed the financial prospects of traveling teams. Indeed, organized baseball exploited local boosterism intently. Fans were expected "to root for the home team" against other nines from rival towns and cities. Barnstorming teams both collaborated with and resisted organized baseball's hegemony. To thrive financially, barnstorming teams needed to entertain because they were always on the road and could not count on the indulgence of hometown rooters. For most baseball fans, that meant they had to play well or at least well enough to challenge the local team and excite its supporters. But playing well was not always enough. There had to be something special about traveling teams. If major leaguers or well-known former major leaguers joined up, a barnstorming team was marketed as both good and special, especially in towns and cities without major league franchises. Otherwise, fans were frequently lured by the relative "otherness" of the ballplayers. For example, various Bloomer Girl nines trekked the United States in order to attract baseball fans not familiar with the idea of women competently playing baseball. The Chicago American Giants, a notable and talented African American baseball team, might schedule a 1914 game in Santa Cruz, California, where fans rarely saw African Americans, let alone African Americans masterfully playing baseball. In Nebraska, an entrepreneur by the name of Guy Green organized a team of barnstorming Native Americans. Subsequently, he assembled a traveling team partly made up of Issei residing in California and advertised it as "Green's Japs." In addition, Green launched a traveling team of Hawaiians in 1913. Seeking to exploit the Hawaiians as exotic, Green concentrated on drawing fans in the rural American Midwest—fans who might be curious about seeing authentic Hawaiians in action.[30]

Hawai'i and mainland promoters of the Travelers hoped to exploit the team's talent and their exoticized novelty. Yet whether by choice or not, the Travelers offered more than just their baseball expertise or their real or presumed Chinese ancestry. Mainland observers noted that they entertained spectators before the game by engaging in "shadow ball"—a performance in which the participants acrobatically threw and caught an invisible ball. During the game, they avidly coached one another in various languages while occasionally and humorously ridiculing opponents and umpires. Several of the Travelers, moreover, were skilled musicians and singers, entertaining select fans at parties and other social gatherings with their repertoire of Hawaiian music and "American rag."[31]

For the thousands of mainlanders who gained admission to Traveler games, expectations were largely cultivated by a mixture of Orientalism and primitivism. In Europe and North America, Orientalism and primitivism inspired cultural practices that depicted nonwhite people globally as substantially, and most likely inherently, incapable of mastering the virtues and even the vices of Western civilization. However, we should mine these cultural practices for their contradictions. On the one hand, they articulated the kind of arrogance that justified European and American imperialism, as well as such horrors as Jim Crow, the Chinese Exclusion Act, and the Indian Removal Act. They argued that materializing out of Europe, Western civilization created the modern world of factories, railroads, airplanes, automobiles, skyscrapers, telegraph lines, immunizations, machine guns, and baseball. At best, those who did not naturally share in the inheritance of Western civilization could mimic modern behavior. At worst, they not only failed to evolve the capacity to reproduce the triumphs of the West but also were dangerously resistive to Western hegemony. Nonetheless, Orientalism and primitivism harbored a critique of Western modernity. Whether mid-nineteenth-century transcendentalists or early twentieth-century antimodernists, some intellectuals wondered whether a world of factories, railroads, airplanes, automobiles, skyscrapers, telegraph lines, immunizations, machine shops, and modern sports competition merited all that much celebration. Perhaps people who had stalled or been stalled in their cultural advancement were somehow happier because they were closer to nature, to spiritual truth, and to one another.[32]

Entrepreneurs such as P. T. Barnum and Buffalo Bill Cody recognized that Orientalism and primitivism sold. Regardless of whether inspired by a sense of superiority or curiosity, nineteenth- and early twentieth-century Americans, Barnum and Cody believed, wanted to gawk at exotic "Orientals" and "primitives." This was not just because the objects of their gazes might be conjoined twins like the famed Thai brothers of Chinese ancestry, Chang and Eng Bunker. And it was not just because they enjoyed hooting at the grunting and cavorting "Wild man of Borneo." Rather, Barnum exhibited a small group of Qing dynasty Chinese of both sexes and various ages. All these persons had to do was act normally from their perspectives, and the members of this "Chinese family" would, he expected, convince onlookers that they were witnessing something very exotic and freakish. Likewise, many years later, Buffalo Bill Cody would market the American Indians in his employ as whooping savages but also present them engaged in rather mundane activities as well because he knew that to many Americans, Indians exuded exoticism just because they were Indians.[33]

Orientalism has a geographical foundation, originally referring to people who were born in or were perceived as able to claim descent from those born in regions of the world located east of Europe. Scholar Edward Said traced its historical origins to a widespread intellectual response to Western imperialism encountering and colonizing Egyptians, Persians, South Central Asians, and East Asians. Said described Orientalism as "a Western style for dominating, restructuring, and having authority over the Orient." In Orientalism, race combined with culture to essentialize "Orientals" as not only irrevocably different from Westerners but also inferior in significant and often irreparable ways.[34]

Rudyard Kipling put the matter tragically well when he wrote "East is East, and West is West, and never the twain shall meet." Yet like many Orientalists, Kipling acknowledged the individual Asian's capacity for decency, courage, and intelligence. Westerners, he declared, would never understand Asians or vice versa. Westerners needed to assert whatever technological and military superiority they had gained over Asia to protect themselves from those Asians who lacked the capacity for decency but might claim courage or crafty intelligence in abundance. More generously, Westerners needed to assert their superiority and shoulder the "white man's burden" to teach Asians and other nonwhite peoples at least the rudiments of Western civilization, including, for American imperialists, sports such as baseball. Claiming the West as the norm and Westerners capable of a wide variety of behaviors, Orientalism ideologically boxed in and stressed the singular exoticness of quite diverse Asian peoples, as well as Middle Eastern and North African peoples. It proved handy not just for imperialists but for marketers of Asian performers and performances in Europe and North America. In the nineteenth and early twentieth centuries, white Americans may well have been convinced that seeing Asians was strange enough but seeing them do seemingly unexpected things like playing baseball.[35]

That the Travelers came from Hawai'i evoked primitivism as well as Orientalism. The haoles who took charge of the islands' political affairs in the 1890s rationalized their political and legal legitimacy by claiming that Hawaiians were too primitive for self-government in a world journeying toward the modernity of the twentieth century. While primitivism fastened on the racial and/or cultural deficiency of the people who had inhabited the Hawaiian Islands for hundreds of years, it frequently lingered in the same environment that bred the notion of the noble savage in North American white-Indian relations. Antimodernist intellectuals in the West warned against the deadly plunge into a cultural realm ruled by technology and the profit motive. They praised the craftsmanship of the traditional artisan and summoned the premodern, magical worlds of hobbits and magical rings. They often insisted that the primitives still existing as the twentieth century dawned had much to teach in terms of humanity's relationship to nature, to spirituality, and to one another. And just as there was no harm in remembering fondly one's youth, they argued, there seemed no harm in remembering the existent legacy of humanity's youth.[36]

For capitalism's promoters, it would not do for people to sink too deeply into premodernism. Civilized people should spend considerably more time working than surfing and should take aspirin rather than consult a shaman. Still, promoters on both sides of the Pacific profited if they convinced mainlanders that they could safely revisit humanity's past by vacationing in Hawai'i or, if one had neither the time nor the hefty bank account, purchasing a sheet of supposedly authentic Hawaiian music and a ukulele. Thus, just as Hawai'i was incorporated into the U.S. empire, it was increasingly commercialized. Business interests on the islands and the mainland merchandised a version of traditional Hawaiian culture unmenacing to mainland whites—a quaintly exotic, soothing, and reinvigorating culture. That is, moments spent with nature and nature's children would calm the nerves frayed by modernity and strengthen the body and mind from renewed assaults by time clocks and congested streets.[37]

The Travelers, their island and mainland promoters hoped, would market Hawai'i effectively. They would appear in public as middle-class American young men yet rendered unique by race and culture. Sponsors in Hawai'i furnished them with promotional literature, extolling the virtues of the islands as a tourist's delight, an investor's dream, and a white resident's haven. They would tote ukuleles and express their talents as musicians and singers to remind mainlanders that in Hawai'i the locals represented little threat to white hegemony. In the process, they built on the growing popularity of hapa Hawaiian music—that is, Hawaiian-themed music commodified by white, mainland composers and music publishers. Hawaiian musicians, moreover, toured the mainland at the same time as the Travelers and would, by way of use of such instruments as the steel guitar, help shape the way Americans made music for decades to come. Whether in music or baseball, these performers from Hawai'i conveyed capitalism, and they were also conveyors of racial hierarchy as well as cultural practices challenging that hierarchy. To repeat, American entrepreneurs, such as Barnum and Cody, understood that they could profit from whites willing to pay money to see non-whites perform publicly. However, the circumstances of those performances had to be defined carefully. That is, they might show glimpses of nonwhite humanity, as Cody's "Wild West Shows" did, but they could not seriously challenge white hegemony or the salience of the market.[38]

Athletic performances of nonwhite athletes sometimes proved difficult for white supremacy to contain. "Anthropology Days," staged under the promotional banner of the St. Louis World Fair and Olympiad in 1904, allowed sightseers to view people widely perceived as primitive struggling to master Olympic-style events. The event was an intriguing attempt to marry objective social science to the consumer culture, and the results were predictably ludicrous to many onlookers, convincing them that to reach the highest stages of athletic competition one had to be white and civilized. Yet at the same event, a contingent of female basketball players from Ft. Shaw Indian School in Montana appeared in St. Louis to demonstrate their talent at defeating white teams. While many might have been surprised and even aggrieved to observe young indigenous women mastering a game that demanded athletic finesse, intelligence, and teamwork from its most successful practitioners, they might have taken solace in the belief that white educators had shaped the Ft. Shaw hoopsters into a winning combination—thus confirming the prevailing racial hierarchy and the policy of Indian assimilation.[39]

White supremacists could also scoff, at least in the early twentieth century, that basketball, especially basketball played by young females, was not all that important. But college football and prizefighting were important in the early twentieth-century sports world, and both sports stood out to white supremacists as vital battlegrounds for white males to test and ultimately claim their superiority. Hence when the Carlisle Indian School's football team defeated some of the best college football teams around, and when African American Jack Johnson humiliated white opponents in the ring, white supremacists had some explaining to do.

Gender and racial ideologies intertwined to clarify why physically healthy, white young men were humbled on various gridirons and in prizefighting rings in the early twentieth century. The vaunted superiority of white males in sports such as American football and prizefighting turned on their presumptive manliness. White supremacists, when alluding to sport, typically defined manliness in not just physical but intellectual and emotional terms as well. Thus, to be manly meant harnessing appropriate physical skills, courage, intelligence, and the attribute of sportsmanship. The American Indians who performed for Carlisle were often lauded for possessing some or all of the necessary manly characteristics. At the same time, the popular press often diminished their accomplishments by referring to their deceptive tactics, doing more than just hinting that their victories, like those of American Indian soldiers, came at the expense of fair play. If the Carlisle gridders were truly the equal of the whites they opposed, they would not resort to such trickery as the forward pass and other tactics designed to avoid an honest physical confrontation with their white adversaries.[40]

At least with the Carlisle football team and the Ft. Shaw hoopsters, white supremacists could comfort themselves that American Indian athletic success demonstrated the beneficence of U.S. Indian education policy. The impact of Jack Johnson proved more difficult to brush off. For many white American sports fans in the late nineteenth and early twentieth centuries, the heavyweight champion of the world represented manliness even if individual title holders, such as John L. Sullivan, might fall short of proper manliness outside the ring. Jack Johnson was an African American who not only physically outmatched his opponents but outsmarted and outlasted them as well. Black, as well as other presumptively primitive, athletes were seen by some white supremacists as capable of athletic achievements in events that required short-term speed but not intelligence, courage, or endurance. Jack Johnson confounded such assumptions, rendering it important for racial supremacists to unearth a "Great White Hope" to put him in his place.[41]

To perform as a successful barnstorming team for five years, the Travelers had to walk a tightrope over a racial maelstrom. They could threaten the racial hierarchy of early twentieth-century America—they could do what "Orientals" were not supposed to do and defeat white teams at a game that white American males considered their own preserve. Otherwise, why would people bother to pay good money to see submissive incompetents losing time and again to superior white nines? But the Travelers had to swerve away from too vigorously transgressing America's racial norms. Like subsequent nonwhite barnstorming sports teams, they had to smile their way to victory, demonstrate gratitude to their white hosts, and assure them that it was all a game and that the racial hierarchy, while a bit tattered, remained intact when their local heroes went home humbled by brown-skinned ballplayers.[42]

Organized and Independent Baseball

The Travelers opposed teams residing mostly outside the confines of organized baseball. Eventually, individual Travelers played on such teams based on the East Coast—in Buck Lai's case, for several years. Before and after their Traveler experiences, these ballplayers were aided by the inability of organized baseball to clear away alternatives such as outlaw, semiprofessional, African American, and barnstorming teams. Organized baseball cast a wary eye on such aggregations even though the latter paradoxically could both subvert and reinforce the game's professional establishment.[43]

Since the 1880s, the National Agreement sought to sustain organized baseball's legitimacy. Reflective of modernizing capitalism's tendency toward consolidation in the economic and political spheres, the National Agreement merged the three most powerful professional baseball leagues at the time: the National League, the American Association, and the Northwestern League. By the early 1900s it had spread its wings and encompassed professional leagues from coast to coast and added the American League to couple with the National as organized baseball's two "big leagues." Meanwhile, the National Agreement instituted a three-person National Commission to oversee and enforce the terms of the National Agreement. Profit, but not "free enterprise," manufactured the National Agreement's calling card. Professional ballplayers were banned from "jumping" from one franchise to another. Moreover, team owners and managers were banned from encouraging such jumping. Organized baseball chiefly deployed the "reserve clause" as its major weapon, essentially binding professional ballplayers to the franchises for which they had signed contracts. It was all quite one-sided. Teams could release ballplayers under contract to them anytime they found it convenient, but ballplayers could not leave a franchise while under contract. Otherwise, they faced blacklisting.[44]

Generally, nonwhite ballplayers and entrepreneurs were left alone by organized baseball. But that was hardly reason to celebrate, especially for athletes fully capable of competing effectively against all the white elite ballplayers that graced American and National League teams in the early twentieth century. Since the 1880s, African American ballplayers were barred from organized baseball by an unwritten agreement stipulating that Jim Crow was just as welcomed by whites in the dugout as it was in the schoolhouse and streetcar. If not identified as Black, ballplayers perceived as nonwhite were somewhat more tolerated by organized baseball. Charles Bender and John Meyers, both of whom were notoriously nicknamed "Chief," were standout major league Indian ballplayers in the early twentieth century. As for Latinos, they were well advised not to appear too dark skinned; otherwise they would trip over the color line. A San Franciscan of Mexican ancestry, Vincent Nava was marketed as Cuban when he joined organized baseball in the early 1880s, probably because his skin appeared too dark.[45]

A couple of Hawaiians showed up in organized baseball during the early twentieth century. Barney Joy was a skilled left-handed pitcher who made the trek in 1907 to the San Francisco Seals training camp, where he not only earned a spot on the team as a starting pitcher but attracted fans curious to see a "Kanaka" hurler and eventually attracted interest from major league clubs. The National League's Boston Braves signed him, but reports circulated that Joy was Black. Reports of his African ancestry were denied by the Braves management, but they may have stifled Joy's interest in returning to the mainland in 1908 or the Braves' interest in encouraging that return. Another Hawaiian from Honolulu, John B. Williams, probably surpassed Joy as a pitcher. In 1911, Williams debuted as a pitcher for Sacramento of the PCL, and by 1912 he was the team's ace. A right-handed power pitcher, Williams remained in Sacramento through the 1913 season, but the American League's Detroit franchise signed him for 1914.

Consequently, Williams became the first Hawaiian to play big league baseball. He was, however, not successful as American League batters cuffed him around a little too regularly, and "Honolulu Johnny" was dispatched to the minors, where he lingered for the rest of his professional career on the mainland.[46]

Beyond the erratically expanding borders of organized baseball, independent baseball offered something of a not always comforting haven to ballplayers and entrepreneurs who did not fit the sports professional establishment's mold out of either volition or bigotry. Some players simply saw the temptation of organized baseball as a diversion from making reliable incomes performing steady jobs or running their own businesses. Others were doubtlessly wary of the discipline organized baseball might impose on them. Still others, of course, did not have much of a choice. That is, they were not considered sufficiently light skinned or, for that matter, sufficiently male to play organized baseball at any level. Independent baseball, moreover, furnished Jewish, Black, and, in the case of Buck Lai, Chinese would-be sports entrepreneurs' prospects of running baseball teams to a far greater extent than organized baseball cultivated by a largely white, native-born, Protestant establishment.[47]

Independent baseball offered fans of the game some alternatives as to how they might spend their leisure hours. Organized baseball had covered the map of the continental United States adequately by the early 1900s, although fans in the Far West might wonder why they could not enjoy major league baseball more directly than articles and box scores in newspapers. Still, when the local team was playing away games, especially on weekends, baseball fixes had to be filled, while promoters pondered why stands had to be empty. Moreover, Sunday laws impinged on commercialized professional sports such as baseball. By demanding in some cities and larger towns that businesses close down on Sunday, these laws effectively stilled organized baseball on the one day of the week nearly everyone could count on as a day off. Independent ball games, where spectators were not charged admission but hopefully would generously contribute money to a passed hat, evaded Sunday laws.[48]

Independent baseball nines substantially expressed the disparate ways that early twentieth-century Americans forged communities. That is, they embodied civic, neighborhood, spiritual, class, occupational, and political as well as racial and ethnic pride. They nurtured loyal followings of fans quite willing to spend some time and money watching them take on rivals. However lovable some organized baseball teams could be, they were, after all, made up of young men who other than being uniformly white and nearly uniformly gentile came from all parts of the country and identified with all kinds of social, economic, and political backgrounds. Shuffled off to different franchises during their careers, professionals in organized baseball might find themselves in St. Paul, Little Rock, Jersey City, or Philadelphia. While the lives of independent ballplayers were often quite peripatetic, some early twentieth-century fans could imagine them as envoys of their group consciousness during a tumultuous, transitional period in

American history. Like family and religion, baseball, independent as well as organized, frequently materialized as a "haven in a heartless world."[49]

Independent baseball teams promoted local and corporate capitalism. In Philadelphia, for example, major department stores such as Wannamaker's, Lit Brothers, and Strawbridge and Clothiers sponsored baseball teams in the 1910s. Commercial teams effectively advertised the businesses they represented, especially if they were good. In addition, since some of these sponsors built their own ballparks, baseball could expand their revenue flow. Independent baseball proved quite capable of serving corporate capitalism. The Pennsylvania Railroad established baseball leagues presumably to advertise its benevolence to employees and patrons.[50]

Conclusion

The Travelers traipsed the often blurred boundaries separating organized and independent baseball. Some of the nines the Travelers opposed were minor league aggregations perched on the lower rungs of organized baseball's hierarchy, but they also managed a few dates with teams representing the relatively elite PCL. Further, after they left the Travelers, Buck Lai, Andy Yamashiro, Vernon Ayau, and Alfred Yap competed in organized baseball as minor leaguers.[51]

The minor leagues served a larger, less tangible function than training and warehousing professional ballplayers. However marginal to the success of American consumer capitalism, they helped expand and root organized baseball in America's soul. Yet, independent baseball, as represented by Buck Lai and his Traveler teammates, also carved out niches in American baseball history, however largely unacknowledged for many years by the sport's historians. As millions cheered the exploits of organized baseball and its heroes such as Babe Ruth and Ty Cobb, others cheered the exploits of perhaps physically less gifted ballplayers from the Hawaiian Islands as they traversed the American empire from Honolulu through the heartland of the United States to its Atlantic Coast.

3
The Travelers Take the Field

The *Hawaiian Star* asserted that $6,000 had been raised to finance an all-Chinese team's inaugural tour of the mainland in 1912. Hawai'i's business and sports worlds had earlier combined to finance Duke Kahanamoku's trek to the mainland. Coupled with Kahanamoku's journey, the all-Chinese team's excursion to the mainland, backers hoped, would enhance mainland investment, tourism, and consumption of Hawai'i's cash crops, as well as entice more mainlanders to the islands as permanent residents. But Honolulu's Chinese community also pitched in, seeking to gain respectful representation in a land that fostered pernicious anti-Chinese legislation.[1]

Of course, Honolulu-based backers believed that an all-Chinese team would represent Hawai'i adequately as ballplayers. Even though they lost more than they won on their journeys, the Waseda and Keio University nines boosted the reputation of Japanese baseball on the mainland, and sponsors of the all-Chinese contingent hoped that the ballplayers could at least match the success of the Japanese teams. Indeed, given the ability of an all-Chinese nine to better Waseda and Keio when they showed up in Hawai'i, Hawai'i Chinese merchants, according to Vernon Ayau, speculated that an elite squad of Chinese ballplayers from the islands would make a more positive impression on mainlanders than the Japanese. Unfortunately, En Sue Pung's decision to remain in Hawai'i blindsided the initial Traveler trek. The *Hawaiian Star* claimed that Pung wanted assurances from the promoters that he would not have to paddle back home in a canoe. He reasonably worried about the fiscal foundations of the trip. Unlike all the other ballplayers, Pung had a wife and a growing family as well as a decent job in Honolulu.[2]

Yet, while promoters anticipated that the Chinese barnstormers would reveal themselves as credible ballplayers, they also expected the Travelers to entertainingly advertise Hawai'i. For example, the *Pacific Commercial Advertiser* reported that the ballplayers would parade around the town in which they were scheduled to play a game in "traditional" Chinese blouses and trousers. While doing so, they would wear fake queues attached to their ball caps. They then were supposed to remove the blouses, trousers, and queues and appear as regular ballplayers once they took the field. The Travelers did not seem to have done much of this, unless in jest. But while they did not perform Chinese, or at least mainlanders' version of Chinese, they did perform Hawaiian, or once again a mainlander's version of Hawaiian, by carrying their ukuleles and guitars around the States, singing Hawaiian and hapa Hawaiian songs.[3]

The Honolulu press focused attention on the impending all-Chinese venture during the early months of 1912. The *Hawaiian Star* noted that factions within the Chinese baseball world endangered the approaching trip. The *Star* complained that two groups, including the ultimately successful one headed by Sam Hop, vied for leadership of the various Chinese players in Honolulu. The daily urged abandoning the proposed mainland trip unless the Chinese united. If the trek proved successful, the *Hawaiian Star* later speculated, inspired promoters would authorize another tour in 1913, although it lamented that fans would miss some of Honolulu's best performers in the Oahu Baseball League. Meanwhile, an unrestrained *Honolulu Evening Bulletin* extolled the approaching trip of the Travelers as "baseball history."[4]

At the outset, Honolulu's press expressed little concern about the logistics of moving a dozen or so young men from Hawai'i to the U.S. mainland and then from one part of the mainland to another. Yet scheduling proved troublesome throughout the Travelers' tours. That is, the ballplayers were expected to cover as much of the mainland as possible, but linger longest on the urban East Coast, where they were promoted as exoticized novelties to a population who might respond generously to Orientalism's allure. However, booking Travelers games was complicated and produced frequently road-weary young men. Robert Yap, a Chinese American musician living in Chicago but born and raised in Hawai'i, initially assumed responsibility for scheduling. His brother Edward resided in Honolulu and served as the team's manager. Both Yaps were uncles of future Traveler first sacker Alfred Yap. As team manager, Edward presumably oversaw travel arrangements, lodging, and financial matters for the inaugural journey, while assuming scheduling responsibilities from his brother. As a booking agent, Edward Yap proved either softhearted or inept. Perhaps he was concerned about tiring the frequently exhausted players as they traveled through the mainland. Nonetheless, according to the Honolulu sporting press and at least one of the Travelers, Edward booked a monetarily insufficient number of games by the time the ballplayers reached New York City. The investors of the previously mentioned $6,000 expected a return. Moreover, money was constantly needed for travel, lodging, food, and other expenses.[5]

Writing under the pseudonym of Konohi Fat Choy (KFC), a correspondent to the *Hawaiian Star* and apparently a Chinese barnstormer criticized the team management. The April 24 edition published KFC's concerns that the team would even fail to complete its journey across the mainland owing to a lack of bookings. However, he was told that because of their exoticness, the Travelers might do better on the East Coast. Displaying class chauvinism, he wrote, "In the East... tame Chinamen are a novelty." The May 9 edition published the ballplayer's declaration that the Travelers' "management was unbelievably bum." He confided that substitute ballplayers were left behind to save money on travel expenses.[6]

While they were in New York City, the Travelers ran into Nat Strong. The son of Welsh immigrants, Strong was a creative, ambitious baseball entrepreneur who worked the netherworld of independent baseball—semiprofessional, barnstorming, and mostly African American nines. In the 1890s, Strong started building his empire in independent baseball by assuming the managerial reins of the Murray Hill baseball club out of Manhattan. In the early 1900s, Strong maintained his power base from a lower Manhattan office in the then famous skyscraper called the World Building, so called because it housed the *New York World* newspaper.[7]

To his credit, Strong recognized, as too few white entrepreneurs did, the talent and drawing power of Black ballplayers. Yet he wanted to profit from that talent and drawing power as much as possible—African American managers and players claimed excessively so. Strong would help African American nines schedule games, but he expected what many Black baseball entrepreneurs and ballplayers considered an unfair cut of the action. According to baseball historian Neil Lanctot, Strong and other important white booking agents like Eddie Gottlieb usually got 5–10 percent of the take. Cum Posey, who ran the Negro League Homestead Grays, cared little for Strong but admitted he gave Black teams needed exposure. Lanctot's judgment of Strong is, in any event, severe: "If not an actual 'menace' to black baseball, there is little doubt that Strong was primarily driven by profit and had little interest in developing the industry into a stable institution.... Strong was openly hostile to any organization that might potentially cut his bookings by weaning black teams away from their reliance on independent games with white semi-pro teams." Thus, when Strong, then in his mid-thirties, emerged as the booking agent for the Travelers, the ballplayers were fortunate to find someone who would get games for them, but unfortunate in finding someone who could very well exploit them, although there is no evidence of any discord between the Travelers and Strong.[8]

In 1912, Strong used the clever strategy of convincing local promoters and prospective opponents that the Chinese barnstormers were beatable but respectable enough as ballplayers to entice paying customers. Strong confided to a New London, Connecticut, ball club, "These Chinks can't pole. They're all right on fielding, but they're tramps with the lumber." As it turned out, the Travelers could hit: "The chinks were there with a slap and they nearly got the verdict" against New London, according to one newspaper account. Unfortunately, an error by Lang Akana let in a key run for the home team: "If the chink left fielder hadn't thought he was a Turk instead of a chink and kissed the ground with his back to the sun in the fifth inning," the Travelers might have won.[9]

Called "an exceptionally active man in his line of work" by the *Hawaiian Star*, Strong filled the Travelers' itinerary up nicely—perhaps too nicely. Apparently, the idea was to get the Travelers to the West Coast early enough to take advantage of the college baseball season wrapping up in May and June. Once on the West Coast, they did not linger. That the region was the hotbed of anti-Asian politics in the United States might have motivated the Travelers' short stay in California in addition to the decision to keep them out of Oregon and Washington. More likely, Strong figured that the biggest paydays would come in his neck of the woods—the urban East Coast—and he deemed moving the ballplayers east of the Rockies quickly as vital.[10]

Arriving in California in early to mid March, the Travelers usually opposed Stanford and the University of California in the San Francisco Bay Area. Then, they might play a few games in California's Central Valley. Only once did the Travelers venture to Los Angeles, where in 1914 they beat an Occidental College nine. Because Pacific Coast League teams trained in the Golden State, the Travelers were able to book a couple of games against high-level minor league teams. In San Jose, for example, they were barely beaten by the Salt Lake City nine in 1915, while the Portland Beavers clobbered them a few days later in a game played in the Central Valley.[11]

While the barnstormers enjoyed the sites of the San Francisco Bay Area, they found the weather upon their arrival inhospitably cold. Seeing snow on the Sierras may have been a rare treat for the young men from Hawai'i, but doing so presaged games in elements unknown on the islands. Writing for the *Honolulu Evening Bulletin*, sports editor Laurence Reddington informed readers that the typically expert fielders in Honolulu learned that cold and wet hands made for messy errors in Utah in April 1912. Indeed, March and April weather in the Far West and the prospects of too many sloppily played games and cancellations may have prompted the team to journey through the warmer southwest from 1914 through 1916.[12]

Dizzying travel schedules perhaps proved more lamentable than the weather. Beyond the Golden State, the Travelers played several games a week. Sometimes, this meant a number of games in the same area. Too often, however, it meant catching trains that crisscrossed states and state lines. While he valued the trip to the mainland in 1913, outfielder Sing Hung Hoe did not miss the traveling and the "quick-order dinners at the crowded railroad stations and 'dog houses,' with many curious eyes staring at you." Nor did he profess nostalgia for "the noisy night trains or on the twelfth or fifteenth story of some hotels."[13]

While on the East Coast, the Travelers played most of their games in and around New York City and Philadelphia, although they would roam into western Pennsylvania, upstate New York, New England, and, one year, eastern Canada. By the time the Travelers reached the urban mid-Atlantic, it was late May or early June—a time when college baseball schedules wound down. However, the urban East Coast constituted a hotbed of semiprofessional and talented Black teams. Since Strong was a dominating figure in New York City among teams outside organized baseball's realm, he could easily book games for the islanders, although relatively few games were scheduled against Black nines. In any event, several of the Travelers' games on the urban East Coast drew overflow crowds of 5,000–10,000 fans.[14]

The 1912 Journey

Known in Honolulu as the "all-Chinese," the team was often promoted as representing a nonexistent Chinese University or College of Hawaii. Sam Hop, who trained and then managed the team from 1912 through 1914, maintained to Loui Leong Hop that this was done to soothe mainland colleges squeamish about their undergraduates playing nonstudent teams. Thus, the artifice of the Travelers playing for a trumped-up four-year school was created and sustained by promoters and the players. Publicizing the Travelers as enrolled in a university made further sense given that Chinese students were exempted from the Chinese Exclusion Act. The ballplayers could, therefore, fulfill the desire of Chinese community leaders in Honolulu to represent an emerging middle class, modernizing Chinese diaspora. Still, the publicity surrounding something called the Chinese University of Hawaii confused the Hawai'i sporting press and Hawai'i baseball fans who knew better.[15]

The expected arrival of a baseball team consisting of young men of Chinese ancestry prompted the *Sporting Life* to title a March 1912 story "Not a Yellow Peril." Fans could expect, as the subtitle indicated, "a Chinese invasion of the United States in the near future to which there will be no armed resistance and whose bloodless battles will be fought upon the base ball fields of America." More seriously, the *Sporting Life* asserted that these ballplayers were born and raised in Hawai'i and "that the Chinese in Hawaii are good ball players is a fact well known to the Americans in the West." American military personnel stationed in the Pacific, in particular, understood that Chinese in Hawai'i could master the American national pastime. They found out that "the Chinese boys always take delight in defeating the American teams of the army and navy and the Japanese teams passing through Honolulu when coming to or returning from America." A generally accurate *Sporting Life* story observed that the team represented the Chinese Athletic Club, forged out of students "from the schools and colleges of that cosmopolitan city." In putting together its baseball team, the weekly published out of Philadelphia insisted, the CAC "takes in only the best men of the several school teams." Then, the *Sporting Life* contradicted itself by testifying that "boys coming to America on March 28 are students in the College of Hawaii, an institution of agricultural and mechanical arts." Meanwhile, it notified readers that "Chinese students" in various U.S. cities were readying a "royal welcome" for the Hawaiian visitors.[16]

The 1912 Travelers first stopped in the San Francisco Bay Area. There, they were greeted by a report in the *Oakland Tribune* provocatively and inaccurately headlined "China Sends Team of Stars to Show Us How to Play." The Travelers lost their first game to the University of California, but their performance raised eyebrows. Honolulu's *Pacific Commercial Advertiser* quoted a Bay Area newspaper to its readers—a newspaper that maintained that "the visitors played a fine brand of ball and surprised the spectators by their fast fielding and heavy hitting ability." After their opening game in Berkeley, the *Sporting Life* observed that the visiting ballplayers "are likely to open the eyes of Americans to the athletic ability of Chinese."[17]

As the Travelers moved eastward, they won more often than they lost, and even when they fell short of victory they performed credibly. The University of Utah nine beat the Travelers in the first of two games. And then after falling behind by ten runs in the second game, the Chinese bats exploded for twenty-two runs and a runaway victory. Lai Tin led the way with two grand slams. Chicago's *Day Book* ambiguously promoted an upcoming game between the Travelers and the University of Chicago by declaring, "The yellow peril, which has provided so many chances for jingoes to sling bunk, is menacing the University of Chicago this afternoon. . . . The Mongolians have taken to the game with avidity as have the Jap." The Travelers then met defeat at the hands of the University of Chicago nine. Interestingly, team manager Edward Yap arranged a pregame race between Lai Tin, dubbed with the orientalist term of "celestial" by the *Chicago Tribune*, and a University of Chicago athlete. Perhaps foreordaining what would happen to his team that day, Lai Tin lost the sprint.[18]

The Travelers journeyed to Cincinnati in early May to oppose the University of Cincinnati nine. A reporter for the *Cincinnati Times-Star* claimed to have made "an important discovery" while attending the game: "The Chinese baseball team is no yellow peril." After interviewing the players and manager Yap, the *Times-Star* writer contended, "Yellow Peril! Oh, No! These Chinamen are fellow citizen." They "live and vote under the stars and stripes." Edward Yap, described as a "fairly tall and strong young Chinaman," told the reporter that "we like baseball as much as you native Americans." The *Times-Star* added, "The players can speak English, Chinese, and Hawaiian, but they converse among themselves in clean English."[19]

The Travelers arrived in New York City for the first time in the second half of May. There, they played Fordham at the famed Polo Grounds. The *New*

York Tribune said the host nine was taking the game seriously since the visitors "are fast and hard-hitting." After the game, the *New York Sun* supplied interesting coverage of the ballplayers' New York City debut. The *Sun*'s journalist professed to replicate the team's cheer: "Brackity-de-ax-de ax, Brackity-de-ax-de-ax / Higgity-Hoggity-Higgity-Hog / Chinese Ball Team. Rah! Rah! Rah!" The *Sun* eased any worries readers might have had by stating that the cheer "isn't as terrifying as it sounds when a bunch of leather-lunged Celestials get together and spin it off—only the college yell of the Chinese baseball players from Honolulu." The ballplayers journeyed the mainland, according to the *Sun*, to show that Hawai'i was up to date when it came to matters such as America's national pastime. Even though Fordham emerged the victor, the *Sun* conceded that the game demonstrated the Chinese ballplayers were "more aggressive than most Americans suspect, especially in baseball." The Travelers' command of baseball struck the *Sun* as surprising, while exhibiting the sport's "international popularity."[20]

The *Sun*'s coverage linked the ballplayers to exotic Hawai'i and the no less exotic "Orient." It asserted, perhaps with tongue in cheek, that Chinese playing baseball constituted an important event in world history, "symbolizing a distinct change in the order of things for Mongol feet, never before seen except in a sandal, are now strutting the baseball diamonds in cleats. Orientals, also before pictured in their pajama-like blouses and trousers, are wearing regulation flannel ball suits, and heads adorned with silken caps seen mounting the coiled queues are now protected by long visored caps, over the close cropped hair."[21]

The *Sun* constructed a racialized cultural bridge linking the Travelers to the powerful Native American Carlisle Institute football team, which had downed or lost grudgingly to the best college elevens in the nation: "Deep-seated craft and guile lurks as deeply in the Chinese breast as it does in the redskin's, and the almond-eyed visitors are forever uncorking the most remarkable and unheard of plays at the most inopportune and at least favorable time." That is, the Chinese ballplayers bunted when they should have hit away and hit away when they should have bunted. The Traveler pitchers, according to the *Sun*, did not command great stuff "but manage to outguess and outfigure the batters with alarming regularity." They seemed, moreover, to ignore base runners, while concentrating on the batter. The outfielders "betrayed a deep intimacy of the great American game." As for fielding in general, "the Chinese, agile as wildcats, follow up the ball in wonderful style—in fact, their field work bears on the sensational." As batters, they were not easy to strike out, although the *Sun* advised them to bunt and "place hit" more often than slug the ball for distance. Thus, "the first Chinese college team" to play in the United States was competitive with "American" college nines. And the amazed spectators who watched the game noted "that a speedier game than that displayed by the Chinese could not be desired. They know every angle and their disadvantage is they lack the science imported by professional coaching."[22]

The *Sun* praised the Hawaiians as "true sportsmen." The Travelers appeared to accept umpires' decisions graciously and their own mistakes good-naturedly. They encouraged teammates who had just committed errors. And they deserved admiration for undertaking the longest road trip of any college team. Not very subtly, the daily informed readers that "an amusing accessory of the visitors was their cheering section, which poured out a continual stream of wash talk and laundry advice to their undersized diamond heroes."[23]

While staying in the New York metropolitan area, the Travelers encountered the Ridgewood nine, a formidable semiprofessional aggregation. The all-Chinese nine lost, but the *Brooklyn Daily Eagle* lauded their performance. It reported that Lai Tin and Apau Kau socked home runs and that the former initiated a "scintillating" triple play. All in all, the *Eagle* maintained, "the Orientals conducted themselves with dignity and by their gentlemanly bearing and sportsmanlike playing won the friendship of all." Indeed, New York City warmed up to the Travelers. They were even invited to sing at the prestigious Midtown Waldorf-Astoria Hotel. According to Buck Lai, Lang Akana led the team in rehearsing for the event. Apparently, the concert's promoters asked the ballplayers to sing Chinese songs, but they only knew tunes composed in Hawaiian. Thus, while they performed the Hawaiian compositions to much applause, Lai declared the New York City press insisted they sang Chinese lyrics.[24]

The Travelers attracted attention in part because they were novel and therefore easy for the press to demean, but also because they were stunningly good at baseball. In early June 1912, a Buffalo newspaper promoted an upcoming game between "pigmies" and "giants." "Little Apau," who was not really all that short, would pitch for the "sallow-skinned followers of Confucius." The Travelers lost to the Simon Pures nine, 4–1. Still, the *Buffalo Courier* praised Lai Tin as "a very clever third baseman" and blamed a rain-soaked field for slowing down the visitors on the base paths. Moreover, it quoted an individual the *Courier* identified as the Chinese manager, who understood that fans on the mainland figured on seeing a "joke nine" when his team came to town. However, he hoped that the Travelers exceeded their expectations. Later in June, a manager of a Schenectady nine had the opportunity of booking either the Boston Red Sox, one of the best teams in the major leagues, or "the famous Chinese baseball team." Even though the talented Red Sox were World Series bound, the *Schenectady Gazette* asserted that either choice would prove equally compelling to fans. In late July, the *Binghamton News* announced the coming of the Travelers, claiming that the management of the local ballpark had gone to great expense to stage the event, which included a pregame parade around town and to the ballpark. In September, the Travelers were in Flint, Michigan, where they lost to the Flint independent nine, 3–0. However, the *Flint Journal* declared that the locals had to play well, "for the orientals put up a hard battle in every department."[25]

Race shadowed the Travelers in 1912. Canada embraced Chinese immigration restrictions as fervently as the United States. Thus, when the Travelers appeared at the Canadian border in order to play a game in Canada, they were initially turned away because they did not possess documents demonstrating U.S. citizenship. More seriously, the Travelers encountered the kind of humiliating discrimination widely suffered by African Americans. The *Sporting Life* reported late in August that the Chinese ballplayers were barred from a hotel in Pennsylvania. This marked the first time that they had been accorded such treatment, according to the *Sporting Life*, reminding us that while racialized as inferior in white America, the racism the Travelers experienced was less pernicious and systematic than would have been faced by a traveling team of African Americans. A hotel in Franklin, Pennsylvania, in the northwestern part of the state denied accommodations to the ballplayers even though, the *Sporting Life* insisted, they were "well-educated and have been entertained by some of the best people." The weekly added that the Chinese took out their anger on the local team, 14–4, before finding a place to sleep in nearby Oil City.[26]

The Travelers returned to the Midwest later in the summer. In Cleveland, the Chinese ballplayers confronted invidious press coverage. After a victory over the Tellings nine, the *Cleveland Plain Dealer* told readers that the Travelers' "coachers gesticulated like a bunch of monkeys" while yelling instructions "in Chinese, Japanese, Portuguese, Hawaiian all of which they can use with equal facility." At the same time, the *Plain Dealer* disclosed that individual Chinese ballplayers did not seem to mind letting mainlanders know about the kind of structural discrimination people of Chinese descent faced in the United States. Utility player Mon Yen Cheung was quoted condemning the Chinese Exclusion Act. Betraying a desire to forge an identity of class privilege not unusual for economically advantaged racialized minority group members, he maintained that even though it was aimed at Chinese immigrant laborers, the law affected all people of Chinese ancestry. Even if professionals and merchants, Chinese immigrants still had a hard time getting into America, the ballplayer contended, unless they bribed U.S. officials.[27]

Viewing the Travelers as island missionaries, Hawai'i's newspapers seemed pleased with the impression the Travelers were making. In June 1912, the *Hawaiian Gazette* hailed the shining press reviews accorded "the Honolulu Chinese team" on the mainland. The *Pacific Commercial Advertiser* in August declared the Travelers "a valuable promotion asset to Hawaii," asserting that in the mainland press, "talk about the Travelers and the Honolulu Chinese boys easily takes the palm these days. The boys seem to be everywhere." Without comment, the *Advertiser* cited an article from a Homestead, Pennsylvania, newspaper. The article addressed the musical talent of many of the ballplayers, assessing them as an "entertaining lot." At the same time, these U.S. citizens displayed "Oriental ways," nurtured in their "Oriental home." The author swallowed the fiction of the Chinese University of Hawaii, insisting it offered many competitive sports to students. As well, the Travelers apparently told the author that Hawai'i's population exhibited racial diversity and that Hawaiians were happy as Americans.[28]

Captain Albert Akana returned to the islands earlier than his teammates. He told the press that his employer granted him only a six-month leave of absence and he had to make sure he would have a job when he got back. Generally, he professed satisfaction with the journey to the mainland. Like KFC, though, he expressed discontent over the lack of funding for the team, declaring that the Travelers had to work hard to book enough games to keep the tour of the mainland financially afloat. He also complained about some of the team's opponents. Akana insisted that if the Travelers won the first of a series of games against a mainland opponent, the latter would too often seek strengthening by bringing in ringers. Such cheating led the Travelers to ultimately utilize Chinese and Hawaiian to vocalize signals to one another. Opponents may have thought such tactics were unfair, but the Travelers believed that they were not always treated justly by the home teams.[29]

The 1913 Journey

While the 1912 team won more games than it lost, Sam Hop and Nat Strong wanted to strengthen the Travelers. At the same time, a few key players preferred to stay home after a rigorous tour of the mainland. Some new names, then, joined the 1913 roster. Among the additions was a player who possessed indigenous but no apparent Chinese ancestry—Fred Markham, sometimes known as Denny. Possessing a Chinese father and a Hawaiian mother, Henry Kuali proved one of the hardest hitters on the team. Another key recruit was a talented Maui-based pitcher, Foster Robinson, who could claim Chinese descent on his mother's side. However, these three athletes presented marketing problems for Hop and Strong. If the nine presumably represented the Chinese of Hawai'i in one way or another, their surnames presented a problem. Thus, on the mainland, Markham was promoted as "Mark," Kuali became "Ah Lee," and for a while Robinson was called "Aheong."[30]

The Travelers stayed busy before relatively large crowds of spectators in 1913. Before June, they concentrated on whipping one college nine after another. When they shut out the University of Missouri, 2–0, the school newspaper extolled the visitors' skill in all aspects of baseball but pointed out they demonstrated a tendency toward "grandstanding." One observer of the Missouri game was quoted as asserting that the Travelers were the only "foreign" team that could hit. Vocal communication between the ballplayers amused and surprised spectators because they used varied languages and exhibited command of baseball slang, "rendered odd" because of a "Chinese twang."[31]

The 1913 Travelers encountered more trouble with professional nines than with college teams but, even so, usually performed credibly. A week after they took down St. Mary's College in California in their first game on the mainland, they arrived in Wichita, Kansas, to play a professional team known as the Wichita Jobbers. The Travelers got off to a fast start but eventually fell to the professionals. The correspondent who wrote the account of the game for the *Wichita Eagle* blamed the loss on the visitors' weariness from constant travel and their lack of a regular catcher in the lineup. The correspondent added that the Travelers looked better than college teams in the area and with a good night's rest might have upended the Jobbers. Happy he made the 1913 journey, outfielder En Sue Pung reported back home his pleasure with the large crowds attracted to the Travelers' games against independent professionals in New York City. He and his mates beat the Long Island nine, 8–2, before 3,000–4,000 people. In the process, Pung proudly asserted, the Travelers overcame the pitching of former big leaguer Andy Coakley. After the game, Pung maintained, the victors were treated to an "old fashioned Chinese dinner" by a couple of apparently well-off Columbia University students of Chinese descent.[32]

As planned by Strong, the Travelers immersed themselves in the independent baseball of the urban Middle Atlantic region. When the Travelers arrived in Wilmington, Delaware, in July 1913, a local newspaper could only surmise that they came as foreigners, dubbing them as members of the Hong Kong University. The account assured readers that they would find ballplayers who exhibited both the familiar and the exotic: "With the exception of their facial expressions, they look very much like Americans and dress in the American style." The *New York Evening World* acknowledged the ballplayers' stay in the city with an insulting, orientalist cartoon reproduced in the *Star-Bulletin* of July 30. The cartoon showed "pigtail Chinese" trying to play baseball. These ballplayers represented Chinese laundry operators and workers in the big city "on strike" from their usual occupation in order to take up the sport. The cartoon's caption reads, "Chinese Team Has Ruined New York's Laundry Business." The *Honolulu Star-Bulletin* could only speculate that "Chinese athletes of class were a novelty back east."[33]

In 1935, Buck Lai remembered a 1913 visit to Philadelphia, where the Travelers opposed a highly regarded semipro aggregation called the Stetson Hatters, sponsored by a company based in the Quaker City that manufactured the large-brimmed hats known best as worn by males in the West. Any visiting team that came into the Hatters' park and won were promised Stetson hats. He and his teammates, Lai recalled, wanted those hats. He also remembered that the Philadelphia fans appeared surprise that the visitors lacked queues. By the eighth inning, the Travelers held on to a one-run lead, but the Hatters loaded the bases with no outs when Apau Kau was brought in to pitch. Apau Kau's first couple of pitches seemed ominous from a Traveler standpoint as they landed wide of home plate. The base runner on third must have thought so too as he displayed a cavalier attitude that nothing would happen to him except to score the next run. Apau Kau and Lai, then, worked a neat pickoff play at third. The surprised base runner fled to home plate, where he was easily tagged out. The runner on second then moved to third, telling whomever would listen that he was not as gullible as his predecessor. Apau Kau, then, walked the bases full to presumably set up a potential double play. Instead of a double play, Apau Kau picked the overconfident runner off third and got the batter he was facing to pop up. Not resigned to serving white people's needs, the Travelers happily left the ballpark with their hats.[34]

The Travelers were supremely successful in 1913. From a won-lost perspective, they claimed a stunning 105 victories out of 144 games. In August the *Pacific Commercial Advertiser* lamented tongue in cheek that the Travelers "win so often it is really getting monotonous to the Hawaiian lads." From a promotional perspective, New York City honored the Travelers with a banquet at a Mandarin restaurant on Broadway in Lower Manhattan. According to the *Advertiser*, many of the city's dignitaries attended the event. Indeed, a photo of the banquet published in the *Advertiser* shows many well-dressed white people dining with the Travelers.[35]

Honolulu's other major newspaper appeared even more supportive of the barnstormers. An editorial in the *Honolulu Star-Bulletin* in May 1913 started by acclaiming the Travelers' victories on the mainland, but then took an interesting twist demonstrating the newspaper's allegiance to an early twentieth-century version of racial liberalism. Responding critically to a California state legislator's support of a law aimed at barring Asian immigrants from owning farmland in the state, the daily declared, "We have seen some freak arguments in favor of the California Alien Land Law but here is one that deserves to rank with the superlatively weird." That is, a representative from Fresno pointed out that the Travelers' dominance in baseball presaged what would happen if Asians became too comfortable in the Golden State; they would dominate California agriculture just as the Travelers were dominating America's national pastime. A few months later, sports editor Lawrence Reddington enthused that the East Coast was getting thoroughly schooled on Hawai'i thanks largely to the Travelers. Reddington wrote, "The boys are for Hawaii first, last, and always and whenever they catch an attentive ear, especially if said ear is attached to a member of the press fraternity they cut loose a lot of good stuff." Reddington allowed that Hop and his ballplayers were throwing around a great deal of "hooey" about the fictional Chinese University of Hawaii. But if Traveler promotional efforts bent the truth, Easterners deserved it because they "kept shipping missionaries to the 'heathen Chinese', but now the shoe is on the other foot and a dozen Chinese missionaries are preaching the gospel of Hawaii's prosperity to the New England 'natives.'" After the Travelers returned to the islands, the *Star-Bulletin* published an anonymous letter to the editor claiming that the Travelers not only helped put "Hawaii on the map but this year they have painted it in glaring colors. How many Americans on the coast and middle western states knew anything about Hawaii before previous to the Chinese invasion?"[36]

The 1914 Journey

In 1914, Hop added two Nikkei, brothers Chinito and Tsuneo Moriyama, and a Hawaiian, Luther Kekoa. The Moriyama brothers would play as "J. Chin" and "T. Chin," while Kekoa would be known as "Ako" or "Aki." The next year, the Travelers' Chinese identity was further diluted by the presence of Andy Yamashiro, who would play as "Yim." Possessing Hawaiian ancestry, pitcher George Bush and outfielder James Aylett would also make the journey in 1915. Bush's surname would appear in the box score as "Bo," while Aylett would appear as "Let." Looking back thirty years later, James Moriyama indicated that he and his brother found their pseudonyms humorous. The growing diversity of the Travelers did not sit well with at least some Honolulu Chinese, who understandably believed that the team represented them as well as all of Hawai'i. Indeed, this issue of whether Hop's traveling nine embodied Honolulu's Chinese community provoked controversy before the 1914 trek began.[37]

As 1914 dawned, Honolulu's baseball world expected the Travelers to make a third trip to the mainland. However, it was not certain that key Chinese teammates would head eastward with them. In February 1914, the *Pacific Commercial Advertiser* advised that both Lai Tin and En Sue Pung might stay on the islands for "personal reasons." In Lai Tin's case, the *Advertiser* maintained, his mother objected to seeing her son depart for another long journey to the mainland. Hoping to calm the storm swirling around his team, Hop overconfidently assured the local sporting public that matters had been straightened out and that all key Chinese members of the Travelers would journey to the mainland with the rest of the team. Meanwhile, spokespersons for Honolulu's Chinese community claimed that because of players such as Markham, the Travelers no longer represented them. They wanted an authentic Chinese nine to promote them in Honolulu and elsewhere. Thus, the *Advertiser* published a report that Lai Tin and other Chinese such as Lang Akana, Kan Yen Chun, En Sue Pung, and Vernon Ayau not only would remain home but ultimately report to a new team sponsored by the Chinese Athletic Union (CAU). As it turned out, Lai Tin, as well as Akana and Kan Yen Chun, did stay in Honolulu. En Sue Pung and Ayau, nonetheless, voyaged to the mainland with Hop.[38]

Mainlanders did not seem to notice the emerging diversity of the Travelers. U.S. immigration authorities waylaid the visiting ballplayers on Angel Island in the San Francisco Bay. The anti-Asian immigrant politics legitimized by the Chinese Exclusion Act and the embrace of xenophobia in general by many Americans sustained U.S. government efforts to investigate arrivals at newly constructed facilities at Angel Island. We do not know how outraged the ballplayers and Sam Hop were that U.S. authorities did not let them into San Francisco. At the very least, they were angry enough to not let things play out. They contacted Prince Kalanianaole, the lone and nonvoting Hawaiian delegate to the U.S. Congress, and H. W. Wood, Hawai'i's commissioner to the Pan-Pacific Exposition then taking place in San Francisco. These gentlemen protested to U.S. immigration authorities that the detained men were all citizens, eight voted, and six served in Hawai'i's National Guard. What may have swung matters in the ballplayers' favor, according to some press reports, was that En Sue Pung enjoyed a reputation as Hawai'i's Ty Cobb. Their American pedigree supported, the Travelers were allowed into the United States.[39]

As the 1914 tour progressed, the media accepted and double downed on a simplistic, all-Chinese narrative of the Travelers. The *Washington Herald* noted "another Yellow Peril" journeying through the mainland, maintaining that "a Chinese baseball team from Hawaii has been licking all the white teams on the Pacific Coast." Around the same time, an Iowa newspaper proclaimed the arrival in Muscatine of the "Chinese University of Hawaii traveling baseball team." It added that the "celestial aggregation" proved that "native Chinese" could master "Uncle Sam's pastime." After seeing the local team taken down by the Travelers, Indiana's *Kokomo Tribune* published the following, geographically distorted verses:

A ball club of heathen Chinese
Came touring the land of the free
With Hop Sing in the box
They trimmed up our Sox
Just mowed 'em right off at the knees. . . .
So here's to the lads of Hong Kong
in the land of chopsticks and gong
They're no outfit of simps, but a game bunch of imps
And we hope they'll be back before long.[40]

Honolulu's two mainstream newspapers diverged in their coverage of the Travelers in 1914. More supportive of the CAU's "stay at home Chinese," the *Pacific Commercial Advertiser* expressed disillusionment with Hop's "near Chinese" contingent. In April, the *Advertiser* derided the cover story the Travelers played under. The daily asserted that Sam Hop seemingly deluded himself into believing in the existence of a Chinese University of Hawaii by the way he touted it to the press, declaring himself the school's physical director. Moreover, the *Advertiser* disparaged the Moriyama brothers for apparently accepting their imposed Chinese identity.

With pleasure, however, the *Star-Bulletin* reported on mainland journalists' befuddlement by the Travelers' talent and inability to conform to stereotypes. The *Star-Bulletin* cited the case of Adelle Rogers, famed female reporter for the *Los Angeles Evening Herald*, who expected the ballplayers she interviewed to speak nothing but a mangled English, which she had practiced before interviewing the Travelers. She anticipated, additionally, that they would show up wearing kimonos, queues, and feathers. Instead, she found them "educated, occidentalized, and American tailored." Reminding us that there is nothing straightforward about how racialized gender has worked in history, she gushed, they "resembled a masculine fashion show." One Traveler exemplified to her the "most gorgeous exponent of an American fashion show. He wore a purple-blue suit, cut high over a silk-striped shirt." To the first Traveler she interviewed, Rogers remarked, "You velly much fine Chinese ballplayers." To this and other similar inquiries, the player asked, "What can I do for you?" Moreover, she described a Traveler as a "coffee colored youth" carrying a ukulele case. Still, he managed to counter her affected pidgin English questions in "perfect English."[41]

The East Coast press admired the 1914 Travelers' skills as ballplayers. In anticipation of the Travelers encountering the Morrisville nine, which competed in the very good semipro Delaware River Valley League, the *Trenton Times* advised local fans to expect plenty of good baseball and entertainment. The *Times* depicted the "Chinese" ballplayers as entertaining, full of "pep," and coaching in "Pigeon." A Morrisville, New Jersey, newspaper raved about the visitors from Hawai'i after they lost to the hometown semipro nine. Spectators, the newspaper maintained, expected "a circus attraction" but surprisingly witnessed "one of the fastest battles staged in this city this year." Consequently, they "concluded that baseball is not a national game but international in scope." The Travelers won the crowd over, but as racialized foreigners: First, "the Chinks amused the spectators by a series of juggling stunts that served to put them right by the crowd." Then, the Travelers got serious with the first pitch and shocked fans in attendance with their talent. "Never in the history of local baseball has a home crowd been so cordial towards a visiting attraction, and so nasty to the home clan," added the daily.[42]

As in previous years, the 1914 team played several games in and around New York City and Philadelphia. The Travelers attracted the largest crowd of the season in the Philadelphia suburb of Media even though the game was played on a Wednesday. In West Philadelphia late in the summer of 1914, the islanders opposed the Victrix nine, sponsored by the Roman Catholic Church. An attendance of 4,000 watched the game and displayed, according to one press report, "no little amount of surprise" at witnessing "the defeat of a formidable local team by the 'Yellow Peril.'" In the process, the visitors exhibited a command of inside baseball, dropping pop-ups to make double plays and using the squeeze bunt effectively. On the base paths, "the baserunning of the Chinamen was to many an enigma, the cunningness, speed and agility, bewildering at times the players and spectators." An even larger overflow crowd of 6,500 in Philadelphia witnessed the Travelers take care of a nine representing the Strawbridge and Clothier's department store. According to one press observer, the visitors amazed fans in "the manner in which [they] streaked around the bases" and made the home team's catchers look "foolish." For example, they "pulled off a pretty delayed double steal." As for New York City, the *Brooklyn Daily Times* declared in 1914 the "Chinks were great favorites . . . due to their wonderful playing."[43]

The Travelers' future looked bright when they returned to Hawai'i in the fall of 1914. Sam Hop reported to the Honolulu press that the team had won ninety-six games, lost sixty-one, and tied four. He added that the record would have been even better had ace Foster Robinson not gotten hurt in May. The Travelers drew well, Hop boasted, especially in Philadelphia. Nat Strong showed up in Honolulu in December, delighted with the Travelers as a business venture. Speaking before the city's Ad Club, he hailed the Travelers as one of Hawai'i's "best promotion assets." While in Honolulu, Strong praised Hawai'i's ability to prepare players like Lai Tin. On the islands, he proclaimed, the third sacker and his teammates could play all year round unlike most mainland ballplayers. Acknowledging the ample number of "orientals" playing and supporting baseball on the islands, Strong maintained that the game "westernized" them, while adding that it was odd to see the more "traditional" of them root at ball games.[44]

The 1915 Journey

Sam Hop remained on the islands when the Travelers made their fourth trip eastward in 1915. Accordingly, Lai Tin and Apau Kau shared command of the team. Returning to the Travelers in a capacity of authority, the third sacker referred to himself as William Lai Tin in a letter to the *Pacific Commercial Advertiser*. Writing from the West Coast, he informed folks back home that the Travelers were enjoying themselves and had "played before good crowds, seen the fair [San Francisco's Pan-Pacific Exposition], and hoped to have a successful season."[45]

The Travelers played two games in the San Francisco Bay Area in the first mainland stop of the 1915 tour. While watching the Stanford game, "American" fans, according to the *San Jose Mercury*, saw something startling. Second sacker "Chin" ranged far to his right to grab a grounder. Chinito Moriyama figured he could not throw the runner out from where he was. So, he tossed the ball to shortstop Vernon Ayau, who with his momentum moving toward first base was able to gun down the runner. A few days later, the Travelers lost a close game to the PCL's Salt Lake City nine, 3–2, before a capacity crowd in San José. Apau Kau shut down the Salt Lake City bats for most of the game. Consequently, the *Salt Lake Telegram* praised "Kau, the Oriental pitcher," while claiming that "the Orientals are good fielders but light with the stick"—although, given the score, they were not all that much less effective than the Salt Lake batters. During the game, the San José crowd seemed stunned when Lai Tin slid aggressively into second base, knocking down a Salt Lake City infielder. The idea of a nonwhite "celestial" forcefully confronting a white athlete near ground zero of America's anti-Asian movement apparently distressed at least some San José fans, but not to the extent that anything untoward happened. Indeed, most San José spectators backed the guests from Hawai'i.[46]

On the field, the 1915 journey proved a triumph for a team that had become essentially a mixture of Chinese, Japanese, and Hawaiians. Yet the identity of the Travelers as all-Chinese stuck. Lehigh University's 1915 yearbook referred to the Travelers as "semiprofessional chinks." Rex Mulford, a correspondent to the *Sporting Life*, noted the Travelers' command of baseball. After they beat a Xavier University nine, Mulford acknowledged that the Travelers "cleaned up on the

Saints." Observing that a good crowd watched the game, Mulford added, "The Celestials from the romantic isle know how to play the game. They are magnificent fielders, pretty good hitters, and fast runners." Like other observers of the Travelers, Mulford maintained that while they "coached in their own tongue... they are masters of the English language as well as the American game." A week later Mulford informed *Sporting Life* readers that the Travelers had beaten a tough semipro opponent in Cincinnati, the Shamrocks:

> Those Chinese invaders have been lingering hereabouts and "cleaning up" in a remarkable manner. They ran down to Lexington and beat the Kentuckians and then came back and twice put the Shamrocks out of the running, and the "Shams" are considered some pumpkins in these baseball parts. A new "Yellow Peril" to baseball hopes has thus been turned loose. The visit of these collegians from the University of Hawaii created no little comment and interest. In one of the games one of the celestials tapped a base runner on the wing, and as the play was within the empirical visual range the Judgment was "out." A Shamrock protest was made that the runner had not been touched. Of course, there was no reversal of the decision, but the Chinese left fielder called out: "Hit him on the head next time!" thus proving that even the proverbial suave manners of the Chinese have felt the martial spirit of the diamond contest.[47]

While the Travelers performed in and around Cincinnati, Apau Kau visited the offices of the *Cincinnati Enquirer*, most likely to drum up interest in the barnstormers among the residents of the Ohio city. The *Enquirer* maintained that the pitcher examined the newspaper's register and immediately recognized the then famous names of prizefighters John L. Sullivan and James Jeffries, entertainers Eddie Foy and George M. Cohan, and pitcher Christy Mathewson. He told the *Enquirer* that he particularly enjoyed baseball and boxing. Aware of how dangerous the world had become by 1915, Apau Kau supposedly proclaimed that if the United States ever entered the war, "Chinamen in Hawaii would fight for the stars and stripes." Describing Apau Kau as "pretty husky" and cosmopolitan, the *Enquirer* fell for the pitcher's description of the players as students of the nonexistent "Chinese University." Apparently, he also insisted that he and his teammates were "rank amateurs" who made expenses, but all other money earned by the Travelers went into a "university fund." Called "the celestial manager" of the Hawaiian team, Apau Kau insisted that he and his teammates were "bonafide [*sic*] students," proved by the annual turnover in the team's makeup.[48]

While the Travelers visited Carbondale, an industrial town in northeastern Pennsylvania, a reporter for a local newspaper interviewed William T. Lai, described in the *Carbondale Leader* as team captain. The extensive piece resulting from the interview initially attempted to honor the Travelers as a whole. "Except for a Mongolian cast of continence by no means accentuated," the ballplayers looked like typical American young men fresh from an American college campus: "They speak English perfectly, with an oriental tang, which make it as mellifluous in their mouths as Italian in that of an educated Roman . . . The twelve young men . . . are lithe in build, graceful in movement, gentlemanly in demeanor, and democratic in intercourse."[49]

Moving on to Lai Tin's interview, the reporter maintained that the Traveler declared that the team represented a then nonexistent "University of Hawaii." Lai stressed that the student body consisted primarily of "Chinese, Hawaiians, and Americans," all of whom lived in equality with one another. "Racial prejudice," according to the third sacker, did not abide in Hawai'i nor, he promised, would it. Interestingly, Lai failed to mention Japanese, Koreans, and Filipinos in his tale of the University of Hawaii.[50]

Lai had much to say about Hawai'i. He claimed that the islands' Chinese population consisted largely of nuclear families dedicated to the trades. In doing so, he probably wanted to disassociate Chinese on the islands from the stereotyped "bachelor laundryman" so denigrated but often needed on the mainland. As for the islands' natives, he lamented that they were disappearing. Reflecting on what he considered an "anthropological phenomenon," Lai maintained that whenever "superior" or more "progressive" races invade, the indigenous people vanish or get absorbed by the more powerful. Still, he asserted that the "native population" managed to survive on the islands, engaging in agriculture and fishing, as well as living "in perfect harmony with the intruders."[51]

Lai Tin appeared amused by mainland "immigration" to Hawai'i and how those migrants refer to the continental United States as the "old country." To a significant extent, Lai Tin conceded America shaped life in Hawai'i. In Honolulu, the city cops exhibited a "fussiness" one might encounter in a mainland metropolis, while the English language significantly reigned as did English-language newspapers such as the *Honolulu Star-Bulletin*. However, he protested that "Honolulu is not, of course, an American city, and no transformations of a material order can make it one, because it has a physiognomy of its own."[52]

Lai Tin then transported his exploration of Hawai'i in ways evoking the recent work of historian Gary Okihiro but also the model minority narrative of recent years. He averred, "We are as much natives of the Pacific as we are of the islands. I mean the ocean is part and parcel of our lives." However, the real "natives" of Hawai'i "are as much at home in the sea as you are on dry land . . . as they should be for the Pacific is a generous benefactor to them." Prompted to discuss education on the islands, Lai Tin proclaimed that Hawai'i's public school teach English to "natives, Chinese, and Americans," once again ignoring other ethnic groups. Presumably referring to the Chinese, Lai Tin also informed the reporter that "we" also learned Chinese and Hawaiian, with the latter fading owing to American occupation. Elaborating on the education of Chinese in Hawai'i, he declared that while tending to favor an education that would advance their commercial activities, they also pursued the liberal arts. In any event, Lai Tin insisted that Chinese, even in pre-revolutionary China, value education.[53]

Notwithstanding the possibility that the *Carbondale Leader*'s reporter put words in his mouth, Lai Tin enacted well his role as a promoter of Hawai'i, while articulating an early twentieth-century version of cultural pluralism. The islands' sugar and pineapple industries might not have been pleased as he failed to boost Hawai'i's primary agricultural commodities. However, the islands' burgeoning hotel and travel industry should have applauded a narrative that rendered Hawai'i inviting to prospective tourists and even permanent visitors. Lai Tin, indeed, understood the Travelers' objective of displaying the islands as both comforting and exotic to mainlanders. He also understood the Travelers' other objective of representing the Chinese diaspora in a similar manner to a nation doubtful of the benefits of immigration, especially Asian immigration—that while distinctive, Chinese people were not in Honolulu or Philadelphia to steal jobs from whites or lure their children to opium dens. Rather, they could play a productive role in American society. In the process, Lai's elision of Japanese, Koreans, and Filipinos from his discussions of Hawai'i may not have been so much an attempt to demean them, especially given how important Nikkei were to the Travelers in 1915, but a pronouncement on how he identified himself—as a blending of Chinese, Hawaiian, and American.

In New York City, the Travelers opposed many of the best independent nines around. Early in July, the *Brooklyn Daily Standard* enthused that the Travelers were the greatest drawing card in baseball outside of the big leagues. "Never before," the *Brooklyn Daily Eagle* trumpeted, had so many people watched a ball game at Sea Cliff Park on Long Island. A crowd of 5,000 people saw the Travelers win handily, 10–4. The *Eagle* correspondent observed lines of automobiles conveying fans to the game.[54]

Toward the end of the 1915 tour the Travelers played two games against the African American Lincoln Giants. During their 1912 trip, a mainland-based piece published in the *Decatur Review* accused the Travelers of racial discrimination. The story asserted, "The color line has been drawn in a great many cases but this one may be tied, but not beaten. The Chinese baseball team that came over here with a great reputation was challenged by the Lincoln Giants of New York recently. The answer came back from the yellow boys that they drew the color line and would not mingle." To be sure, the Chinese may well have been motivated by racism, although they often played highly competitive games against the strong Black 25th regiment nine during Honolulu's winter season. However, another factor could have been that the white owners of the Giants were rivals of Nat Strong, who, in turn, discouraged his Chinese clients from playing them. In 1914, the possibility of playing the Lincoln Giants arose again, and once more the Travelers proclaimed reticence. Nonetheless, according to the *Honolulu Star-Bulletin*, New York City's Chinese Merchants Association pressured the Travelers and, presumably, Nat Strong to schedule the Lincoln Giants. Indeed, the

Travelers faced the Lincoln Giants in their last game in New York City before returning to Hawai'i, winning 6–2.[55]

In 1915, however, the Hawaiians were slated to oppose the Giants on three successive weekends in September. Playing at Olympic Field on Fifth Avenue and 136th Street in Harlem, the Travelers fell to the home team, 8–2. The Black-run *New York Age* titled its story of the game, "Lincoln Giants Take Chinese Cues [*sic*]." The *Age* estimated that the crowd of 7,000 was the largest to see a Giants home game in months. And while they did not do well on the field, "the Chinese team of the University of Hawaii" exhibited a pregame shadow ball "that earned them rounds of applause." The next weekend, the Giants encountered Apau Kau at his best. He mowed down Giants batters in a 5–0 victory. Once again, the stands were filled. The *Age* generously reported "the Orientals played a flashy brand of ball that kept the 7,000 fans on edge from start to finish." Unfortunately, the rubber game was canceled because of inclement weather and was not rescheduled because the Travelers needed to depart for Cuba before returning to the islands.[56]

Cuba offered the ballplayers from Hawai'i tough opponents, composed of many professionals possessing ample mainland experiences themselves—mainly performing with and against top-flight African American ballplayers. According to Cuban baseball historian Jorge S. Figueredo, the Travelers were not expected to do well, but proved stronger than Cubans anticipated. Calling himself William Lai Tin, the Travelers' "team captain" dispatched correspondence to the *Honolulu Star-Bulletin* in early November admitting that the barnstormers should have done better in Cuba but had to cope with illness inflicting key players. Indeed, Lai Tin pointed out that health reasons compelled Apau Kau to leave Cuba early for New York. He also mentioned that Markham was not returning to Hawai'i with the team but would remain on the East Coast to attend Temple University's business school in Philadelphia. Lai Tin's praise for Markham was unstinting, asserting that he had caught 156 of 157 games in a "big league" manner during the 1915 tour.[57]

A few days later, another, more detailed story authored by Lai Tin appeared in the *Honolulu Star-Bulletin*. Lai Tin acclaimed Cubans' love of baseball and maintained the Travelers enjoyed visiting various historical and cultural sites on the island. And even though they faced talented nines such as the Almendares, powered by Cristóbal Torriente, one of the great sluggers of his era, they held their own. Lai Tin expressed pride in what the Travelers had accomplished not only on the Caribbean island but throughout their many months on the mainland. He insisted that the Travelers' 5–7 record in Cuba was comparable to, if not better than, what mainland big league teams had done against formidable Cuban nines. In all, the 1915 Travelers won 102 games, lost 52, and tied 1 under a variety of imposing conditions, Lai Tin contended. Subsequently, Lai Tin informed the *Star-Bulletin* that the Cuban fans were the best he saw during the 1915 journey.[58]

Another 1915 Journey

Meanwhile, skilled Hawai'i Chinese ballplayers were so plentiful in the 1910s that in 1915, while the Travelers, with Lai Tin, Apau Kau, and Vernon Ayau in tow, headed for the mainland, an all-Chinese nine, sponsored by the CAU, trekked to Asia. Emerging from the desire of Honolulu's Chinese community to attain representation in the Oahu League for an all-Chinese nine, the CAU contingent had performed well in 1914 while the Travelers were off to the mainland. The *Pacific Commercial Advertiser*, taking a shot at the Travelers, claimed the CAU nine truly represented Honolulu's "Chinese population," while "Sammy Hop's aggregation will get little credit when they return to Honolulu." After the CAU team shut out the Portuguese, 5–0, in April 1914, the *Advertiser* reported that the 1,000 fans in attendance voiced pleasure in witnessing a nine constituted entirely by players possessing at least some kind of Chinese ancestry. Moreover, captain Lai Tin was cheered loudly as he took his place in the batter's box. When a University of California team visited Honolulu in 1914, it lost twice to the CAU nine in memorable games in which Lai Tin starred. Thanks to these games, the *Advertiser* declared, "Chinatown is talking nothing but baseball." And even though Lai Tin rejoined the Travelers in the spring of 1915, CAU organizers and players undertook an ambitious journey westward.[59]

According to former Traveler pitcher Luck Yee Lau, China extended an invitation to the CAU to ship its team eastward in order to eventually represent the nation in the Far Eastern Games. Fostered largely by the international reach of the YMCA, the Far Eastern Games surfaced in the 1910s as the Asian version of the Olympics, which, at this time, was largely confined to athletes from Europe and the Americas. China, Luck Yee Lau declared, did not have a ball team that could compete with the Japanese or the Filipinos. Thus, those in charge of China's athletic representation cast their eyes on Hawai'i. In addition, Luck Yee Lau wrote, "Manilla people" wanted to see a Chinese team from Hawai'i in action in the Philippines. "So," he declared, "we of Hawaii combined the trips and went forth last spring to cross bats with our distant friends of the Far east."[60]

Much was expected of the journey of these young men to Asia. The *Honolulu Star-Bulletin* represented the trip as a powerful example of "sports evangelism." As the team was supposed to appear in both China and Japan, the *Star-Bulletin* even speculated that the ballplayers could ease tensions between the two nations. The *Star-Bulletin* gloated over how baseball, as played by the CAU nine, as well as the Travelers, promoted the islands. An editorial in the *Star-Bulletin* boasted that because of island teams appearing on both the U.S. mainland and the "Orient," "Hawaii is uniquely advertised abroad." Providing context to all this was that Hawai'i's economic elites hoped to bolster trade with China and Asia in general.[61]

The CAU contingent performed excellently in Asia, winning twelve games, losing three, with one tie. Race and ethnicity, however, made getting into the

Philippines problematic. Because of the Chinese Exclusion Act, the ballplayers from Hawai'i had to convince U.S. authorities in the occupied Philippines of their U.S. citizenship status before they were allowed in. In Manilla, an organization called the Oriental Club presented the Chinese ballplayers with the Hancock Cup in recognition of their fine play in the Philippines. The CAU's triumphal trek westward was celebrated by the Honolulu business community. The Honolulu AD Club, for example, feted the ballplayers with a banquet upon their return.[62]

The Travelers' Last Journey

Lai Tin clearly held the team reins as the Travelers made their last journey to the mainland in 1916. He also seems to have taken a hand at booking and advertising. In late 1915, he corresponded with mainland newspapers, advising them of the Travelers' approaching return in 1916, and promising they would materialize as "a faster team than ever." Yet the 1916 squad was not as good as Lai Tin anticipated. While the 1913, 1914, and 1915 Travelers won far more often than they lost, the 1916 version triumphed less frequently. Still, for a team that was constantly on the road, the 1916 Travelers could take pride in winning more than half their games. The team included even more players of non-Chinese ancestry. Three Nikkei contributed to the Travelers' success as did several Hawaiians. There were even two haoles on the squad—Bill Inman and Roy Doty. Inman at least was born and raised on the islands and generally played under his own name. Doty, who was a relative newcomer to Hawai'i, played under the name of "Dot." Doty recalled in 1951 that he was recruited to replace hard-hitting first sacker Hoon Ki Yim. It is not clear how many mainland fans, opponents, and sportswriters were actually fooled by these "yellowface" performances, but until the very last game of the Travelers, mainlanders referred to them as Chinese.[63]

During the early part of the 1916 journey, Lai Tin reported back to Honolulu on the team's progress. He admitted to abetting a perhaps good-humored effort to dupe the mainland press into believing in the reality of the "Chinese University . . . of Hawaii." After walloping Howard Payne in Brownwood, Texas, 14–6, Lai Tin and other Travelers extolled the institution they supposedly represented. Lai Tin maintained that students competed in various sports such as baseball, basketball, football, and swimming, although he stressed that football was not easy for Chinese University gridders because of the warmth they experienced during Hawai'i's autumns and winters. Several years later, Bill Inman recalled puffing up the Chinese University of Hawaii on the mainland. He remembered telling reporters that he and his teammates sought to raise $60,000 on the mainland to build a university gym. Inman insisted to the press, moreover, that he served as the university's football coach.[64]

One of the more interesting pieces of press coverage of the 1916 Travelers could be found in the *New York Telegram* late in the summer. Claiming the role of a "skeptic," the *Telegram*'s correspondent went to Harlem's Olympic Field to watch a "weird" game pitting the Lincoln Giants against a "Chinese" nine. Before a crowd of 3,500, the Travelers topped the Giants, 10–6, but the major theme of the *Telegram*'s article was the author's astonishment at the performances of the nonwhite ballplayers. This author must not have been a keen follower of local baseball in New York City. Otherwise, even if racist, the author would have known that the Travelers and the Lincoln Giants were very capable nines. Still, the correspondent wondered why the Travelers spoke English competently, while also asking, "Whoever heard of negroes and Chinese playing baseball as it should be played?"[65]

Occasionally, the mainlanders realized that Inman and Doty did not quite fit into the narrative of the Travelers as Chinese. When Inman pitched against the University of Texas nine before a large crowd in Austin, the *Austin American* called him "the 'white' Chinese hurler." After watching a Travelers game, a reporter for the *St. Louis Post Dispatch* concluded that two-thirds of the visiting ballplayers were Chinese, a couple were part-Hawaiian, and one was an American, born and raised in Hawai'i. After the Travelers beat a York, Pennsylvania, nine before 4,000 spectators, the *York Daily* noted that Inman, patrolling the outfield for the game, looked like Jim Thorpe. In promoting a game pitting the Travelers against the Taylor ABC's, the *Indianapolis News* described Inman as an "American." Indeed, it was probably at the same game that spectators figured out that Inman and Doty were white and "razzed" them more than their Traveler teammates.[66]

Whether in large cities such as New York or Philadelphia or small towns, the Travelers still attracted good crowds and press in 1916. In mid-April, the *Commerce Journal* noted that the largest attendance ever at the local park watched the "Chinese University of Honolulu" beat the East Texas Normal College nine, 5–1. The town closed down its businesses so that residents could take advantage of the "rare treat" of seeing a baseball team from "Celestial Country." Nine hundred locals showed up and were not disappointed as they witnessed "a clever bunch of athletes . . . [who] . . . put up a clean article of ball." The *Brooklyn Daily Eagle* pointed out that in a ballpark nestled on the border between Brooklyn and Queens, "no better baseball has ever been offered Ridgewood fans than was the case when . . . the Bushwicks trimmed the Chinese, 3-0." The *Sporting Life* acclaimed the barnstormers' performance on the mainland. The "Chinese," the weekly opined, had won most of their games against college teams. And while playing in and around Philadelphia, they had topped their opponents in ten of thirteen games, including victories over tough semipro nines. As the tour wound down, the Travelers headed westward. A crowd of 6,000 watched the Travelers hold their own against the formidable ABC's in Indianapolis. The barnstormers lost both ends of a doubleheader, but the *Chicago Defender* complimented Traveler players such as Lai Tin, praised by the distinguished African American weekly as a "fielding star."[67]

In-Between Tours

When the Travelers returned to the islands between tours, they were expected to play as a team and as individuals on Hawai'i's baseball diamonds, which could remain quite active while mainland diamonds were swamped with mud or covered with snow. Lai Tin, for example, played for a multiethnic nine called the Stars after the 1912 tour but subsequently performed for all-Chinese and not so all-Chinese Traveler teams. The fact that Lai and his mates were relative celebrities in Hawai'i's baseball world rendered them valuable gate attractions but also targets of rival teams composed of different racial and ethnic groups.

Belying the narrative of Chinese submissiveness, Sam Hop's demands for gate money provoked controversy in the Honolulu press between the 1912 and 1913 tours. Comparing the then all-Chinese Travelers to Black boxer Jack Johnson, Hop declared that the heavyweight champion would not fight without a guarantee of over half the gate money and neither would the Travelers play one of many ethnic, multiethnic, and service teams in and around Honolulu. Critics considered Hop and the Travelers too presumptuous. One moaned that they "stood out for the hog's measure" of the gate receipts.[68]

Largely, however, the Travelers had their way with local teams. A "picked nine" of the supposedly best non-Traveler ballplayers in Honolulu was organized to take on Hop's aggregation. However, this team lost "while the Chinese, as usual, played like a well-oiled machine," according to the *Star-Bulletin*. The one team that effectively challenged the Travelers represented the all-Black 25th regiment stationed on O'ahu. A product of the U.S. military's deference to the segregation of Black soldiers, the 25th traveled the wave of American imperial expansion, helping suppress, often unenthusiastically, American Indian and then Filipino/a resistance to Manifest Destiny and the white man's burden, although not always enthusiastically.[69]

Led by future Hall of Famer Wilbur Rogan, the 25th regiment nine tested the talents of all-Chinese and ethnically mixed Traveler teams. According to the *Pacific Commercial Advertiser* late in 1915, the Travelers and the 25th had become "ancient rivals." News of a game between the Travelers and the 25th reached the *New York Age*, which published an account of a hard-fought game before a packed crowd at O'ahu's Schofield Barracks. The 25th edged the Travelers 4–3 by using the latter's game of "inside baseball," advancing base runners by way of numerous sacrifice hits.[70]

Journeys' End

Despite their relative notoriety, the Travelers ended their journeys to the mainland after 1916. Perhaps the novelty was fading, although the Travelers still drew fans. The run-up to American entry into World War I may have played a role in potentially diverting mainland interest in watching the barnstormers in action.

Indeed, at a 1927 reunion of the team, former Travelers complained the war "jammed things up." More serious were the reports of personal fractures dividing the Travelers. More serious still was that several key members of the Travelers remained on the mainland after the 1916 trek. Lai Tin, Andy Yamashiro, Apau Kau, and Fred Markham decided to live in or around Philadelphia, perhaps hoping to land jobs in organized baseball. Alfred Yap, the hard-hitting infielder who joined the 1915 tour through September, had earlier made a home on the East Coast as a student at Lehigh but did not seem to hang out with Lai, Yamashiro, Markham, and Apau Kau. And, after coming back to Hawai'i in the fall of 1916, Vernon Ayau was signed to a minor league contract in December 1916 to join the Seattle Giants of the Pacific Northwest League.[71]

Even though they eventually broke up, the Travelers represented a source of pride to followers of the national pastime in Hawai'i. Honolulu newspapers such as the *Honolulu Star Bulletin* regularly reported on their games on the mainland while also shedding light on the doings of Traveler ballplayers individually and collectively on Hawai'i's ball fields between trips. The *Star-Bulletin* acclaimed the team it called the "Chinese Travelers" in the winter of 1915–1916. The ballplayers, the *Star-Bulletin* declared, had advertised Hawai'i more than any other "aggregation of athletes" from the islands—only the renowned Duke Kahanamoku matched their fame on the mainland. The *Star-Bulletin* added that "each year the ball tossers from Hawaii play hundreds of games in every section of the country and hundreds of thousands of people have watched them play."[72]

The team also proved a source of pride to those elements of the Chinese diaspora inhabiting the U.S. mainland. Whether the team was largely Chinese in ancestry or not, the Travelers gained support from often beleaguered Chinese American communities on the mainland. En Sue Pung offered the *Honolulu Star-Bulletin* insights into how well Chinese communities in the west received the Travelers in 1914. He estimated that 200 "Chinamen" witnessed the Occidental game. After the game, Chinese merchants in Los Angeles honored the ballplayers with a midnight "Chinese supper" even though the Travelers had earlier enjoyed a "haole dinner." In Tucson, En Sue Pung wrote, 500 Chinese appeared for the game against the University of Arizona. Many of these spectators were small-scale shopkeepers and restaurant owners. And Pung, as did probably many of his teammates, took delight in the Chinese spectators "opening up a bottle of champagne to celebrate our victory over the haoles." In El Paso, the Travelers were greeted by an owner of a local Chinese restaurant. Migrating to the border city from Honolulu, this restaurant owner treated the ballplayers to a noon meal before their 3:30 P.M. game. It was at that game that the Travelers encountered an El Paso fan who demanded they show their "references" proving they deserved his time at a ball park. After the Travelers easily conquered the home team, 12–4, Pung exulted that he and his teammates tendered the skeptical El Paso fan plenty of "references."[73]

The young men who traveled the American empire possessed fond, but mixed, memories of their experiences. Sam Hop, who ran a chop suey restaurant in Honolulu in the 1920s, reminisced for Loui Leong Hop, a sportswriter for the *Honolulu Star-Bulletin*. He remembered that he and his players consistently eluded the mainstream media's simplistic perceptions of them. After a game against Vanderbilt, a reporter queried him with a ridiculous Chinese accent. Hop answered in conventional American English and, according to the former baseball manager, the interrogator fled in confusion. Sam Hop also addressed the insults dogging the players, explaining that terms like "Yellow Peril," "Chinks," and "Chinamen" offended them, although they learned to harden themselves against such epithets.[74]

Former Travelers remembered their journeys to the mainland for the press. In 1928, the amused Moriyama brothers recalled to Loui Leong Hop that Apau Kau persuaded them to play with the Travelers as the Chin brothers. They also recalled an opposing college team served the barnstormers smaller and deadened balls when they were at bat, while the Traveler pitchers threw official balls. For a while, the Travelers found it hard to square up on the balls pitched to them, but when they discovered the ruse, they got the deadened balls thrown out and, riled, unleashed their bats in a rout of the home team. En Sue Pung remembered the trials of playing baseball on a variety of mainland ball fields. During a reunion banquet of Travelers in 1940, En Sue Pung recalled playing center field during a game at Stamford, Connecticut. The outfield was so hilly, the great athlete maintained, he could not see either the left or right fielder. Luck Yee Lau, like Sam Hop, remembered the insults as well as the good times. He told *Honolulu Advertiser* columnist Bill Pacheco in 1946 of a degrading promotion for a game that the Travelers played at some unnamed location. The former pitcher declared that a large figure of a stereotypical Chinese man was installed with its eyes pointed in the direction of the ballpark. This, Luck Yee Lau insisted, "infuriated the boys." Later, at the ballpark, he recalled a man who came over to the bench and verbally abused them as "Chinamen," vowing the Travelers would lose easily. Instead, according to Luck Yee Lau, a riled up nine beat the locals easily, 16–1. Vernon Ayau, he maintained, rubbed salt in the locals' wounds by calmly cradling grounders hit in his direction and then whipping balls over to first base just in time to get batters out.[75]

Mainland journalists published their memories of the Travelers. Lank Leonard, a syndicated columnist and cartoonist, remembered the Travelers in 1928. In an article focusing on Buck Lai, Leonard recalled seeing the barnstormers in Port Arthur, New York. They staged quite a show, he reminisced, playing "shadow ball" before the game and persuading him that "those Chinks were natural entertainers and 'Buck' Lai was one of the best." Leonard stated that since the Travelers spoke perfectly good mainstream English, their conversations with one another on the field in "Chinese" were simply a device to render them more intriguing to spectators. Yet, Leonard insisted, while the Travelers enjoyed clowning, they also played superior baseball.[76]

Conclusion

While largely forgotten today by keepers of America's baseball historical lore, it is worth remembering that the Travelers encountered treacherous racial frontiers as they negotiated the varied terrains of the American empire. To be sure, the cultural borders they encountered were not as well patrolled for them as for Black ballplayers, but "racism's traveling eye" still followed them as they chased after flyballs and pilfered bases. In the process, the Travelers demonstrated a complex cultural citizenship embracing American, Hawaiian, and Chinese identities, countering those seeking to restrain them in racialized iron cages.[77]

4

Crossings of Baseball's Racial Fault Lines, 1917–1918

• •

The Travelers' relative fame and on-field success launched at least moderate shock waves throughout the American empire's baseball world from the East Coast of the mainland to the Hawaiian Islands and beyond. In the process, they promoted the globalization of baseball while traversing hazardous racial borderlands. However, during America's run-up to World War I and the war itself, racism and xenophobia escalated as calls for cultural homogeneity accelerated. Thanks in part to the movie *Birth of a Nation*, the Ku Klux Klan enjoyed an unholy renaissance. Madison Grant's racist and xenophobic *Passing of the Great Race* emerged as a best seller and fed into the already much too popular eugenics movement. Former president Teddy Roosevelt and contemporary president Woodrow Wilson despised one another, but they also agreed to despise as well hyphenated Americans—those immigrants and their offspring who shunned the melting pot. And while American capitalists might appreciate how immigrants filled their labor needs, they also feared that they brought anticapitalist ideologies with them to the United States. Typically, while anti-immigrant politics circled around European immigrants, they landed hardest on nonwhite immigrants, banning immigration from much of Asia as well as the Pacific Islands in 1917. That same year, moreover, a bloody anti-Black riot erupted in East St. Louis. If Americans were told World War I was about making the world safe for democracy, democracy did not seem very safe in America.[1]

Organized Baseball Reaches Out

Lai Tin, who over time became better known as William Lai, Bill Lai, and, of course, Buck Lai on the East Coast, seemingly surfaced as the hub around which ex-Travelers such as Apau Kau, Vernon Ayau, Fred Markham, and Andy Yamashiro circled. Before making a permanent home on the East Coast, Lai entertained a prior opportunity to play professional baseball on the mainland as early as 1915. As mentioned previously, Lai Tin lingered in Honolulu to lead a formidable Chinese Athletic Union (CAU) team rather than join the 1914 mainland tour. In June 1914, the University of California nine arrived on the islands, where it opposed the CAU aggregation in two tightly played, well attended, and prominently publicized games. Lai Tin, handling shortstop, stood out as his team edged Cal twice. The *Star-Bulletin* gushed, "If every ball player would run out hits the way Lai Tin does there would be a lot more runs scored. 'Tin' goes to first at full speed whether his chances are good or bad." Several months later, in December 1914, readers of the *New York Times* learned about the Cal games. The *Times*'s correspondent praised Lai Tin's swiftness and flawless fielding. Calling him a "speed demon," the correspondent added, "Lai Tin, the leader of the Chinese team, who plays shortstop, worked his players so well that they seemed the strongest in both defense and attack."[2]

The decision of the *Times* to publish an account of Lai Tin's accomplishments against Cal several months after the fact may not have been coincidental. Around the same time, the American baseball world discovered that both Lai Tin and Lang Akana had been recruited by elite organized baseball franchises. The Portland Beavers of the Pacific Coast League sought Akana, while the big league Chicago White Sox quested after Lai Tin. Curiously, the Portland Beavers' decision to give Akana a tryout seemingly aroused more animus than the possibility of Lai Tin playing in the American League against the likes of Ty Cobb. This may have been because the West Coast was more drenched in anti-Asian politics than the Midwest and East Coast. In any event, a threatened player boycott in the PCL helped force the Beavers into passing on Akana. Lai Tin's failure to show up at the White Sox spring training camp in Paso Robles, California, proved more mysterious.[3]

Mired in mediocrity and facing competition for Chicago's baseball dollar from the National League Cubs and the upstart Federal League Whales, the Chicago White Sox franchise was owned by Charles Comiskey. Always on the lookout for another dollar, Comiskey perhaps hoped that Lai Tin would bring his team more public attention and patrons curious to see a ballplayer of Asian parentage donning a major league uniform. Moreover, the White Sox were considering moving the regular third sacker, Buck Weaver, to shortstop. So perhaps third base was available to the skilled Lai Tin.[4]

Mainland professionals who visited the islands during the winter of 1914 and 1915 caught sight of Lai Tin and Akana as well as other ballplayers in Hawai'i.

For example, a team of major leaguers advertising itself as the All-Americans arrived on the islands in late 1914. Leading that team was one of the best right-handed pitchers of all time, Grover Cleveland Alexander. With Alexander on the slab, the big leaguers beat a team called the Oahu All-Stars, 4–1. Yet when the All-Americans faced the CAU team, Lai Tin proved troublesome to Alexander, whacking a triple and another hit. The all-Chinese nine with Apau Kau on the mound and batting four for four barely lost to the All-Americans, 5–4. One mainland professional subsequently told the *Sporting Life* the all-Chinese harbored "great" fielders but inadequate hitters. Yet John Bliss, a former major league catcher for the St. Louis Cardinals, praised Akana and Lai Tin as well as catcher Kan Yen Chun. Bliss indicated that Akana was not ready for the PCL but needed a year in the lower division, Northwestern League. Kan Yen Chun was a nice catcher, Bliss admitted, but too physically light for professional baseball on the mainland. Lai Tin, Bliss contended, possessed all the big league tools. He could field, run, and hit.[5]

The mainland sporting press extended a measure of courtesy to Lai Tin. The *Washington Post* informed readers, "In the event of Lai Tin fulfilling expectations he will enjoy the unique honor of being the first Celestial to play on a National or American League team." Lai Tin was also boosted as "one of the best shortstops in the Far East," where apparently one could locate the Hawaiian Islands. A story published in the *Albany Evening Journal* lamented that Native American pitcher Chief Bender was headed to the Federal League, organized as an ill-fated opposition to the baseball establishment. If he had stayed with the Philadelphia Athletics, Bender could have faced "Lai Tin, the new Chinese infielder of the White Sox." Such a confrontation "would have provided a spectacle of race conflict not provided elsewhere." A somewhat respectful *Sporting Life* claimed that "if all is said about Lai Tin is true there is no doubt he can make it." And writing under the pseudonym of "Sportsman," a journalist for the *Baltimore Afro American* weighed in on the signing of a "Chinese" by the White Sox. Without naming Lai Tin, Sportsman averred that the ballplayer in question hailed from Honolulu and was recruited by organized baseball because of his skill set and not because he could be marketed as an exotic novelty. Sportsman "hoped that African Americans would be extended the same courtesy"—a "courtesy" withheld for a few decades.[6]

Some journalists sought to squeeze humor out of Lai's signing and, in particular, his name. The *Sporting Life*'s Rex Milford wrote, "Now that the White Sox have corralled that Honolulu Chinaman—Lai Tin—every paragrapher in Balldom will be ringing the challenges on the possibility that Tin will be canned." Frank Menke, a well-regarded sportswriter, urged readers to consider "the complications that would come in case Mr. Tin horned into a regular job." When readers of the *Lima Daily News* on January 10, 1915, found out about Lai Tin's recruitment by the White Sox, they became privy to an imaginary argument between the Chinese ballplayer from Hawai'i and an umpire: "Ow, Owee, Whatee malla you? You all time givee ploor Chinee worst from itee! way outsidee! way outsidee!" In the monthly *Baseball Magazine*, William Phelon observed that the recruitment of "the Chinese wonder . . . has caused ripples of merriment." While calling Lai Tin a talented player, Phelon wrote that he was the nephew of "Pie Tin" and a close relative of "Tin Horn." Even one of baseball's greatest pitchers got into the act. In February 1915, a column under Christy Mathewson's byline asserted that when "the new Chinese player" joined the White Sox, Comiskey could "depend on the laundry patronage of Chicago." That is, if an umpire made a close call against the "Chinaman," he could well expect "a shower of flatirons . . . accompanied with a conversation that reads like a laundry list."[7]

Meanwhile, Akana lost the struggle to play PCL baseball. A disappointed *Honolulu Star Bulletin* condemned Portland and the PCL: "Narrow racial prejudice or possibly the fears that if the bars are let down someone will lose his regular job, threatens to work a grave injustice to Lang Akana, the local ball player." The *Star-Bulletin* further confided its support for Lai Tin: "The local fans are thoroughly disgusted over the whole affair [with Akana] and will be pulling hard for Lai Tin to make good with the White Sox. If he develops into a star the Portland management may have a few regrets coming."[8]

For those rooting for Lai Tin to make baseball history, he sadly failed to show up at the White Sox spring training camp at Paso Robles. And it is not entirely clear as to why. One story published in a mainland newspaper and cited by the *Pacific Commercial Advertiser* claimed that the White Sox "were restrained from signing him by the objection that chinamen are not eligible for the American League." The *Stockton Evening Mail* reasoned that Lai Tin required more "seasoning" to suit the White Sox. It was also purported that Lai Tin himself preferred to give the White Sox the brush-off because he did not want to be the only person of his ethnic background playing for the Southside franchise, seeking instead the company of the 1915 Travelers. A *Brooklyn Daily Standard* piece claimed that Nat Strong, while in Honolulu during the winter of 1914–1915, had seen the unsigned contract offered by the White Sox, as well as a similarly unsigned contract tendered to Apau Kau by the Philadelphia Athletics. Lai, according to Strong, entreated the White Sox management to recruit other Travelers. Strong maintained that the White Sox were only interested in Lai, but the infielder and Apau Kau desired playing on the mainland with at least a few "fellow countrymen." Significantly, En Sue Pung reportedly warned Lai Tin and Apau Kau away from organized baseball and its embrace of racism. Other Travelers attracted or were at least rumored to have attracted the interest of mainland professional franchises. Among these were Foster Robinson, Kan Yen Chun, En Sue Pung, Fred Markham, and Vernon Ayau.[9]

The *Honolulu Star-Bulletin* suspected as well that racism restrained organized baseball from employing Chinese and other ballplayers from Hawai'i. In July 1914 it reported that the Oahu League had sought recognition from organized baseball as a minor league. However, the *Star Bulletin* declared, organized baseball's "adherence to the color line" raised the "bars of race" against the Oahu League. The PCL's A. T. Baum told one reporter that "no negroes or Orientals" were allowed as players. It made sense, then, to the *Star-Bulletin* that since the Oahu League would not exclude its "very best players," who were Japanese and Chinese, as well as the standouts on the all–African American 25th regiment nine, organized baseball would not only turn its back on expanding to Hawai'i but also fail to diligently recruit En Sue Pung and Vernon Ayau.[10]

Gathering on the Mainland

Lai Tin's decision to remain on the East Coast after the 1916 tour seems to have been motivated by love as much as anything else. As a Traveler, Lai Tin had fallen for a white Brooklyn resident named Isabelle Reynolds, whom he met at a church social. The couple would marry and live in the Philadelphia area. Significantly, in states such as California, antimiscegenation laws outlawed such weddings, while throughout the nation marriages uniting a nonwhite male and a white female were, even if legal, widely frowned upon. And while Lai Tin marrying a white woman might have been deemed more acceptable among their white neighbors than if an African American male married Isabelle Reynolds, the couple still treaded a highly treacherous racial frontier. In the process, they perhaps demonstrated what scholar Sheryll Cashin calls "cultural dexterity," which she defines as "an enhanced capacity for intimate connections with people outside one's own tribe, for seeing and accepting difference rather than demanding an assimilation to an unspoken norm of whiteness."[11]

Eventually marrying a white woman himself, the fellow who invariably defended the infield to Lai Tin's left on the Travelers merits recognition as the first Chinese American to play organized baseball. Unlike Lai Tin, Vernon Ayau returned to Honolulu after the Travelers' 1916 journey. During the winter of 1916–1917, Honolulu was visited first by a team of mainland professionals assembled from various franchises and then by the PCL's Portland Beavers, training in the city. Local ballplayers offered keen competition to the mainlanders, and Vernon Ayau's work at shortstop shone. Called the All-Americans by the Honolulu press, the mainland professional nine defeated a team of Hawai'i-based all-stars, 5–1. Ayau and other former Travelers were on the Hawaiian all-stars nine, as well as Black 25th regiment stars Wilbur "Bullet" Rogan and Home Run Johnson. Bill Leard, manager of the Seattle Giants of the Northwestern League, was impressed with Ayau and signed him to a contract, although the mainlander remained decidedly silent about inking a superb ballplayer such as Rogan. One mainland correspondent who had seen Ayau play declared he glittered as the best shortstop outside of the big leagues and that only an "unwritten law banning Mongolians" could prevent him from making good. Against the Beavers, Ayau not only sparkled in the field but demonstrated some hitting promise, smacking a homer to help an all-Chinese team edge the PCL club, 9–8.[12]

In 1917, the Northwestern League possessed teams in Washington, as well as Montana and British Columbia. Moreover, it encompassed a region that had fervently and even violently shunned people of Asian ancestry. Unsurprisingly, then, the Pacific Northwest offered an ambivalent welcome to Ayau. The Seattle Giants hoped they had found not only a skilled shortstop but an exotic novelty to entice more customers. Thus, according to an *Oakland Tribune* report, Bill Leard expressed disappointment that Ayau appeared insufficiently "oriental." Indeed, the shortstop, Leard complained, could not even speak Chinese. Yet a newspaper in Portland voiced the opinion that Ayau was too "oriental" for the Northwestern League. One of the towns in the league, it emphasized, was Great Falls, Montana, where white workers had once thrown a Chinese immigrant into a local river during a strike in the late 1800s. The *Portland Telegraph* could not guarantee Ayau's security "in case he ventures into the forbidden land." The *Honolulu Star-Bulletin* countered by praising Ayau as "a player of good habits." Moreover, it predicted that he "should become a popular star with the Seattle team." The *Portland Oregonian*'s Roscoe Fawcett, furthermore, celebrated Ayau's signing by Seattle, declaring that it proved the "cosmopolitan" character of American baseball.[13]

The sporting press interviewed the shortstop soon after Ayau arrived in Washington. He expressed confidence that other Chinese in Hawai'i would play professionally on the mainland. Among those he mentioned as professional prospects were Lai Tin, Apau Kau, and Kan Yen Chun. Seemingly forgetting that Andy Yamashiro stood out as one of the better batters on the 1915 and 1916 Travelers teams, Ayau insisted that the Chinese were more likely to carve out careers in baseball than "Japs," because they hit better. Notably, Ayau criticized organized baseball's construction of the color line for barring the talented Rogan.[14]

Initially, the Seattle Giants seemed willing to give Ayau a fair chance. The *Seattle Post-Intelligencer* admitted that Ayau was "handicapped" in making the Giants. But it was also convinced that Bill Leard and Giants fans were open-minded. Royal Brougham, a sports columnist with the *Seattle Post-Intelligencer*, claimed that Ayau was "making good at short" in mid-April 1917, while gaining support from Seattle's Chinese community. When the season started in May, Ayau sparkled in the field as shortstop. Against Vancouver in early May, Ayau made the play of the day for the Giants, knocking down a hard line drive and then throwing out the batter. But after a few weeks the Giants released him, claiming that "the little Chinese" could not hit Northwestern League pitching. Apparently, as well, Ayau suffered back problems but the *Seattle Star* did not expect he would have any trouble finding a position with another Northwestern League team.[15]

Ayau dawdled in the Pacific Northwest, shining in semipro ball in Seattle and Portland. Late in May, Ayau performed for the Northwest Steel Company in Portland. In his first game in Portland, the *Portland Oregonian* opined that Ayau could have drawn more fans if the public had been given proper notice. As it was, he exhibited a "snappy" game at short. The Northwestern League called on

Ayau's services again when the Tacoma franchise recruited him. The *Sporting News* pronounced Ayau a "success" for Tacoma and reported, rather ominously for those fearing Asians taking jobs away from European Americans, that Tacoma had to release a white player to make room for Ayau. Russ Hall of Montana's *Anaconda Standard* asserted that the Tacoma management "produced a Chinaman for an infielder. He is Ayau . . . and the grinning celestial plays the game a whole lot better than some of the white men" tried earlier in the season. The *Anaconda Standard* called Ayau "a little Chinaman who does things in the pinches." Still, Ayau did not stay long with Tacoma, for whom he generally held down third base. According to the *Anaconda Standard*, Ayau had performed consistently, but pressure from the league's Great Falls' franchise compelled Tacoma to release "the yellow third sacker." The *Standard* concluded, "Thus endeth the diamond career of a smiling Chinaman [who] saveys the white man's sport pretty well." The *Seattle Times* added that the "clever little Hawaiian third baseman" had been "kidded" by Tacoma teammates who told him he might get thrown into the river when the team got to Great Falls. Ayau, according to the *Times*, decided to remain in Tacoma, "where the worst that could come to him is to be taken for a ukulele artist." Ayau, however, persisted in trying to find a job in the Northwestern League, eventually landing at shortstop for the Vancouver franchise. Unfortunately, Ayau's stay in the Canadian city did not last long as the U.S. entry into World War I spelled doom for many minor leagues. The Northwestern League was no exception, folding in mid-July. According to Baseball-reference.com, Ayau batted only .203 in 133 at bats while in the Northwestern League.[16]

In late July, the *Seattle Times* reported that Ayau lingered on the mainland: "His desire for a dish of good old poi was not as strong as his desire to play baseball." Thus, invited "by Lai Tin, a fellow Oriental," Ayau struck out for independent ball on the East Coast. Reportedly, Lai Tin could have reunited with him in the Northwestern League. Chinito Moriyama told the Honolulu press in early May that he had received a letter from Lai saying that the third sacker had gotten an offer from Spokane. Lai expressed disinterest, claiming he held a good job in Philadelphia and was playing independent ball in the region. Given Ayau's fate, Lai Tin probably made the right decision.[17]

Andy Yamashiro deserves celebration as the first person of Japanese ancestry to play organized baseball in the United States. Apparently persuaded by Lai Tin, Yamashiro remained in the Philadelphia area rather than return to Honolulu. In the fall of 1916, he received national press attention as a member of the Temple University football team. Represented as an exotic in football gear, Yamashiro, according to the media, hoped that Temple would launch him toward a dental career. The *Philadelphia Public Ledger* declared Yamashiro the first "Chinese football player" to earn a regular spot on a college football team. The daily recognized that "Yim" was not Yamashiro's real last name but explained that it was difficult for student cheering sections to give three cheers of "yeah" and then "Yamashire [*sic*]."[18]

Yamashiro never became a dentist, but in the spring of 1917 he started what proved to be a short-lived career as a full-time professional ballplayer. Widely perceived as Chinese because of his fictional surname of Yim, he roamed the outfield for the Blue Ridge League's Gettysburg Ponies. Yamashiro batted a respectable .291 in ninety games, winning plaudits for his speed. Furnished with a D classification, the Blue Ridge League clung to the lowest rung of organized baseball's ladder. Still, several future major leaguers initiated their baseball careers in the Blue Ridge League, which comprised franchises in towns in Maryland, West Virginia, and Pennsylvania. People of Asian ancestry were few and far between in the municipalities served by the league; thus Yamashiro had to have been seen, to quote historian Ronald Takaki, as a "stranger from a different shore." Accordingly, life was not always easy for Yamashiro in the Blue Ridge League. Maryland's *Frederick Post* declared that the "little fellow acts like a gentleman and should be treated as a gentleman." However, the *Post* lamented that opposing fans too frequently abused the "little Chinaman."[19]

Yamashiro, nonetheless, often excelled in a Gettysburg Ponies' uniform. In a game against Chambersburg in mid-May, the Nisei lifted a ball over the center fielder's head and scampered around the bases for an in-the-park home run. The *Chambersburg Public Opinion* averred, "Yim was touted as a fast runner. His press agent did not exaggerate a bit." After taking the lead in a double steal, Yamashiro inspired the *Public Opinion* to label him an "aggressive opponent." In another game against Chambersburg in May, Yamashiro hit a double and then made a "great" and "agile" headfirst slide to score the winning run. Around the same time, the *Hanover Evening Sun*'s "Bill's Corner" hailed Yim's popularity in Gettysburg and predicted he would collect accolades throughout the league. The anonymous columnist praised the outfielder's versatility, stressing his powerful bat. The columnist asserted, "It sure is worthwhile to catch Yim in action." When Gettysburg downed Chambersburg again the next month, Yamashiro, according to a *Philadelphia Inquirer* correspondent, "furnished the thrills of the game." Meanwhile, the *Honolulu Star-Bulletin* noted that "the old boy from the land of Cherry Blossoms" shined for Gettysburg.[20]

Yamashiro played independent baseball in the Philadelphia area before the 1917 Blue Ridge League season and after it prematurely folded owing to the exigencies of World War I. In April 1917, he covered center field for Roxborough in a game against Midvale, getting a hit and scoring a run in a game matching nines representing different Philadelphia neighborhoods. In September 1917, Yim played for the Delaware County League's Media team. Competing outside league competition, Media lost a doubleheader against the famed Bacharach Giants, an all-Black team based in Atlantic City. Yim got a hit in both games. Meanwhile, "Yim, the famous Chinese player," took some at bats for a nine sponsored by Lit Brothers—a popular department store in Philadelphia.[21]

While performing beyond organized baseball's realm, Lai Tin created a fine reputation in East Coast baseball in 1917. Nonetheless, the press accounts of Lai on and off the field were often misleading. In May 1917, the *Philadelphia Inquirer* printed a piece on "L.W. Lai," prompted by the increased call for military recruits after the U.S. declaration of war. This story depicted its subject as a mechanical engineer employed by the Pennsylvania Railroad. Lai was further described as a graduate of the "College of Hawaii," for which he was a champion broad jumper and sprinter. The *Inquirer* also remembered that he recently played on the touring "Chinese team." The story's gist was that Lai had been recruited into the "Ninth Regiment" of engineers and was himself actively recruiting others into the military. Indeed, in Honolulu, the *Star-Bulletin* confided in June 1917 that "Lai Tin is going to France as part of the 9th regiment engineers."[22]

This and other related stories' erratic efforts at accuracy did not totally elude reality. Lai had not entered the military at the time, although he conceivably took a hand in recruiting others. But Lai had registered for the draft. Calling himself William Tin Lai, he gave his address to the draft board as 1421 Arch Street in Philadelphia, the location of the Central YMCA. Although born in Hawai'i and therefore a natural citizen of the United States, Lai is described as "naturalized" on the registration card, which further claims Lai was a clerk for the Pennsylvania Railroad, single, and "racially Mongolian." In terms of physical appearance, Lai was called tall, medium built, with black hair and brown eyes.[23]

For much of 1917, Lai and Fred Markham performed for Upland of the challenging Delaware County League. Based a bit southwest of Philadelphia, the Delaware County League was loaded with talented ballplayers, many of whom were former and future major and minor leaguers. Indeed, the great Frank "Home Run" Baker played at one time for Upland, and many of the league's teams opposed talented Black nines in the area with some success. Newspapers in and near Philadelphia introduced Markham and Lai as newcomers to the Delaware County League during the spring of 1917. In April 1917, the *Philadelphia Inquirer* announced that Upland had signed "Mark, the big Chinese University catcher and Lai, another of the celebrated Chinese players." Published out of Delaware County, the *Chester Times* extolled Lai as "one of the fastest runners in the country." As summer progressed, the press in and around Philadelphia occasionally shone spotlights on Lai and Markham. In August 1917, the *Trenton Evening Times* averred that Mark, who caught for "the famous Chinese team," had strengthened Upland, as had Lai, "another Chinese."[24]

Lai kept his friends back home in Honolulu abreast of his experiences in far-off southeastern Pennsylvania. The *Star-Bulletin* got ahold of a letter he sent with a clipping describing an Upland game. Future Hall of Famer Chief Bender pitched for Upland and Markham caught. Lai, according to the clipping, sparkled in the game. A month later, the *Honolulu Star-Bulletin* published a photo of Lai with Chief Bender. The caption declared Lai "one of the greatest Chinese players in baseball." It added that "Bender from one section of the world, and Lai from another is an example of what baseball is doing in the world today." Despite organized baseball's concerted efforts to marginalize Native Americans,

Latinos, Asians, and Pacific Islanders, while excluding Blacks, the game's supporters throughout the American empire persisted in portraying the game as cosmopolitan and egalitarian.[25]

Eventually Vernon Ayau joined Lai and Markham in Upland's lineup. On August 26, the *Philadelphia Inquirer* reported the Delaware County League statistics that had hitherto been kept. It claimed that "Lai, the classy third sacker of Upland, called the Ty Cobb of the Delaware County league, holds the base running honors." In September, the *Inquirer* ran a photo article on the Upland nine. The team roster was shown with Lai standing next to Ayau in the back row. "Marks" was seated in the front row. The text praised both Markham and Lai by labeling them as "classy Chinese," although no mention was made of Ayau. In late September, Chester upended Upland, 3–1. Even so, Lai, according to the *Chester Times*, excited fans with a fielding gem at third while knocking in Upland's only run with a double.[26]

Meanwhile, in mid-August, the *Honolulu Star-Bulletin* praised the playing of Markham, Ayau, and especially Lai in Delaware County. Regarding Lai, the *Star-Bulletin* celebrated the good press accorded the infielder. It boasted that a Philadelphia paper called Lai better than former Philadelphia Athletic great Frank Baker. Considering that the latter put together a Hall of Fame career that included leading the American League in home runs for four years and a lifetime .307 average in thirteen years, that was high, albeit exaggerated, praise. As for Ayau, Lai wrote to the *Star-Bulletin*, praising the shortstop's contributions to Upland.[27]

In October, Upland played a series of playoff games against Chester. On October 7, Upland beat Chester, 4–0. Lai batted two for five and scored a run. Hailed by the *Chester Times* as "Upland's great catcher," Markham shone, too, batting two for four and stealing a base. In another playoff game, Chester edged Upland in extra innings before a crowd that included Connie Mack, head of the American League's Philadelphia Athletics, and the National League's Philadelphia Phillies' manager, Pat Moran. At third, Lai helped "pull . . . off a lightning double play" to stifle a Chester rally. Additionally, Lai got two hits and scored one of Upland's two runs. Both Mack and Moran, the *Philadelphia Inquirer* declared, appeared smitten by Lai's performance.[28]

Upland's baseball schedule did not keep Lai busy enough. In August, he, Ayau, and Markham performed for a Millville, New Jersey, nine. Midway through the month, Lai led Millville to a victory over Bridgeton. Accompanying an account of the game, the *Bridgeton Evening News* published a respectful cartoon of "Lai, the Hawaiian star, handling some difficult chances." After a game against Vineland, the *Evening News* enthused that the three ballplayers from Hawai'i played "sensationally" for Millville. The *News*, in particular, admired Markham's throws down to Ayau to catch Vineland base runners. A hundred miles away from Philadelphia, Lai and Markham found time to play for the Brooklyn Bushwicks, the notable independent team named after a neighborhood that bordered Brooklyn and Queens. For most of Lai's long career with the Bushwicks, they played at Dexter Park, a multipurpose facility sharing space with a hotel, dance hall, carousel, swings, shooting gallery, and bowling alley. Co-owned by Nat Strong, the Bushwicks generally played one or two games a week on Sunday and typically at home. Attendance was usually high for Bushwick games, and owners Strong and Max Rosner made money, in part, by luring visiting teams with guarantees of $500–$600 per game but steadfastly denying them percentages of the gate.[29]

In March 1917, the Brooklyn sporting press alerted readers that Lai and Markham would join the Bushwicks. The *Brooklyn Daily Eagle* announced Lai's signing, calling him a "clever Chinese player." At that time, the Bushwicks had not yet moved into Dexter Park and were playing home games at a site called Wallace's Ridgewood Grounds in Queens until it burned down. The *Brooklyn Daily Standard Union* welcomed Lai and Markham. It claimed that Lai would bring into Ridgewood a good number of friends he made while playing with the Travelers in New York City, appraising the third sacker as "the greatest drawing card ever seen at Ridgewood." As for Markham, the daily hailed him as the "peer of catchers playing independent baseball and the equal of many major league catchers." A few days before opening day, the *Standard Union* insisted that the two "Oriental cracks" had just arrived from the Pacific Coast to play for the Bushwicks. Around the same time, Markham had registered for the draft in Philadelphia. His registration card indicates that he was an unemployed accountant and racially Malay, a designation typically preserved for natives from places such as the Philippines and Indonesia.[30]

Lai and Markham performed well for the Bushwicks. On April 22, 1917, the Bushwicks inaugurated their season before 3,000 fans at Ridgewood. The *New York Sun* marked the occasion of Lai and Markham wearing Bushwick uniforms by declaring that for the first time in the state's history "two Chinese ballplayers" played on the same team as whites. Early in June, the Bushwicks split a doubleheader with the all-Black Brooklyn Royal Giants. The *Brooklyn Citizen* criticized Markham's catching but praised the overall fielding of "the other Chink." On June 10, the Bushwicks split a doubleheader, winning one game from a New London, Connecticut, team but losing to the African American Philadelphia Giants. Lai was the hitting star of the first game, collecting three hits and three stolen bases, inspiring the *Brooklyn Daily Times* to dub him "a slugging demon." The *Brooklyn Citizen* was more taken with his fielding, stressing that Lai's glove work was "easily the highlight" of the doubleheader. Meanwhile, Lai corresponded with the *Star-Bulletin*, assuring locals that he and Markham were key members of the Bushwicks. Indeed, Lai's all-around play for the Bushwicks continued to spark admiration in 1917, overshadowing Markham's solid but less exciting productivity. Late in August, Vernon Ayau debuted with the Bushwicks. The *Eagle* described his work at shortstop as "brilliant" as the Bushwicks took on the Brooklyn Royal Giants in a doubleheader. Lai's fielding too won commendation by the daily as did Markham's work at catcher.[31]

In Honolulu during the fall of 1917, the *Star-Bulletin*'s Riley Allen wrote he had returned from the mainland, where he met with Ayau, Markham, and Lai in Philadelphia. They told him they were satisfied with their baseball lives on the East Coast. At the same time, Allen urged readers in Hawai'i to take pride in how the three represented them on the mainland. Allen focused on the Hawaiian "Denny" Markham. He contended that Markham had "developed into a high-class catcher," as well as a good hitter. Markham's ballplaying services, Allen asserted, were in demand, but the Hawaiian was determined to use baseball to finance his schooling at Temple so that he could become a certified public accountant. Not all former Travelers on the mainland had congregated in the Philadelphia area, Allen confided. Hawaiian George Bush had landed a job as an assistant foreman at Henry Ford's auto plant in Dearborn, Michigan. Allen subsequently penned an editorial in the *Honolulu Star-Bulletin* that reflected the beliefs of too many haole public opinion makers on the islands. In a vein familiar to minority groups in America down through the years, Allen complained that Hawaiians tended to think they were owed a living rather than working hard to sustain themselves. More should follow the lead of Markham, whose diligent pursuit of an education exemplified a "progressive Hawaiian."[32]

Lai and the Philadelphia Phillies

Standing out among some of the best ballplayers outside of organized baseball, Lai was given an opportunity to play for the Philadelphia Phillies in the spring of 1918. The Phillies had finished a respectable second place in the National League in 1917. Yet World War I might well have contributed to the Phillies looking at alternative sources of talent as many major league–caliber ballplayers were thrust into either military service or war-related work. Moreover, some Phillies were reluctant to agree to the contract offers sent to them by the team's front office. As for Lai, perhaps knowing that several of his former teammates lived in and around Philadelphia made it easier for him to join the Phillies than was the case previously with the White Sox. Late in March 1918, readers of the *Washington Post* discovered the following story headline: "Chinese Player Gets Trial with Phillies." The story testified that "Billy Lai, the Chinese lad," was in the Phillies' training camp in St. Petersburg, Florida. It added that Lai had been "a sensation" while performing for Upland, where he "led the circuit in baserunning."[33]

Lai's presence with the Phillies elicited a great deal of press commentary. The *Brooklyn Daily Eagle* published a photograph of Lai Tin in a Travelers' uniform. The title of the corresponding text was "Oriental Phenom Gets His Chance." The *Eagle* reminded readers that Lai had been participating in local independent baseball, maintaining that since the Phillies' roster was hard-hit by several contract holdouts, Lai's chances of making the Phillies were not all that remote. Moreover, it averred that based on what he had heard about Lai, manager Pat Moran considered the infielder big league material, because while Lai's hitting was suspect, he got on base often by way of walks, and once on base he could unsettle the defense with his dynamic base running. A piece in the *Sporting News* asserted that "with the Chinaman Lai Tin and the Indian Tincup" on the Phillies, the Philadelphia franchise had an "all-nations" squad. Readers of the *Lima Daily News* discovered that "'Billy' Lai, the Chinese third baseman from Honolulu, who is getting a trial with the Phils, is a crack ukulele tinkler." Columnist Jack Vance wrote that umpires would have a hard time with Lai, as "you can't understand what a Chinaman says, let alone what he thinks." A brief piece published in the *Des Moines Daily News* on April 7, 1918, was titled "Hail the Chink." It declared that manager Pat Moran might be on to something by turning Lai into a Philly. "The Chinese third baseman" would draw fans curious to see "the oriental" in action.[34]

On the first day of the Phillies' camp, Lai, according to the *Philadelphia Public Ledger*'s Robert Maxwell, attracted a great deal of attention. Maxwell described the ballplayer as ambitious and confident enough to "expect to prove his worth in the first five minutes of practice." Lai indicated to the press that he always wanted to play in the big leagues. Moreover, he thought he could make the Phillies, telling the press that he hit the great Grover Cleveland Alexander well in an exhibition game in Hawai'i some years earlier. Maxwell confided that Lai was one of the fastest men baseball had ever seen and could handle his infield duties well. Yet, Maxwell added, some observers actually doubted that Lai came from Hawai'i, because he did not tote around a ukulele.[35]

Lai's performance in the Phillies' preseason games proved lackluster. In any event, former boxing great turned sportswriter James J. Corbett counseled readers that "Lai Tin, a Chinese," impressed Moran. Corbett described him as a "crack infielder," very fast, but weak at bat. Still, Moran could keep Lai around for a while, Corbett speculated. "The Celestial," he declared, would boost attendance. In Honolulu, Riley Allen possessed a letter from Fred Markham claiming that he too had been offered a contract by the Phillies but turned it down to pursue his education. Lai, Markham insisted, was the fastest player on the Phillies' spring training roster and would make good.[36]

Lai, however, would not make good with the Phillies. The May 23 edition of the *Sporting News* announced that "Billy Tin Lai, the Chinese infielder," had been released by the Phillies to the Eastern League. As for why Lai did not make the Phillies, mainland newspapers pointed to Lai's hitting as a problem. The *Honolulu Star-Bulletin* commented that Lai had hit well during spring training but began to slump as the Phillies neared opening day. In any event, Moran was happy enough with Lai to want to keep him close at hand. So, Lai, described by the *Star-Bulletin* as a "big leaguer in every sense of the word," was sent to the relatively nearby Bridgeport Americans.[37]

Over the years, assorted organizations known as the Eastern League inhabited the world of professional baseball. The one that Lai joined in 1918 was established in 1916 with franchises in Connecticut, Maine, and Massachusetts, while Providence, Rhode Island, began to host a franchise in 1918. Within organized baseball's hierarchy, the Eastern League was classified as a B league. That is, it was relatively high on organized baseball's food chain. Nonetheless, the Eastern League was considered a decided step below the most elite minor league organizations, such as the PCL, the American Association, and the International League.

Reuniting with Lai on the Bridgeport Americans was Andy Yamashiro after the latter's good year at Gettysburg in the D-level Blue Ridge League. He was living in Philadelphia between baseball seasons. Early in 1918, the *Honolulu Star-Bulletin* published a photograph of him demonstrating jujitsu at Jack O'Brien's Health Studio in that city. The Nisei also played with the Bushwicks in the beginning of their 1918 season. Indeed, Yamashiro, Markham, and Ayau appeared in the Bushwicks' opening game lineup in early April 1918. The latter two continued to perform for the Brooklyn nine after Yamashiro departed for Bridgeport, where both he and Lai got off to fast starts for the Bridgeport Americans. The latter was often called "Bill" or "Willie" by the Eastern League press, while the former continued to be identified as Chinese in ancestry and possessive of the surname of Yim. On May 26, Bridgeport took on Springfield, and, according to the *Bridgeport Telegram*, "the Chinese players for the locals . . . shine[d]." On May 29, the *Bridgeport Telegram* reported that sweltering heat was the topic of the day as the Bridgeport nine faced Waterbury. Still, Lai and Yamashiro, "the Chinese players," did not mind the warm weather as they sustained their excellent performances. Lai, called "the Celestial third sacker," and player-manager Paul Krichell pulled off a double steal that was the highlight of the game. On June 2, Bridgeport beat Providence, and "the Chinese players of the locals, Bill Lai at third and Andy Yim in right, had another field day each."[38]

Lai, according to the *Bridgeport Telegram*, attacked the game. It opined that "Bill Lai is full of pepper and . . . always in action." Perhaps not a consistently great fielder, he often had phenomenal plays at third. He excelled most, the *Telegram* testified, at hitting and base running. The *Telegram* concluded that Lai evinced prowess of both power at bat and the ability to beat out infield hits. He was also a "quick thinker" who pressured opposing catchers while on base. "So far," the *Telegram* asserted, "catchers have been practically powerless to intercept the Chink." The daily further described him as the "prize pepper box" of the Eastern League. The *Telegram* found him belying the stereotype of the passive Asian, as he was constantly "chattering and moving in some direction." At the same time, the *Telegram* contrasted Lai to "Andy Yim, the Chinese right fielder," who appeared a "stolid type."[39]

In correspondence to Hawai'i, Lai articulated his joy in organized baseball during the summer of 1918. In July, the *Honolulu Star-Bulletin* reported that the ballplayer had written one of his sisters that the Eastern League posed few problems for him. For example, he boasted of his hitting and stealing twenty-four bases in his first twenty-five games, adding he could have stolen more had he not been slowed down by a charley horse. The next month, Lai wrote home proclaiming that both he and Yamashiro found Bridgeport fans appreciative of the skills they consistently exhibited as ballplayers.[40]

As the season progressed, Lai and Yim continued to generate generally favorable press, at least in Bridgeport. Around mid-June, the *Telegram* reported that "Andy Yim, the Chinese right fielder," and Lai serenaded their teammates with Hawaiian music and songs on a road trip to Hartford. The next day, the *Telegram* ran photos of Lai and Yim under the headline "Our Chinese Puzzles." Subsequently, the *Telegram*'s T. F. Magner lamented that Eagle manager Paul Krichell quit over a dispute with the Eastern League president. Krichell's baseball acumen was clearly demonstrated to Magner when he signed Lai and Yim, who not only helped the Americans but were "the only two Chinese playing professional baseball."[41]

World War I troubled Lai's Eastern League season. Early in July, the *Philadelphia Public Ledger* reported that "Billy Tin Lai" was the first local player to come under the government's "work or fight" edict—an edict aimed at mollifying a public wondering why athletic young men played baseball while others headed for European battlefields. Consequently, sportswriter Magner worried about Lai's draft status and exulted when the Philadelphia draft board informed the ballplayer he would not have to report for military duty. Lai had successfully argued that he should continue civilian life because he had a wife and child. Magner insisted that the Bridgeport nine could not afford to lose "easily the best third sacker in the league."[42]

To be sure, the hiring of Lai and Yamashiro provoked controversy. The *Sporting News* pointed out that "Billy Lai" and "Andy Yim" inspired objections from the Providence and New Haven franchises. It asserted that Bridgeport could hardly be blamed for using "the two Chinese players." They were, after all, "two of the fastest players to wear a Bridgeport uniform" and doing their "level best" to keep Bridgeport a contender. The protesters may not have wanted the "Celestials" in the Eastern League, but the *Sporting News* stressed that no regulation existed preventing "Chinamen" from playing in organized baseball any more than Cubans—"Negroes," yes, but not "Chinamen." Meanwhile, at least some Black ballplayers on the East Coast expressed understandable exasperation, wondering why the color barrier was lifted for Lai and Yamashiro but not for them.[43]

Back in Honolulu, the *Honolulu Star-Bulletin* and *Pacific Commercial Advertiser* reported on Lai's fine ballplaying on the East Coast. The Star-Bulletin assured readers that "New England sportswriters [were] going wild" over the young man from Hawai'i. The Star-Bulletin quoted Roger Ferri of the *Providence News* that Lai was "too fast" for the Eastern League. The *Star-Bulletin* added that Yamashiro maintained the reputation of island baseball as well. The *Advertiser* described Lai as the "big sensation" of the Bridgeport nine, while "Yim" emerged as a "big sticker."[44]

World War I shut down the Eastern League's season in August. Summarizing the local ball club's 1918 season, the *Bridgeport Telegram* celebrated the contributions of Lai and Yamashiro. Fans, the daily declared, would "certainly miss Bill Lai and Andy Yim, the two Hawaiian ball players." Emphasizing their foreignness, it insisted that Bridgeport baseball lovers had taken to Lai and Yim from the start, finding them "perfect gentlemen, well educated to the American way of things, and always in the game until the last." Lai, especially, was applauded as the swiftest base runner that the Eastern League had seen in years.[45]

Before heading back to the Philadelphia area, Lai and Yamashiro competed in an exhibition game for Bridgeport against the National League's Pittsburgh Pirates. The Americans triumphed against the big leaguers in extra innings, 2–1, with both Lai and Yamashiro standing out. Pirate manager Hugh Bezdek particularly admired Lai, whom he could see in the big leagues. The Chinese American was, according to Bezdek, faster than most in the majors and too fast for the Eastern League. The *Telegram*'s Manger warmly described Lai's triple against the National League club. It "was a pretty blow and gave the fans a chance to see how fast the Hawaiian youngster can round the paths when he wants to." The *Pittsburgh Press* noted as well that "the heathen Chinese, Billy Lai and . . . Charley [*sic*] Yim . . . helped scuttle the Pirates."[46]

A decade later, Ed Sullivan, the future renowned television personality but at the time a syndicated sports columnist, remembered witnessing "Buck Lai, the little Hawaiian-Chinaman," play in Bridgeport in 1918. Writing at the time that Lai tried out for the New York Giants, Sullivan wondered why it took so long for the big leagues to afford the infielder an opportunity. In 1918, Sullivan testified that Lai was "the fastest man in any league," and faster than any big leaguer active ten years later. Lai, Sullivan insisted, stuck out as the only ballplayer to "SCORE FROM SECOND on a squeeze play." The Eastern League, Sullivan divulged, possessed plenty of talented ballplayers, several of whom rose to the major leagues, but Lai was not one of them. The columnist declared, "Lai might have made the big league grade that year if the team had been friendly to him." By that, Sullivan seemingly avers, the Bridgeport franchise blocked Lai's way to a major league career. While team management may have held disparaging views of Lai's racial identity, it is hard to believe racism would motivate the franchise to keep Lai around especially since major league teams were obligated to pay Bridgeport for his services. Indeed, perhaps his Bridgeport employers liked Lai too much given his popularity with local fans.[47]

Lai and Yamashiro continued to play baseball after the 1918 Eastern League schedule prematurely ceased. Lai made his way to Chester, Pennsylvania, where he worked at a shipyard. In September 1918, the *Philadelphia Inquirer* reported that "Billy Tin Lai, the sensational Chinese player," joined the Hog Island baseball team. In late August, Lai covered shortstop for Hog Island when it beat the Reading Steel Casting Company. The *Reading Times* declared, "The Chinaman is a wonder on defense." On September 22, 1918, a crowd of 8,000 watched Hog

Island play the Chester Shipping Company. With Lai at third for Hog Island, the magnificent Hall of Famer George Sisler played first base for Chester. As for Yamashiro, he seemingly bounced around the greater Philadelphia region. In mid-August, the right fielder slugged a home run for Wildwood in a game against Olney. He also appeared in the lineup of a team representing the Nativity Catholic Club in the Philadelphia area's Suburban League.[48]

Fred Markham kept busy in independent baseball in New York City and Philadelphia. In June 1918, the *Chicago Defender* reported that Markham caught two games of a doubleheader for the Bushwicks against the Royal Giants. The next month saw Markham with the Chester Shipbuilding team. Playing against Camden, "Fred Mark" as a catcher made "perfect pegs" to nail Camden base runners. He proved peppery and an "active" backstop, according to the *Chester Times*, as well as a good hitter, lashing out two doubles.[49]

World War I

In the weeks after World War I ended, the *Brooklyn Daily Eagle* announced Apau Kau's battlefield death during the waning days of combat. It declared he had been undefeated as a pitcher for the Lit Brothers department store nine in Philadelphia, while also hurling semipro ball in New York City. Wherever he went, *Eagle* readers learned, the young man from Hawai'i cultivated popularity and success. Apau Kau not only pitched effectively for a semipro team representing Lit Brothers but also worked for the popular department store, selling ukuleles and teaching customers how to play the instrument.[50]

Historian Gary Okihiro writes that during the early decades of the twentieth century, "Hawaiian musicians toured the United States and Europe as 'colored artists,' and their music and dance advanced and complemented the commerce-driven dreams of tropical paradise, gentle breezes, swaying palm trees, and moonlight on water." Hawaiian music and dance had fostered a receptive audience among mainlanders since the late nineteenth century. As mentioned earlier, the Travelers sought goodwill for Hawai'i not only through baseball but also through the musicianship of many of the players. However, according to Okihiro, San Francisco's 1915 Pan-Pacific Exposition significantly expanded the market for Hawaiian music and dance. A Honolulu-based magazine designed to promote tourism, *Paradise of the Pacific*, gushed that as a result of the exposition, "everywhere you go, in music halls, vaudeville shows, hotels, cafes, and cabarets Hawaiian dance music is played and Hawaiian songs are sung." Indeed, Hawaiian Luther Kekoa, who often shut down opposing batters for the Travelers as "Ako," remained on the mainland to play ukulele in what the *Harrisburg Patriot* called in July 1917 "a Hawaiian vaudeville skit." Another Hawaiian who once pitched for the Travelers, George Bush, was not just a foreman but also a musician at the Ford plant in Dearborn, Michigan. His boss, Henry Ford, had attended the Pan-Pacific Exposition and became entranced with a group of

Hawaiian musicians. He recruited them to work and play at his plant. Subsequently, they were known as Ford's Hawaiians. Apparently, Bush ended up joining Ford's Hawaiians in 1917, before getting drafted into the military.[51]

Apau Kau, whose name was frequently misspelled by the local press, handled the duties of a semiprofessional pitcher on the East Coast admirably. The *Philadelphia Inquirer* declared, "Appau was in great form" in early July when the Lit Brothers shut down the Ketterlinus team, 16–0. Meanwhile, Apau Kau connected to the folks back home in Hawai'i. He wrote to one resident of Honolulu that Philadelphians "are crazy about Honolulu." According to the *Honolulu Star-Bulletin* in the summer of 1917, he had written to the Hawaiian promotions committee, identifying himself as head of Lit Brothers sporting goods department. Apau Kau promised that if the committee sent him promotional literature, he would gladly distribute it around a receptive Philadelphia.[52]

The fall of 1917 witnessed Apau Kau whisked away from the baseball fields and ukulele lessons toward the meat-grinding battlefields of Europe. In September 1917, the *Philadelphia Public Ledger* announced that "Sam Apau, the brilliant Chinese pitcher for Lit Bros," had been given a farewell dinner by friends. The young man from Hawai'i, drafted into the army, was due to report to Camp Meade in Maryland. The next month, the *Public Ledger* published a photograph of Apau Kau. The caption described him as "the only Chinese at Camp Meade" and a "star pitcher" for Lit Brothers. Also in October, an organization called the Ardsley Club staged a dance at the Martel's Club, located on North Broad Street in Philadelphia. The *Public Ledger* remarked that "Apau Kau, noted Chinese pitcher, who is in training at Camp Meade will be in attendance to greet his many friends."[53]

Despite his racial identity, Apau Kau must have impressed his army superiors, who invited him to attend officer's training camp. The *Philadelphia Public Ledger* asserted in April 1918 that the "popular star of the Lit Brothers" surfaced as a celebrity at the Camp Meade officer's training camp. The only person of Chinese ancestry at the camp, Apau Kau joined its football team. Nonetheless, Apau Kau exhibited growing restiveness at the training camp. He feared he would linger "in school" for a year and fail to get over to Europe to help in the "big push" to conquer the Germans. Thus, Apau Kau decided to ask his superiors if he could reclaim the life of an "enlisted man." Meanwhile, according to a wire story, Apau Kau happily received a package from Honolulu containing a ukulele, which he played often in camp. Readers of the *Lebanon Daily News* discovered that the former pitcher "is giving the real 'wickey, wackey, woo' music now." With his new ukulele, Apau Kau was able to perform in a Christmas concert at Camp Meade.[54]

Attaining the rank of sergeant, Apau Kau was deployed to the maelstrom of World War I Europe early in July 1918 with Company E of the 315th Infantry on a ship called *America*, embarking from Hoboken, New Jersey. In August 1918, a wire story appeared in the *Pittsburgh Press* announcing that not only Apau Kau but Vernon Ayau and Alfred Yap were serving in Europe. The former teammates wrote to Fred Markham that they were "delighted" with their army experience. In October 1918, the *Honolulu Star-Bulletin* informed readers that a not-so-delighted Apau Kau complained to his sister by mail that after three months in Europe, he had yet to see any action. With two brothers also serving in the U.S. military, "the husky pitcher," the *Star-Bulletin* predicted, would do well lobbing grenades at the enemy. Two months later, Andy Yamashiro broke the news of Apau Kau's death to the Philadelphia press. The sergeant was reportedly leading his men when he caught a fatal "hun-bullet" during the latter stages of the Meuse-Argonne offensive, which began in late September and ended in early November. Ultimately successful, the American Expeditionary Forces would suffer over 26,000 soldiers killed and nearly 96,000 wounded as a result of the offensive.[55]

Apau Kau's bravery won esteem from the people of Hawai'i. In early May 1919, the *Honolulu Star-Bulletin* acknowledged that Honolulu's Chinatown honored "one of the best known of Honolulu's young men." During the late winter of 1922, Apau Kau's body was returned to Hawai'i from Antwerp, Belgium, via New York City. Upon the occasion of Apau Kau's burial in Honolulu, the *Star-Bulletin*'s Riley Allen declared that when the pitcher died in Argonne, he "played the game . . . for the team"—the American team. Allen added, "Apau Kau, a Chinese by blood, American citizen by birth, and by absolute and willing allegiance to the Stars and Stripes, will be buried tomorrow afternoon with full military honors. . . . To those honors, Hawaii adds its pride that Apau Kau is one of its 'boys'—a product of this territory where all races mingle and the boys and girls of many bloods are moulded [*sic*] into loyal Americans."[56]

The *Honolulu Advertiser* reported that Apau Kau's funeral in Honolulu was well attended by dignitaries as well as former teammates. The *Advertiser* also published a tribute to Apau Kau written by journalist Sunny K. Hung. While in Philadelphia, Hung visited the Lit Brothers, where he found on the second floor a bronze tablet honoring the department store's former employee. Interestingly, he also learned that the white soldiers in Apau Kau's regiment, while unanimous in their distaste for people of Chinese ancestry, liked him, and he would often serenade them with his ukulele. Later in the decade, Hawai'i's Chinese veterans organized an American Legion post called the Kau-Tom post to honor two of their number who did not return from World War I to the islands—Apau Kau and George Bung Tom.[57]

Vernon Ayau and Alfred Yap were luckier than Apau Kau. In May 1918, Vernon Ayau played his last games for the Bushwicks before joining the military. Early in the month, he emerged as the hitting star against the Philadelphia Giants and the Cuban Stars. Like Apau Kau, Private Ayau was sent to Europe on a ship leaving Hoboken in early July 1918. He was attached to Company F of the 316th regiment. The *Honolulu Star-Bulletin* reported that Ayau had written to his mother from France, assuring her "we are here to fight for liberty and democracy and square our debt to France." In October 1918, the *Star-Bulletin* reported that Ayau received further training in France and earned a promotion to corporal. Sunny K. Hung, subsequently, declared that Ayau had gotten more than a taste of battlefield action as he emerged a relatively fortunate victim of toxic gassing. Winding up in an army hospital, Ayau, according to Hung, had a tearful and what ultimately proved final meeting with Apau Kau.[58]

Alfred Yap arrived in Europe before Apau Kau and Ayau. When Yap enrolled at Lehigh University in 1915, the *Syracuse Herald* predicted that he would prove a good prospect for the school's baseball team. Indeed, Bucknell University's newspaper pronounced Lehigh's Yap as one of the best hitters in college baseball in June 1916. In the summer of 1916, he performed excellently for a nine representing Philadelphia's Strawbridge and Clothiers department store as the *Philadelphia Public Ledger* commended "Yap's . . . fast fielding" in a Strawbridge and Clothier victory. A week later, Yap got a key hit to help his team beat the Travelers. Sportswriter Walter F. Dunn remarked that Yap wanted "to show his former associates" what he could do. In June 1917, Yap excelled in center field for the Bethlehem Steel Company's nine against Wilmington. Some weeks later, he played third base and center field for the Lehigh Stars. In a game against the Saucon Cross nine, he batted cleanup and knocked in a run.[59]

Yap enlisted in Philadelphia in August 1917. He was attached to ordnance and shipped to Europe late in November 1917. While in France, he wrote home, claiming he enjoyed "seeing air fights and other excitements." While reflecting on the World War I experiences of Hawai'i's Chinese ballplayers like Yap, Ayau, and Kau, the *Honolulu Star-Bulletin* proclaimed a month before the conflict ended, "When it comes to a drive or in a pinch these athletes will not fail to uphold the honor of Hawaii in swatting the Huns." In the fall of 1918, Private Yap would see action in the Argonne. Surviving the hell that consumed too many others, he would remain in the service until July 1919. That Yap, as well as Apau Kau and Vernon Ayau, saw action during World War I represents the experiences of perhaps a surprising number of American soldiers possessing Asian ancestry serving during the war.[60]

Conclusion

Fortunately, Ayau and Yap made it back to the mainland, where they would rejoin other former Travelers playing baseball for pay. None of them may have been good enough to reach the highest echelons of organized baseball in America. But opportunities existed for these talented ballplayers to cross racial frontiers and play somewhere under baseball's cosmopolitan canopy. Yet whether those opportunities were plentiful enough to woo them away from Hawai'i permanently proved another matter.

FIG. 1 Steamer Unloading Sugar on Honolulu Dock
Sugar was king in Hawai'i before and after the U.S. takeover. The steamer in this photograph is loading sugar in the Honolulu harbor ostensibly to take to the U.S. mainland. Courtesy of Library of Congress Prints and Photographs Division: Reproduction Number: LC-DIG-npcc-30929 (digital file from original neg.).

FIG. 2 Duke Kahanamoku, c. 1910s
A superb aquatic athlete, Hawaiian Duke Kahanamoku was seen by Hawai'i as an athletic missionary to mainland investors, tourists, and potential residents. Courtesy of Library of Congress Prints and Photographs Division: Reproduction Number: LC-DIG-ggbain-10653 (digital file from original neg.).

FIG. 3 Hawai'i Chinese Baseball Team, c. 1910
Chinese Honoluluans proved adept baseball players and avid fans as early as the 1900s. Standing in the middle of the top row in his street clothes is En Sue Pung, probably the most famous athlete of Chinese ancestry at the time. Vernon Ayau, who gained a reputation as an acrobatic shortstop, is seated second from the right. Courtesy of Library of Congress Prints and Photographs Division: Reproduction Number: LC-DIG-ggbain-08356 (digital file from original neg.).

FIG. 4 Sam Hop, c. 1909
Before taking the reins of the Travelers, Sam Hop was an all-around athlete and athletic promoter in Honolulu's Chinese community. *Pacific Commercial Advertiser*, March 1, 1909.

FIG. 5 Lai Tin, c. 1914

Known as Lai Tin as a young ballplayer in Honolulu, Buck Lai emerged as one of the best ballplayers on the Travelers as well as team leader. Courtesy of Library of Congress Prints and Photographs Division: Reproduction Number: LC-DIG-ggbain-18122 (digital file from original neg.).

FIG. 6 Lang Akana, c. 1914

Possessing Chinese and Hawaiian ancestry, outfielder Lang Akana was one of the more powerful hitters on the Travelers but shunned by organized baseball largely because of its inherent racism. Courtesy of Library of Congress Prints and Photographs Division: Reproduction Number: LC-Dig-ggbain-18236 (digital file from original neg.).

FIG. 7 “Chinese Team Has Ruined New York Laundry Business,” c. 1913
While the mainland press could be relatively respectful of the Travelers, it also luxuriated in derogatory representations of them, such as this cartoon appearing in a 1913 edition of the *New York Evening World* and reprinted in the *Honolulu Star-Bulletin*. *Honolulu Star-Bulletin*, July 30, 1913.

FIG. 8 The Travelers and Nat Strong, c. 1914
A prominent promoter of independent baseball in New York City, Nat Strong employed exploitative methods that stirred controversy in the East Coast's Black baseball community. However, in 1912 he became an assiduous promoter of the Travelers. This photograph of the Travelers (who are unsure as to where they should be looking) was taken during their 1914 visit to New York City. Nat Strong stands second from the right, next to Sam Hop. Standing in the very back are, left to right, Apau Kau and Fred Markham. Kneeling to the far left is En Sue Pung, and Vernon Ayau is on his left. Courtesy of Library of Congress Prints and Photographs Division: Reproduction Number: LC-DIG-ggbain-16148 (digital file from original neg.).

FIG. 9 Chinese Travelers, 1915
The Travelers, as semi-celebrities, posed for many team photos. In this one they were apparently posed from tallest to shortest. Fred Markham (far left) is obviously the tallest, but Vernon Ayau (far right) is not so obviously the shortest. Lai Tin stands fourth from the left, Al Yap stands to his left, and Apau Kau is next. The Moriyama brothers are to Ayau's immediate right, and Andy Yamashiro stands fifth from the right. *Philadelphia Evening Ledger*, August 16, 1915.

FIG. 10 Lai Tin, c. 1915
Known increasingly on the mainland as William Lai, Lai Tin achieved fame as a ballplayer for the Travelers and had his photo published in various newspapers across the United States. *Philadelphia Evening Public Ledger*, August 16, 1915.

FIG. 11 Andy "Yim," Gridiron Pioneer, c. 1916
After the Travelers' tours ended in 1916, Andy Yamashiro enrolled at Temple University in Philadelphia in pursuit of a dental career. While there, he was recruited to join the football team. Known as Andy Yim on the mainland, he attracted publicity as a very rare college gridder of Asian ancestry in the fall of 1916. *Pacific Commercial Advertiser*, November 22, 1916.

FIG. 12 Charles "Chief" Bender and Buck Lai, c. 1917
In 1917, Hall of Fame and American Indian pitcher Charles "Chief" Bender played with Lai Tin and Fred Markham in the semipro Delaware Valley League's Upland franchise. *Honolulu Star-Bulletin*, July 25, 1917.

FIG. 13 John McGraw and Pat Moran, c. 1916
In 1918, Pat Moran of the Philadelphia Phillies gave Lai Tin a tryout for his major league team but cut him and sent him to the minors. Ten years later, John McGraw of the New York Giants did the same thing. Courtesy of Library of Congress Prints and Photographs Division: Reproduction Number: LC-DIG-ggbain-21535 (digital file from original neg.).

5
Peripatetic Pros, 1919–1934

In 1920, opportunities to earn some money playing baseball were ample in the mid-Atlantic region of the U.S. mainland. There were innumerable, albeit racially segmented, independent nines representing towns, urban neighborhoods, businesses, and athletic clubs, as well as all-Black franchises such as Harlem's Lincoln Giants and the Brooklyn Royal Giants. The ballplayers these teams recruited were frequently provided with shares of gate receipts from the game. And while few could make a living playing independent ball, if they performed in a couple of games or more a week during baseball season and combined the earnings from those games with the money they made from full- or part-time jobs, they might do all right. Still, one had to be alert to those opportunities and willing to travel fifty to one hundred miles to get from game to game. And, assuredly, being white helped. Buck Lai, more than his former Traveler teammates, proved able to keep himself quite busy playing baseball for pay despite, and perhaps to some degree because of, his race and ethnicity.

However, it could not have been easy for Buck Lai. Post–World War I America was probably more racist and xenophobic than during the war. Suspicion of European immigration was heightened by a "Red Scare," fostered by the communist takeover of Russia and the presence of European-born radicals widely suspected of hoping to do the same in the United States. A postwar economic slump aggravated social tensions as the labor market swelled with veterans returning to civilian lives and expecting jobs awaiting them. Moreover, despite African American active service and support during the war, violent racist uprisings against Blacks occurred in Chicago, Washington, D.C., and Tulsa, Oklahoma, while lynchings of African Americans, many of them young men in uniform, pervaded the South. Indeed, the Klan grew into a national phenomenon, calling not only for the suppression of nonwhites but also for significant levels of immigration restriction. Madison Grant's *The Passing of the Great Race* underwent additional printings and yielded other racist, xenophobic tripe such as Lothrop Stoddard's *The Rising Tide of Color against White World-Supremacy.* And, significantly, the U.S. Congress paid attention, passing the Johnson-Reed Act, a highly restrictive immigration law in 1924.[1]

The relative acceptance of the Travelers as a team and as individuals did not budge the needle for Americans of Asian ancestry in general. If anything, the Travelers probably convinced Americans that the U.S. colonial takeover of Hawai'i was just. As for Asian immigrants on the Pacific Coast, they had to live with state laws denying them ownership of farmland. And for Asian immigrants throughout the empire, they had to live with a naturalization law denying them citizenship. In 1924, the Johnson-Reed Immigration Act not only significantly barred immigration from southern and eastern Europe but totally denied it to immigrants ineligible for citizenship—Asians, namely Japanese and Koreans, not barred by the Chinese Exclusion Act and the Immigration Act of 1917 banning immigrants from South and Southeast Asia.[2]

Bridgeport

After succeeding in Bridgeport in 1918, Buck Lai apparently found a niche in organized baseball. When the war ended in the fall of 1918, the Eastern League, like many professional leagues, was ready to tackle a full-scale schedule of games in 1919. Indeed, the Eastern League ascended to an A classification, the second-highest rung on the minor league ladder. At the same time, doubt circulated about Lai's return to Bridgeport. According to the *Hartford Courant*, the "Hawaiian-Chinese third baseman" found a good job at a Hog Island shipyard, working as a foreman in charge of one hundred men. Calling Lai one of the two best third sackers in the Eastern League, the *Courant* assured readers that he would don an American uniform for the 1919 season. Upon learning of Lai's return, the *Bridgeport Telegram* welcomed "the celebrated Hawaiian-Chinese (or, do you say it, 'Chinese-Hawaiian')." Soon after the 1919 season began, Bridgeport's new manager, Ray Grimes, decided to experiment with Lai at shortstop. The switch did not work out well. *Bridgeport Times* sportswriter Roger Ferri complained that Lai was a "clever" ballplayer but miscast as a shortstop. A report in the *Sporting News* agreed that "Billy Lai" did not belong at shortstop, "even though he has some class at third base." Eventually, Lai returned to third. The *Bridgeport Times* cheered the move, calling Lai "one of the headiest and best hitting infielders in the league"—a sentiment echoed by Jack Egan, a veteran and respected baseball man as a player, umpire, and manager. After watching Lai as manager of the Providence Grays, Egan testified that the Hawai'i Chinese ranked as one of the best infielders he had ever seen.[3]

Andy Yamashiro's Eastern League stint in 1919 proved distressingly brief. In April 1919, the *Hartford Courant* maintained that Yim, reportedly working as a salesclerk for the Lit Brothers sporting goods department, would follow Lai's lead back to Bridgeport. Moreover, the *Courant* confided that Bridgeport fans enthusiastically awaited the return of Lai and Yamashiro. Yamashiro, however, departed from Bridgeport by the time the league season officially started, thus angering many local fans. Roger Ferri insisted that Yamashiro was not given a chance by Bridgeport, although he did not explain why. Instead, the Nikkei got into nineteen Eastern League games for Hartford, batting .253 in the process. The *Hartford Courant* welcomed Hartford's acquisition of the "speedy Chinese right fielder." In late May, the *Courant* declared that when New Haven visited Bridgeport, Yamashiro was "roundly applauded" every time he stepped to the plate by fans who believed their team had mistakenly let the Nisei go. In response, he managed a triple against his old teammates. A few days later, the *Courant* hailed Yamashiro's hitting in a losing game against Bridgeport. In late June, however, the outfielder was released for poor playing. The exact nature of Yamashiro's poor play went unexplained, although conceivably after courting controversy in 1918 the Eastern League decided to stick with just one Asian.[4]

Lai squeezed in a few semiprofessional games in the Philadelphia area during the 1919 season. He drove in the only run with a sacrifice fly for the Vineland, New Jersey, nine as he covered shortstop for the winning team. Former Travelers were in both dugouts. Listed as "Ayou" in the *Philadelphia Inquirer*'s box score, Vernon Ayau guarded second while Yim roamed the outfield for Vineland, and Alfred Yap handled first base for the losing Millville, New Jersey, nine. A crowd of 5,000 watched the game. Lai, as well as Ayau and subsequently Yim, appeared in a Du Pont Dye League game in September 1919.[5]

Calling "'Hawaiian Bill Lai,' . . . the most reliable of fielders," the *Bridgeport Telegram* was pleased with Lai's reappearance in Bridgeport in the spring of 1920. Before the season began, the *Telegram* announced that the Bridgeport management expressed delight that the "Chinese-Hawaiian" would enter his third year with the Americans in good condition and ready for the coming year. Early in May, Lai slugged a home run that helped doom New Haven. The *Bridgeport Telegram* cheered "good old Bill Lai, Chinese Hawaiian and American, who is noted for starting game-winning rallies." In early June, the *Telegram* acknowledged Lai's popularity among Bridgeport fans. Injured and unable to perform in a game at home, Lai took over one of the coaching boxes. As he did so, hometown fans gave him an ovation. Later in June, injuries struck the Americans' infield. Manager Ed Walsh, a Hall of Fame pitcher, consequently switched "the oriental" to shortstop, where the *Telegram* considered him out of place. In one game, the "usually reliable" Lai committed a key throwing error.[6]

In August 1920, the *Telegram* published a rumor that Walsh had been trying to drive "Bill Lai" out of the Eastern League—a rumor that the former pitching ace for the Chicago White Sox denied, insisting that Lai intended to retire anyway. Walsh's opposition to Lai may not have been racial as he apparently rubbed many of his players the wrong way. Eventually, Walsh softened his opposition to Lai returning to Bridgeport in 1921. And the *Telegram* claimed that Lai was "playing the same brilliant ball that caused the fans to sing so loudly his praises a year ago." On August 17, Bridgeport swept a doubleheader from Albany. Lai managed a key hit in the first game and his fielding sparkled, too. Using a relatively new nickname for the infielder, the *Telegram* enthused, "Buck Lai was on the job every minute of both games." At the end of the Eastern League season, Lai stood out in a doubleheader in mid-September, making several nice plays at third and rapping a couple of hits. According to Eastern League statistics published in *Sporting News*, Lai's 1920 season amounted to 118 games, 441 at bats, 11 doubles, 4 triples, 1 homer, and 27 stolen bases. He batted .265.[7]

Ed Walsh did not return to Bridgeport in 1921, but Lai would. However, as of February 1921, Lai's intentions of playing in the Eastern League remained in doubt. The *Sporting News* claimed that new manager and veteran minor leaguer Gene McCann's "International infield" appeared to be breaking up, because "Buck Lai, the Chinese second baseman, [*sic*] has decided to quit baseball." The reason was that Lai had a good job in Philadelphia, while "a baby has been born to Mrs. Lai and the father thinks he should stay home and watch the Celestial grow." In March, however, the *Springfield Republican* reported Lai's return to Bridgeport. Initially, it asserted "Bucky Lai, the Oriental third baseman," considered retirement and going back to Hawai'i. However, he apparently got the hunger for organized baseball when he read about the exhibition games in the South, and "Bridgeport feels better now that Bucky is coming back." When Lai showed up to play his fourth year in Bridgeport, the *Bridgeport Telegram* rejoiced, declaring him as fast as many big leaguers.[8]

Bridgeport baseball followers continued to appreciate Lai during the 1921 season. The *Bridgeport Times* applauded him as "a fine chap personally and a player who plays the game until the last man is out." There were, however, too few highlights in Lai's somewhat shortened, injury-riddled 1921 season in Bridgeport. One was his hit down the third base line that capped a comeback rally for the Americans against Springfield. In August, Lai roamed sometimes inefficiently in right field for Bridgeport, and his batting dropped off so much that the *Telegram* conveyed surprise when he slugged a bases-loaded triple against New Haven midway through the month. In September, Lai's tenure with the Americans was finished, and the Bridgeport franchise gave him permission to report to a job with the Pennsylvania Railroad before the season ended. Apparently, Lai was of little use to the team because he suffered a hand injury when he caught a line drive bare-handed. The injury benched him for a while, and when he returned he could not hit. A *Bridgeport Times* sports columnist fretted that Lai may not recover from his injuries. Still, he declared that "Buck Lai will always retain a green spot in the memory of local fans. He was a sterling ballplayer and a fine chap off the field." Playing in only about half of Bridgeport's games in the 1921 Eastern League campaign, Lai batted an anemic .229.[9]

Independent Baseball

Lai's stint with Bridgeport was over, but he concentrated on independent baseball in the mid-Atlantic region. Semiprofessional, company, neighborhood, religious, and Black nines were active from early spring through the fall and kept Lai busy. That Lai would find steady employment with a variety of teams, although he possessed a nonwhite identity, suggests the cosmopolitan potential of baseball for all but Blacks and women. As a Pennsylvania Railroad employee, Lai plied his skills in the Pennsylvania Railroad League in the late summer and fall of 1921. In October 1921, Lai hit cleanup and guarded third base for the Philadelphia Terminal nine, winner of the Eastern Division title of the Pennsylvania Railroad League, as it defeated Columbus for the league championship before an impressive 12,000 spectators at Philadelphia's Shibe Park. Lai rapped two hits, including a double.[10]

Lai's former Traveler teammates made names for themselves in independent baseball on the East Coast as well. Yamashiro, however, headed west to Bay City, Michigan, after his brief stint with New Haven. Toward the end of June, Yamashiro batted two for three in a game against Battle Creek. A report printed in the *Rochester Democrat* claimed "Bill Yam" excelled with Bay City. Then racism caught up with Yamashiro, since the team's manager "did not like the Mongolian's looks . . . [and] . . . so he had to go." After returning to the Philadelphia area, Yamashiro rapped a couple of hits for Millville in a game against the all-Black Hilldale nine from Chester County. In August 1919, the Logan Square nine, representing a neighborhood that includes Philadelphia's iconic city hall, beat Connie Mack's Athletics in an extra-inning exhibition game, 3–2. An Atlantic City crowd of 5,000 watched former major league pitcher Lefty Liefeld still the Athletics' bats. He received help from three Hawai'i-born ballplayers on his team. "Mark" as catcher got two hits—a double and a single. Ayau played shortstop and got a hit. And "Yim" scored the winning run on a passed ball. The next month, Yamashiro played center field for the Vineland nine as it beat the West End club. Batting behind Yamashiro was Ayau, who started at second base. Representing a town in southern New Jersey best known for its surrounding poultry farms, Yamashiro singled and scored a run, while Ayau went hitless but got on base enough to score two runs.[11]

In 1920, the U.S. Census found "M. Yamashiro" lodging in Penn's Grove, New Jersey, and working as an office clerk. Close to the Du Pont factory at the time, Penn's Grove is located on the eastern shore of the Delaware River in southern New Jersey and was also the home of Vernon Ayau. In May 1920, however,

Yamashiro journeyed to northwestern Pennsylvania, where he smacked a double for the Oil City team as it edged Carnegie Steel, 7–6. The next month he was in Vineland's lineup when it easily downed the Merrill Athletic Club nine, 14–6. After getting a hit in three at bats, Yim, according to the *Philadelphia Daily Inquirer*, departed for Hawai'i. The next year, the *Bridgeport Times* reported that the outfielder had sent a letter to Lai, informing the minor league third sacker that he was playing baseball in Hawai'i. Keeping up the ruse of Yamashiro's ethnicity, either Lai or the *Times* claimed that the former Eastern Leaguer busied himself coaching "Chinese teams."[12]

Pitcher Luck Yee Lau headed to the mainland after World War I to reunite with Lai and other former Travelers in the Philadelphia area. In January 1920, the *Honolulu Star-Bulletin* announced that Luck Yee Lau planned on attending college on the East Coast, where he hoped to play semipro ball. Late in September of that same year, the *Pacific Commercial Advertiser* noted that the pitcher had returned to the islands, insisting Lau had shone on the mainland. Yet Lai remembered that Lau too often grooved pitches to East Coast semipro batters. Luck Yee Lau, indeed, toed the rubber in the Philadelphia area, although how effectively remains in doubt. Early in July, Benjamin Gilbert, who managed the Camden Athletic Club nine, announced that he had signed both Luck Yee Lau and Fred Markham. Gilbert claimed to have seen the Hawai'i-born hurler and boasted he commanded a "barrel of smoke." In mid-July, Luck Yee Lau's "splendid pitching" spurred Camden to a victory over the Kaufman Pros. A few days later, Lau pitched ineffectively for Camden against the Cuban Stars before a large crowd. On July 23, the *Philadelphia Public Ledger* ran an advertisement publicizing the appearance of "Phenomenal Chinese pitcher Lau" hurling for Highland Park against Rochdale in a Delaware County Suburban League game. Shortly thereafter, Luck Yee Lau would be on a boat to Hawai'i.[13]

Vernon Ayau engaged in independent baseball not long after seeing action in World War I. He joined Millville in mid-July 1919 against the Bacharach Giants. Ayau, considered the best player on the team, fumbled a couple of grounders, making life much easier for the able Black team from Atlantic City. Managed by Frank Baker, Upland was shut out by the Bacharach Giants in June 1920. Nevertheless, "Ayan," as the press too commonly called him, fielded well. In early September, "Ayau, the Oriental star," according to the *Reading Times*, stood out for visiting Upland against a local team. He slugged a double and scored a run in the victory. Around the same time, Ayau appeared on the Wilmington, Delaware-based Harlan nine in a game in which Hilldale easily won, 11–3. However, "Ayau, the clever shortstop, looked best for Harlan," stinging the ball three times for hits. Also in 1920, Ayau's and Baker's hitting sparked a victory for Upland in an exhibition game with the New York Yankees. A big crowd watched the game even though Babe Ruth, in his first year with the Yankees, was not in action. In September 1920, Upland was scheduled to play the Bushwicks, which led the *Brooklyn Standard Union* to inform readers that the visitors carried Ayau, "the crack little shortstop and Chinaman [who] is very popular with local fans." Against a South Phillies' nine, which carried Lai, in August 1922, Ayau got a hit and threw out four runners in a losing effort for Upland. In 1923, Ayau covered third base for the South Phillies. The *Shamokin News-Dispatch* mislabeled him the "famous Japanese infielder." More on the mark, the *Camden Morning Post* described Ayau as "the famous Chinese star" when he played for the South Phillies.[14]

Alfred Yap's baseball career on the East Coast lasted a few years after World War I. Yap reappeared in Lehigh University's starting lineup in 1920 and 1921. In 1950, the *Honolulu Star-Bulletin* reported that Yap's homer for Lehigh broke up a no-hitter hurled by a University of Virginia pitcher, Frank S. Tavenner Jr., who would eventually serve as counsel for the House Un-American Activities Committee. Crisscrossing the border between amateur and professional, Yap appeared in the J. J. Dobson lineup in 1921 in a game against the Pencoyd Iron nine from the Philadelphia area. A wool manufacturer, J. J. Dobson fielded a baseball team that beat Pencoyd thanks in large measure to Yap, who handled shortstop and lashed three hits (two doubles and a single). For his last year as a college undergrad, Yap transferred to Delaware University to take business courses. The *Wilmington News Journal* summarized Yap's baseball season at Delaware by asserting that he had "brought glory to" the school through his solid work at third base and in the batter's box, while achieving popularity among Delaware University students.[15]

After graduating from Delaware, Yap got a taste of organized baseball by playing in the Class D Eastern Shore League, made up of nine franchises representing small towns on the Maryland side of the Chesapeake. Yap started the season with Pokomoke, playing shortstop for at least one game. Subsequently, he moved on to the Crisfield franchise, for which he hit effectively, slugging a homer early in August against Pokomoke. In forty-five games for Crisfield in 1922, Yap hardly embarrassed himself, batting .298.[16]

The next year, Yap appeared in the lineup of the Allentown Dukes, an independent team representing a small city in the Lehigh Valley region of Pennsylvania. In early September, the Dukes took on the powerful New York Yankees in an exhibition game before 4,000 local fans. Patrolling first base for the Yanks was Babe Ruth, normally a right fielder. The *Allentown Morning Call* maintained that Yap "received plaudits" for powering a home run over the center field scoreboard. Indeed, Yap collected four hits in all that afternoon. Ruth hit no homers and wound up striking out with the bases loaded in the ninth inning, giving the Dukes a narrow 8–7 triumph.[17]

Known in the mainland's sporting press as "Fred Mark" or "Marks," Hawaiian Fred Markham performed well in independent baseball on the East Coast for several years. In 1922, Markham not only played for the South Phillies but also headed across the Delaware to join the Paulsboro, New Jersey, nine. Markham, according to the *Chester Times*, handled the bat well and, as a catcher, displayed a good arm. In late May 1923, the *Times* reported that Markham broke out of a slump with a couple of timely hits for Chester against the Richmond Giants. His bat was working in a mid-July game against the Baltimore Black Sox, rapping two hits and scoring a run in Chester's victory. In 1924, Markham joined Lai across the Delaware to put in time for Trenton of the Penn-Jersey League. The *Trenton Evening Times* described him as a "capable catcher." In June 1924, the *Evening Times* announced that Markham was released by the local nine, owing to a flagging batting average. The daily said "Mark" had been attending the University of Pennsylvania and was a "brainy ball player" who should find a position with another independent nine. Instead, Markham returned to the islands.[18]

The Peripatetic Lai

Buck Lai kept busy in independent baseball during the early and mid-1920s. In May 1922, a wire story reported "Tin Lai" had announced his retirement from Bridgeport. The story's author wondered whether Lai would open a chop suey restaurant or a chain of laundries. However, a more respectful *Bridgeport Telegram* simply declared that local fans would miss Lai, stressing he "was a great fan favorite." Lai's daughter-in-law, Mary, recollected that he expressed little discontent at never playing major league baseball even though he obviously loved the game. She stressed that her father-in-law did not enjoy long stays away from his family and preferred a steady income from a regular job over the treacherous career of a full-time professional ballplayer trying to make a living in organized baseball. Perhaps if Lai were white and even more talented, he might have thought otherwise. But he was not white, and his baseball talents, while abundant, were not so remarkable as to guarantee anything resembling a durable major league career of several years.[19]

Consequently, Lai took up the peripatetic life of an independent ballplayer in the mid-Atlantic region with more earnestness than his former Traveler teammates. While living in Philadelphia and then relatively nearby in Audubon, New Jersey, he could work at a regular job during the week, play local games along the Pennsylvania/New Jersey border in the late afternoons, and then commute on Sundays into the Brooklyn/Queens area to cover third base for the Bushwicks. Clearly, Lai was not going to get rich doing this, but he would probably make more money than most professionals struggling up and down the minor league ladder in organized baseball, while emerging as a local celebrity competing against some of the best, mostly African American, ballplayers outside organized baseball's fold.

Winter challenged a nomadic professional ballplayer wishing to apply his skills to supplement his family's income. Great athlete that he was, Buck Lai decided to take on professional basketball in the early 1920s. It turns out that Lai seemingly held his own against top-flight professionals. As basketball historians Robert Peterson and Murry Nelson assert, one would have done well to refrain from investing any hard-earned money in professional hoops in the early decades of the twentieth century. Organized leagues were unstable, and the game itself was so rough and tumble that promoters installed cages around the court to protect spectators during games often held at dance and social halls. Hence, basketball players were described as cagers long after ropes and then nothing replaced the cages. Furthermore, because of the fly-by-night nature of organized leagues, many of the best teams, such as the New York–based Original Celtics, barnstormed the East Coast to earn sufficient revenue.[20]

Lai joined one of the more ephemeral, yet intriguing barnstorming teams in the early 1920s—the All Chinese Collegians of Shanghai. The *New York Evening World* published a photograph of Lai in a basketball uniform, noting, "The Chinese cageman is considered one of the cleverest players in the game." It further described Lai as "speedy and [a] good shooter," who "jumps center and plays guard." In December 1921, the squad encountered none other than the legendary Original Celtics at Madison Square Garden. Composed of some of the finest players on the East Coast, the Celtics won, but according to an account published in the *Bridgeport Telegram*, Lai played the best of any of his teammates, holding his own against a tough Celtic George Haggerty. A few days later, the "All-Chinese" five was ridiculed by the *Wilmington Evening Journal* after severely losing to the Wilmington Collegians. Lai apparently shone as one of two on his team who seemed to know what they were doing.[21]

While Lai was perhaps adept at basketball, his forte was clearly baseball. In 1922, the South Phillies employed Lai the most. The South Phillies represented a section of the city largely consisting of working-class Italian and Irish Americans. Baseball historian Neil Lanctot described the South Phillies as one of the best independent nines in the region. When tough African American nines faced the South Phillies, they met a team that included such players as Lai, Herb Steen, and Howard Lohr, who "were marginal major leaguers or career minor league players who preferred stardom and financial security in independent ball to toiling in uncertain obscurity in the minors." Moreover, the South Phillies, Lanctot maintains, encountered teams in the Philadelphia area possessing several former big leaguers while nurturing future big leaguers. In other words, anyone who rose above the ordinary in the Philadelphia hotbed of independent baseball was a good ballplayer by any standards. The press paid attention to independent baseball, whether played in or around Philadelphia. The *Philadelphia Inquirer*, for example, devoted a whole page of its sports section to the games played for pay outside of organized baseball.[22]

Competition between the various independent teams could be fierce and racially vicious. The great Judy Johnson recalled the animosity raging when his Hilldale team visited the South Philly home field. Johnson claimed that journeys into South Philadelphia were like "playing in the middle of Mississippi. They used to buy those little cushions you sit on and if their team lost, they'd throw them at you. To get out of the park, you had to go between the stands, like walking through a tunnel and they'd hang out over the sides and toss stuff at you—bottles, garbage, whatever was handy—and call you all sorts of names."[23]

In July 1922, the *Trenton Evening Times* dubbed the South Phillies the strongest independent team in the region. It asserted that the nine fielded several players with professional backgrounds, including Lai, described by the *Times* as a "Chinese third baseman" and, wrongly, as a former Philadelphia Athletic. Hawaiian teammate Fred Markham also had joined the South Phillies. An impressive 12,000 people crammed into the South Phillies' new Shetzline Park on Broad and Bigler Streets in Philadelphia to mark the opening of the 1922 season. Lai was at third base for the home team on that Saturday in April, getting off to a good start and continuing to excel against white and Black nines throughout the summer.[24]

In 1923, Lai transplanted his baseball prowess to Chester, located on the Delaware River between Philadelphia and Wilmington, Delaware. In March of that year, Lai, dubbed "the flashy Hawaiian" by the *Chester Times*, was signed by the Chester baseball club. Once again, Fred Markham was one of his teammates. Hoping to generate excitement about the acquisition, the *Chester Times* proclaimed Lai "as fast as the proverbial streak of lightning and is a player who will add much color to the local ball tossers." The daily subsequently boasted at the season's outset that "Buck Lai, the Chinese streak of lightning who has delighted fans since coming here from Hawaii, will knock 'em down at third."[25]

The Chester nine campaigned in the Philadelphia Baseball Association, while matching bats and gloves with various African American nines outside of league play. On July 4, Chester split a doubleheader with the Middletown Cubans. Lai went hitless but, according to the *Chester Times*, made two spectacular fielding plays in the second inning of the second game—plays that drew pervasive applause by those in attendance. In mid-July, Chester victimized the Baltimore Black Sox, 9–1, with Lai singling twice and scoring a run against a charter member of the Eastern Colored League. Markham, batting eighth, also singled twice and scored a run. Late in July, Lai got two hits against the Bacharach Giants, while Markham caught. A *Chester Times* reporter noted at the time that Lai possessed an unusual batting stance in that he placed both of his feet on the edge of the batter's box. However nonconventional his batting style, Lai accounted for three of the four runs Chester scored in a game that ended in a tie with the Giants. Lai was spiked in August while trying to tag a Baltimore Black Sox base runner. The *Chester Times* expected the third sacker would sit out a few games. Nonetheless, a few days later, the *Times* averred, the two best non–major league nines in the Philadelphia area battled before a "mixed" crowd of 3,000. Led by John Henry Lloyd, Biz Mackey, and Judy Johnson, Hilldale shut out Chester and Lai, 3–0.[26]

Displaying athletic virtuosity, Lai appeared in an athletic tournament held for railroad employees in the mid-Atlantic region in September 1923. Inspired by often well-meaning paternalism and the not-so-well-meaning desire to stem labor militancy, many industries in the United States resorted to "welfare capitalism" before and after World War I. This encompassed providing workers with a variety of services including the organization of athletic teams, leagues, and competitions. These offerings were fairly successful until the Great Depression caused industries to cut their services to workers when they were not laying them off, and workers to consider more carefully how benevolent their employers were. Representing the Philadelphia Terminal in the track and field events, Lai broke a long jump record and turned in the fastest time in circling the bases. He also appeared as "the Chinese shortstop" for the nine representing the Philadelphia Terminal on the same day as the track meet. Readers of the *Honolulu Advertiser* learned that Lai might have done even better in the long jump had he been wearing a lighter track and field outfit instead of a baseball uniform.[27]

In 1924, Lai went on a hitting rampage for Trenton of the Penn–New Jersey League. Fred Markham, called a "capable catcher" by the *Trenton Evening Times*, started the season in Trenton with Lai, whom the *Times* considered an infielder with "few peers" in independent baseball. The *Times* looked forward to seeing Lai in action, insisting that "Buck Lai, the greatest Chinese ballplayer in the country, should make a wonderful impression," and for the most part he did. At the end of May, Lai and Trenton won both ends of a doubleheader against an all-Black team that sportswriter Harry Coady Lindop dismissed as the "Royal Blue Giants of Havana, New York City or somewhere in between." Indeed, this team was probably the respected Brooklyn Royal Giants. A very unimpressed and nasty Lindop asserted that the "dusky" ballplayers were laughable, especially in the first game. As for Buck Lai, he "was the featured performer in the morning circus." Lindop declared that the "fleet fotted [*sic*]" Lai "always enjoys games in which he can run wild on the 'bases' without fear of consequences and in the morning had all the darkies crossed up." On July 21, Trenton and Hilldale played to a 5–5 tie. Lai socked two homers against the skilled Chester-based nine. Lindop wrote the following in a story titled "Buck Lai Hits Two Homers in Hectic Struggle with Hilldale": "Standing out head and shoulders above his fellow men was Buck Lai, the fleet-footed Trenton third sacker, who first saw the light of day in the far away Hawaiian Islands." Both of Lai's homers were walloped inside the park but deep into left center. On the first home run, according to Lindop, "the bouncing bucko" almost caught up to the base runner ahead of him. As far as Lindop was concerned, Lai proved himself "the popular idol of Trenton." In August, Trenton beat the Cuban Stars, based in northern Manhattan and led by the legendary Afro-Cuban ballplayer Martin Dihigo. Lai batted two for five against Dihigo's pitching, scoring a key run. The next day, Trenton took on an easier foe. Before 2,000 fans, Trenton subdued the Morgan AA nine, 8–1. Buck Lai displayed no mercy, according to Lindop: "The bouncing bucko delights in showing his speed against less-experienced opponents and he ran the bases yesterday with the fleetness of the proverbial deer."[28]

Meanwhile, Fred Markham wrote home to the *Star-Bulletin*. Published in late September 1924, Markham's letter acclaimed Lai as the most popular ballplayer on the East Coast, presumably meaning the most popular non–major league player because Babe Ruth, after all, was powering homers for the Yankees in 1924. Markham, who was playing ball in Allentown, Pennsylvania, at the time, maintained that Ruth's Yankees expressed interest in signing Lai, as well as, more realistically, Philadelphia's Lit Brothers nine. In any event, Markham claimed that Lai did not need the minor leagues as he was making more money in independent ball than most players were making in the minor leagues.[29]

Lai did not try out for, let alone make, the Yankees. But in the mid-1920s, he displayed his skills for Philadelphia's Lit Brothers team, as well as a host of other independent ball clubs in the mid-Atlantic region. In early May 1926, the *Wilmington Morning News* reported he was at third base for Camden, and hailed him as "the peer of the Chinese ballplayers." Lai stood out in his brief stint with Camden. The team competed in the interracial Interstate League, which included predominantly white teams as well as Hilldale and the Bacharach Giants. According to Neil Lanctot, the league folded because white teams representing places like Camden and Chester could not compete effectively against the Black nines. However, Lai, on a predominantly white nine, seemingly more than held his own against some of the greatest ballplayers of the era. In late April, Lai went four for four against the powerful Hilldale nine. Early in May, Lai's bat once again aided Camden against Hilldale as he knocked a double and a single. Within a week Camden downed the Lincoln Giants, and Lai's defense sparkled. In his last game with Camden, "the flashy third sacker" belted a home run and a double, went four for four, and scored four times against Allentown.[30]

Lai's ball playing in Philadelphia inspired one Quaker City sportswriter to declare that "Buck Lai has played the game for all he is worth—and he's worth plenty as a ball player." The writer, cited by the *Honolulu Advertiser*'s E. Z. Crane in 1927, maintained that while Lai was well liked by baseball fans in the Philadelphia area, most of those fans knew Lai as just Chinese and did not appreciate that he was a "real American" mastering the American pastime. The writer also maintained that Lai played his best against the tougher teams such as the Hilldale contingent. The Chinese American possessed enough of a celebrity status in East Coast baseball circles that when he was spotted in deep conversation with Chief Bender at Philadelphia's Shibe Park late in the 1927 baseball season, it was deemed worthy of note by one sportswriter.[31]

While Lai played for various nines usually in the Philadelphia region, he was almost inevitably wearing a Bushwick uniform on Sundays in the spring and summer. In July 1922, Lai, according to William J. Granger of the *Brooklyn Citizen*, "had a busy day at third base" in a doubleheader with the Lincoln Giants. "He made some corking good plays and also did some good hitting," although Lai got hurt in a close play at third. The next week Granger again applauded Lai's sensational fielding. He wrote about a hard grounder that spun the Chinese

American around. However, Lai earned the cheers of the Dexter Park crowd by holding on to the ball and gunning down the batter at third.[32]

In mid-September 1924, the Bushwicks gained a doubleheader split against Hilldale. Lai stood out offensively. He got but one hit in four at bats in the first game, won by the Bushwicks. However, that hit proved important, because after he singled, Lai then pilfered second. Trying to gun the Chinese American out, the Hilldale catcher overthrew second and Lai scrambled to third. He then scored the winning run on a single. In the second game, Lai singled three times in five at bats. A week later, according to the *Brooklyn Standard Union*, "Buck Lai, the Bushwicks' Chinese third sacker," hit a single, triple, and homer against the York, Pennsylvania, nine. For his home run, the crowd at Dexter Park collected fifty dollars to bestow upon the Chinese American ballplayer.[33]

Dubbed "the snappy little Chinaman" by the *Brooklyn Citizen*, Lai proved his worth to the Bushwicks against top-level competition. On July 26, 1925, the Bushwicks split a doubleheader with Hilldale. According to the *Brooklyn Daily Eagle*, Lai "thrilled the crowd with his base running." The third sacker stole three bases, and when apparently caught off first base by a pickoff throw, he cleverly evaded the tag. On May 1, 1926, the *Chicago Defender*, America's most famed African American publication, acknowledged that Lai's three hits helped the Bushwicks subdue Hilldale at Dexter Park. On July 23, 1927, the *Chicago Defender* reported that Lai's double keyed a Bushwick victory over the Royal Giants, 9–4, at Dexter Park.[34]

In the fall of 1927, Babe Ruth and Lou Gehrig paraded slugging skills into the heartland of America after the New York Yankees dumped the Pirates in four straight in the World Series. Ruth, of course, had just hit a then mind-boggling sixty home runs in 1927, and his teammate Gehrig was not that far behind with forty-seven. Before the two Yankees' barnstorming journey began, they played together on a team called the Bustin' Babes at Dexter Park before an estimated 20,000 fans. On October 12, the Bustin' Babes beat the Bushwicks, 3–2. Batting leadoff, Lai got a single in three at bats, although he committed an error that allowed Gehrig to score. Subsequently, the touring ballplayers would head opposing teams dubbed the Bustin' Babes and the Larrupin' Lous.

Even though he was now in his early thirties, Lai attracted notice from elite franchises in organized baseball. In November 1927, the *Chester Times* reported that Lai and another semiprofessional ballplayer had been given a tryout at the Polo Grounds by John McGraw, famed manager of the New York Giants. A week later, readers in Hawai'i learned from the *Honolulu Star-Bulletin*'s columnist Don Watson that Lai wrote to his brother, Lee Lai, claiming that he received a definite offer from the Philadelphia Phillies but was waiting on the New York Giants. As it turned out, McGraw was impressed enough to tender a contract to Lai. The Chinese American would be given one more chance to compete at organized baseball's highest level.[35]

Lai and the New York Giants

It is not clear why John McGraw was willing to take a chance on an over-thirty-year-old rookie of Chinese descent. Ever since Ruth had joined the Bronx-based franchise, McGraw and his Giants were locked in a losing rivalry with the Yankees for New York City's affections. McGraw was always alive to the possibility of getting more people in the Polo Grounds' stands, and he believed that recruiting ballplayers from culturally diverse backgrounds might help. After all, McGraw had tried to sign an African American player, Charlie Grant, while managing the Baltimore Orioles in the early 1900s. In order to do so, however, McGraw promoted Grant as an Indian named Chief Tokohama. Organized baseball embraced American Indians fitfully, but at least they could slip past the color line if sufficiently skilled. However, Charles Comiskey, Lai's potential employer in 1915, called out Grant's Black identity and McGraw backed off. Still, McGraw valued Native American catcher Chief Meyers for many years and had long hoped to engage the talents of a Jewish star to attract fans from New York's Lower East Side. McGraw, consequently, might have considered Lai an ethnic novelty enticing the curious into the Polo Grounds, that cavernous baseball cathedral in Upper Manhattan. But McGraw was more than just a keen businessperson, and he might well have considered Lai more than a potential gate attraction. McGraw had traded away second sacker and superb, but cantankerous, slugger Roger Hornsby, leaving the fiercely competitive McGraw with a diminished infield and perhaps needing Lai as a utility player. As for Lai, he might have been content to play independent ball, but he also might have viewed trying out with the New York Giants as a reasonable risk. If he made the team, he would earn more money in baseball while remaining relatively close to his family. If he did not make the team, he would still have the Bushwicks and more than several other independent nines seeking his services.

Much as when he tried out with the Phillies a decade earlier, Lai's signing by McGraw inspired varied press responses. The *New York Times* wondered how McGraw could have exhausted all the resources of the United States in order to engage the services of a "Chinese infielder." Not acknowledging Lai as a U.S. citizen and an East Coast resident for many years, the *Times* conceded that Lai was a versatile infielder who might help McGraw. The *San Francisco Examiner*'s Abe Kemp predicted that "Buck will 'Lai' in the minors for a year" rather than make the Giants.[36]

Lai's cultural identity and baseball career appeared up for grabs for the mainland press early in 1928. When the *Gettysburg Times* announced Lai's signing, it averred that "he is claimed by some to be Chinese and by others to be a native of the Hawaiian Islands." Maryland's *Hagerstown Daily Mail* ran both a photograph of Lai in uniform and a cartoon of a stereotyped, queued baseball player fielding a grounder. Readers of the *Florence Morning News* encountered a story titled "First of His Kind." Accompanying the brief story was a photograph of Lai, who was described in the piece as "the first Hawaiian-Chinese player on a major league roster." In the Pacific Northwest, the *Seattle Times* pronounced Lai a "novelty"—part Hawaiian, part Chinese. The story purported that if both Jewish American Andy Cohen and Lai made the team, McGraw would have "the most unusual infield in baseball."[37]

Given the *Chester Times*'s familiarity with Lai as at least a good semipro, one would think it would not dredge up the Chinese laundry stereotype. Still, the *Times* insisted that the Giants would accord Lai a tryout on the field and "not on any collars the athletes may bring down for the training season." Lai had accumulated plenty of experience on the ball field, the *Times* averred, arguing that "baseball has it over the laundry as Lai figures it." The veteran infielder had displayed, the *Times* asserted, a weak bat but a good glove in his years in the minors, although Lai certainly hit more than decently in independent ball in Chester, Camden, and Trenton, as well as neighboring communities and had really only one bad year as a hitter for Bridgeport. Because of his age, the *Times* wondered why the Giants bothered, but guessed he was signed to attract "the fan colony" from New York City's Chinatown.[38]

Lank Leonard had much to say about Buck Lai in a syndicated column. A journalist and illustrator, he drew a respectful illustration of the ballplayer, captioned "Chinese diamond star." However, he also penned smaller cartoons, one of which displayed a Chinese man yelling from the stands and captioned, "There'll be plenty of laundry neglected around New York next spring." A second cartoon showed an umpire hit apparently by an axe. Evoking the banal imagery of violent Chinatown tongs, Leonard wrote, "It might be a tough year for umpires if 'Buck' makes good." Emphasizing Lai's Hawai'i as much as his Chinese identity, a third cartoon depicted a group of ballplayers joyfully singing while a Chinese teammate plays a ukulele. Leonard insisted, "The Giants should be a happy family now that Lai's ukulele is on the job."[39]

In his accompanying article, Leonard jested that New Yorkers should not expect prompt laundry service in the spring because the city's Chinese American residents might linger at the Polo Grounds "making oriental wisecracks" at the New York Giants' opponents. "Buck Lai, the old Eastern League Chinaman," would bear responsibility for luring Chinese New Yorkers away from their laundry duties to the Upper Manhattan ballpark. Leonard remembered that the infielder had captained "the all-Chinese team"—a team that struck a chord among mainland baseball fans. Leonard wrote that "the all-Chinese team [was] full of pep, and took delight in giving crowds a laugh by yelling advice in their native tongue." Leonard conceded that the team members were native English speakers, "but they appreciated the part they were playing and made the most of it." Leonard then explored Lai's years at Bridgeport. He insisted that the infielder was not much of a hitter but a swift and intelligent base runner. After Lai's Bridgeport career ended, Leonard accurately reported, Lai worked as a clerk for the Pennsylvania Railroad while playing "twilight" ball in Philadelphia during the week and wearing a Bushwick uniform on Sundays.[40]

The press in Hawai'i, of course, applauded Lai's signing. Columnist Don Watson promised that baseball fans on the islands would follow Lai's venture with the Giants, praising the former resident as a good role model for baseball. A wire story published in the *Honolulu Advertiser* reported that Lai expressed confidence in his ability to make the Giants. Not only did he believe that he could help the Giants' infield, but Lai insisted his hitting had improved since his tryout a decade earlier with the Phillies.[41]

Among the more interesting press responses to Lai's impending tryout with the Giants came from Japanese American newspapers. Based in Seattle, the *Japanese American Courier* often evinced a willingness to reach out to Chinese Americans, despite the grave differences that existed between Japan and China during the 1920s and 1930s. During its first year of publication, the *Courier* ran an article on Lai, calling the infielder a "sweet ballplayer." With the Bushwicks, the *Courier* maintained, "the Oriental whiz-bang . . . became an attraction." Indeed, some fans, the *Courier* insisted, came to Dexter Park only to see "the wonder Chinaman perform." The writer of the *Courier*'s piece doubted that Lai could break into the Giants as a starter. Still, even if Lai failed to make McGraw's nine, fans would remember him as "the Chinese wonder player." The Hawai'i Japanese *Hawaii Hochi* also crossed ethnic borders to inform readers of a UPI report that McGraw's recruitment of Lai was no joke. It declared that the Giants' crusty manger "might be well pleased" with Lai's work at third base, where he could demonstrate his "big time calibre."[42]

Press coverage of Lai's tryout with the Giants proved troubling. A sportswriter for the *New York Daily News*, Roscoe McGowan, journeyed on the train carrying many members of the Giants as well as prospects to the Florida training camp. He noticed Buck Lai, whom he described in orientalist terms "as a slender young man with a distinctly Mongolian cast of features, a considerable accent, a bland and toothsome smile. Whether his smile is of the Bret Harte persuasion this writer has come to no conclusion." Sports columnist Bill Ritt slighted the Chinese American as a ballplayer. He declared that "New York's only Chinese ballplayer, Lai Tin, has been weighed at home plate and found wanting in base hits." According to Ritt, "This naturalized laundryman holds his bat like an ironing board and swings like a ringer." In addition to muffing Lai's citizenship status, Ritt speculated that if "the Giant celestial makes good . . . and gets into the World Series, all soap-and-suds shops will probably close and a national holiday declared in the best washtub circles."[43]

According to a few mainland press stories, Ty Cobb, who worked out with the Giants, and Lai got along famously. The April 1, 1928, edition of the *Philadelphia Inquirer* featured a photo of Cobb ostensibly giving batting pointers to Buck Lai. The photo was titled "Georgia Peach and Chinese Blossom" in an allusion to the Georgian Cobb's nickname. An accompanying article by the

Inquirer's Stan Baumgartner countered rumors that Lai had been cut, which presumably Philadelphians should consider "good news." According to Baumgartner, Lai had just written Nat Strong a letter detailing his progress in the Giants' spring training camp. Lai boasted to Strong that he was "beginning to show old John McGraw what I can do," surprising the Giants' manager in the process. Indeed, Lai speculated that he could make the Giants. He also told Strong he had met with and learned much about hitting from Ty Cobb, whom he hailed as "a prince of a fellow."[44]

Lai was cut, and his future remained murky. Protesting press accounts that he refused the Giants' offer to send him to a minor league in Little Rock, Lai declared to the *Honolulu Star-Bulletin* that John McGraw had no intention of selling him southward. McGraw, Lai stressed, did not wish to deal away the infielders' services outright. Instead, the great manager supposedly wanted to keep Lai close by in case the Giants needed him. Apparently, high-level minor league franchises on the East Coast were potential landing places for Lai while the Giants considered his future.[45]

Meanwhile, columnist Donald E. Basenfelder reinforced and refuted a narrative of Buck Lai's efforts to make the big leagues that fashioned the Chinese American into a Charlie Chan–like figure. In a column published in the *Camden Morning-Post* on March 12, Basenfelder cited without comment the well-known *New York Evening World* sportswriter Bozeman Bulger, who described Buck Lai as, like the famed fictional Honolulu-based detective, struggling with mainstream English syntax and obsequious toward white authority figures such as Ty Cobb. For example, Lai is quoted as observing of Cobb, "Why most wonderful is he." A week later, however, Basenfelder accused Bolger and other New York sportswriters of "picking on Lai for color." He condemned press coverage presenting Lai as not only overly submissive to Cobb and McGraw but also ignorant of U.S. geography, such as the existence of Arkansas. Nor did Basenfelder find credible reports that Lai preferred starting a laundry or returning to Hawai'i to playing in Little Rock. Lai, he declared, held a decent full-time job in Philadelphia and lived with his family in Audubon, and though perhaps respectful of McGraw and Cobb, he expected fair treatment from organized baseball.[46]

As opening day approached, the Giants wondered what to do with Lai, according to sports columnist Mickey Lake. Calling Lai a "chink ball player," Lake reported that the Giants used Lai in an exhibition game against Jersey City, in which he managed two hits. In any event, the Jersey City franchise was convinced that Lai could fill a team need. Shortly thereafter, Frank Donnelly, who served as secretary of the Jersey City Skeeters, in the Double A International League, told the press that his franchise had acquired the "Chinese infielder" from the Giants. Donnelly observed that the Skeeters envisioned Lai as a utility infielder. A few days later, Lai seemingly showed that Jersey City's acquisition was no mistake by starring in an exhibition game against New Haven of the Eastern League. Readers of the *New York Times* discovered that "Buck Lai, the Chinese player . . . filled in cleverly at shortstop." In addition, Lai did well on offense as he was directly or indirectly responsible for all three of New Jersey's runs. After the official season started, Lai got into a few games with Jersey City as a shortstop. In May, according to the *Sporting News*, Jersey City returned Lai's contract to the Giants, although his brother, Lee Lai, reported to the *Honolulu Star-Bulletin* that he had contracted influenza, which curtailed his stint with the Double A club. A few years later, the *Brooklyn Daily Eagle* reported a different story in which Lai almost made the New York Giants. It also quoted the Chinese American as remembering he issued an ultimatum to the Giants—either the big leagues or the Bushwicks. He would not settle for Jersey City. This story may be accurate since, in early May 1928, the *Trenton Evening Times* reported that Lai was back with the Bushwicks, "after some heavy publicity as the only Chinese in the majors." The *Brooklyn Daily Times* added that the "plucky little Chinese player" remained attached to the Giants, but McGraw had loaned him out while pondering the infielder's future.[47]

Back to Independent Baseball

As it turned out, McGraw left him in Brooklyn, but Lai was devoted to the Bushwicks. In April 1929, the *Brooklyn Standard Union* published a photograph of Buck Lai fielding a grounder in a Bushwick uniform. The caption declared the third sacker almost as popular in independent baseball as Babe Ruth was in the big leagues, adding that "besides being an ace fielder, Lai is one of the big guns in the [Bushwick] attack." The next month, the Bushwicks and Hilldale split a doubleheader. The African American *Pittsburgh Courier* reported that Hilldale's great Oscar Charleston and Buck Lai were two of the "hitting stars" of the day. In July 1930, Buck Lai was present at the first night game played in New York City when the Bushwicks hosted the Springfield nine from Long Island. Around this time, the *New York Daily News*' notable sportswriter Jimmy Powers hailed Lai as the "alert Chinese third baseman" when his hitting and fielding keyed a Bushwick victory.[48]

In 1931, the Bushwicks typically opposed a variety of nines. On May 31, the Bushwicks downed a Japanese nine from Hosei University at Dexter Park. Ten thousand fans turned out, and many were angered by an umpire decision going against the Japanese visitors. The *New York Times* insisted that a near riot ensued. Lai, meanwhile, managed a one-for-four performance. The *Brooklyn Daily Eagle*'s Harold Parrott praised the Japanese pitcher, a Nikkei from Hawai'i, Bozo Wakabayashi, who would eventually pitch and manage in Japan's major leagues. In early July, a *Daily Eagle* headline declared "Lai Is Leader in Bushwicks' Double Victory." Indeed, he hit three for five in both victories over the Brooklyn Royal Giants. Among those Royal Giant pitchers trying unsuccessfully to cool down the thirty-seven-year-old "China boy," as the *Eagle* put it, was the eminent Dick Redding. On August 21, Lai energized the Bushwicks' victory over Springfield in extra innings. The Chinese American whacked three hits in five at bats and scored the winning run after beating out an infield hit. The Bushwicks swept a doubleheader from the Baltimore Black Sox in early September. The second game saw the Bushwicks battling from behind to tie the game in the late innings on a Lai single. In September, Lai once again tormented Springfield with three key hits before 14,000 under the lights.[49]

During Lai's last three years with the Bushwicks, he remained a solid performer. In a late September 1932 exhibition game, the Bushwicks encountered the New York Giants, now managed by Hall of Fame first sacker Bill Terry. Played under the lights, the game saw the Giants win, 5–2. According to Jimmy Powers, the attendance of over 20,000 at Dexter Park meant that the Giants-Bushwick matchup drew the largest crowd yet to see a night game in New York City. Lai managed to smack two singles in five at bats and stole a base. Subsequently, Lai's bat and glove sparked the Bushwicks in a doubleheader split against the Pittsburgh Crawfords, one of the more famous Black ball teams of the era, led by Josh Gibson and Satchel Paige. In announcing Lai would continue to play for the Bushwicks in 1933, Powers described the veteran infielder as "half-Chinese/half Hawaiian and married to an 'Irish colleen.'" On opening day of 1933, the Bushwicks were swept by the Negro League New York Black Yankees before 15,000 spectators and special guest James Farley, FDR's postmaster general and Democratic Party powerhouse. After Farley threw out the first ball, Lai proceeded to wallop two doubles in four at bats and score one run in the first game. In the second game, Lai singled in five at bats. On September 21, 1933, a crowd of 8,000 at Dexter Park witnessed Lai make a key hit and score a crucial run for the Bushwicks as they beat the Cuban Stars. Toward the end of the 1933 season, Irwin N. Rosee of the *Brooklyn Times Union* contended that Buck Lai was playing the best ball of his career, despite closing in on forty.[50]

In the fall of 1933, Lai earned press attention from very different spots in the American empire. In mid-October, Irwin N. Rosee wrote that Lai deserved more publicity, declaring that he was the oldest Bushwick in terms of service. Rosee added, unfairly, that Lai was the "only Hawaiian ballplayer who didn't prove to be a pineapple" on the mainland. On the islands, the *Honolulu Star-Bulletin* divulged contents of a letter from Lai, who wrote that he had been offered a chance to join a team that would barnstorm Mexico and Puerto Rico, as well as various parts of South America. Lai said he turned down the deal because he was not offered enough money to make it worthwhile for him to leave work. And while he did not say so openly, one can well imagine Lai's trepidation of endangering his employment status in the midst of the Great Depression.[51]

The 1934 season marked Lai's last with the Bushwicks. Even so, co-owner Max Rosner insisted to sports columnist Bill McCulloch that Lai was, at forty, a "physical marvel" and, without qualification, one of the best third sackers in the country. Early in June, the ballplayer whom William J. Granger of the *Brooklyn Citizen* called the "Chinaman" smacked a clutch triple to help the Bushwicks beat the Black Yankees in the second game of a doubleheader. On August 19, the Bushwicks played a doubleheader against a team headed by onetime Brooklyn Dodger ace Dazzy Vance. In the second game, with Vance on the mound, Lai managed three singles in five at bats, driving in three runs. Because of tension developing between the Bushwick management and mid-Atlantic Black nines, Strong and Rosner started to bring in Southern Negro League teams to Dexter Park. Among these nines was the Birmingham Black Barons, which the Bushwicks swept in two games. Lai singled in five at bats in the first game and then powered up with three hits in five at bats and three runs batted in during the second. On August 26, a *Brooklyn Daily Eagle* columnist named "Shortstop" proclaimed that Lai "starr[ed] as a boy and a man for the last fourteen years" as a Bushwick. During an unusual midweek game on September 19, Lai drove in the winning run against the Farmers nine. A *Brooklyn Times Union* writer proclaimed, "It isn't the first game Lai has won and I hope it will not be his last. He is a grand campaigner."[52]

After several years playing for the Bushwicks, Lai was paid a tainted tribute by Irwin N. Rosee upon the occasion of Lai's return to Dexter Park in 1935 with a team of barnstormers from Hawai'i. Rosee described Lai as a "suave easterner" whose baseball career expressed "an interesting tale, as fascinating almost as some of the fabulous yarns which come drifting out of the East." Rosee reminded readers of Lai's stint with the Travelers, after which "Buck stayed with the Bushwicks for fans to know him, kid him, and even love the slant eyed fellow on third base."[53]

Beyond Brooklyn, Lai continued to surface on various diamonds, mostly in the Philadelphia area. In 1928, Lai played for Philadelphia's Corley Catholic Club. When the Allentown contingent lost to Corley, Lai's bat was credited for its downfall. Starting at shortstop, he whacked a triple that drove in the winning run. In June 1929, the South Phillies edged the Bacharach Giants, 5–4. The *Philadelphia Inquirer* extolled Lai's "brilliant work" for the winning team during the game. A few months later, the South Phillies beat Chester, with Lai slugging a double and scoring a run. In late August 1930, Lai tripled to spur Philadelphia's Mayfair Athletic Association nine to a victory. A couple of weeks later, Lai batted three for four and knocked in two runs for the Philadelphia Terminal nine when it blanked Altoona Works, 5–0, at Wildwood, New Jersey. Early in September 1931, Lai's "trusty bat" helped secure a victory for the South Phillies over a nine from Southwestern Philadelphia called the Bartram Artisans. In 1933, Lai journeyed away from his geographical comfort zone by joining a team representing a state hospital in Middletown, New York, in the Hudson Valley region. Meanwhile, Lai helped coach an American Legion youth team representing his hometown of Audubon, New Jersey, in 1931.[54]

By playing for the Bushwicks and other independent nines from March to the fall, Buck Lai could augment his regular income. The *Brooklyn Daily Eagle*'s Frank Weitekamp cited Max Rosner as his source in purporting that the better semipro players in 1934 made $200 a month, and Lai was assuredly a better semipro. Given that the average yearly income in the United States in the 1930s was $1,368, Lai's pay as a semipro would have been envied by many Americans. That he also worked for the Pennsylvania Railroad in 1934 helped. Indeed, Weitekamp added that unlike other Philadelphians on the Bushwicks, he got a discount on train tickets to New York City because of his job with the "Penn railroad."[55]

In Lai's America of the early 1930s, the Great Depression stalked middle-class stability. If able to promote themselves effectively as colorful, unique, and capable, independent traveling baseball teams could draw fans, hungry for diversion during the Great Depression. The supposedly all-bearded House of David barnstormers come to mind, as do nines based on diverse and often exoticized racial and ethnic identities. Most likely hoping for economic autonomy, Lai took over management of a traveling aggregation called the Orientals, composed of Filipinos and reportedly other ballplayers of Asian descent in the spring of 1931.

Inspired by the white man's burden and coveting greater access to Asian markets, the United States used the Spanish-American War to liberate the Philippines from Spain in 1898 and then bind it to its expanding empire. Filipino resistance to American imperialism was bitter and the consequences deadly as 4,000 American military personnel died in the Philippine-American war in the late 1890s and early 1900s, while thousands more Filipinos died directly or indirectly as a result of the war. As in any war, brutality ran the show for both sides. However, American military actions in the Philippines proved so heavy-handed that an American congressional investigation ensued and prominent anti-imperialists such as Mark Twain condemned the massacres of innocent Filipinos. Historian Paul A. Kramer calls what happened in the Philippines a "race war," and certainly it seemed so to many American supporters of the war who saw it as a way of expanding Anglo-Saxon horizons.[56]

But as the United States cut down guerrilla warfare in the Philippines, the need to pacify the islands took precedence. Filipino "savages" became America's "little brown brothers," although it seemed easier for the United States to express patronizing warmth for the Philippines' more Hispanicized and Christianized population than its "primitive," non-Christian people. American imperialists such as Dean Worchester, consequently, hoped that American sports such as baseball might render Filipinos more amenable to colonization. He expressed joy that the sport seemingly made inroads among less westernized Filipinos, weening them away from what he deemed unacceptable pastimes.[57]

Some Filipinos mastered baseball surprisingly well by the 1910s. In 1913, a team of Filipinos toured the United States around the same time that the Travelers experienced their second journey to the mainland. The team's on-the-field success did not equal that of the ballplayers from Hawai'i, although they fostered curiosity. One press account asserted that the ballplayers belonged to different "tribes" and were "obliged to speak in a tongue other than their own to carry on a conversation among themselves." The Filipinos opposed semiprofessional and college nines, losing much more than they won. Still they could "put . . . up a pretty good article of ball." While a bit north of San Francisco, the Filipinos defeated a Santa Rosa nine, 8–4. And, as Buck Lai knew, Filipino immigrants forged competitive baseball teams in Hawai'i in the 1910s. Brought to Hawai'i's sugar and pineapple plantations to provide the inexpensive, reliable, and controllable labor force no longer supplied by Chinese, Japanese, and Korean workers, Filipinos eventually made up the second-largest ethnic group on the islands, next to the Nikkei.[58]

Press accounts of Lai's Orientals surfaced in the late spring and summer of 1931. In May 1931, the *Harrisburg Telegraph* reported that the Orientals were scheduled to appear in the central Pennsylvania city. The article advertising the game insisted that Lai had played three years with the New York Giants and that a "Jap pitcher" named Kresi would probably take the mound for the visitors. The next week, Lai's nine appeared in Shamokin, Pennsylvania. Calling Lai the only "Oriental baseball player to ever crash the big tent," the local newspaper revealed that the Chinese American had culled players from the "defunct" University of Manila nine, which had been touring the United States, while asking contacts in Hawai'i to ship him some island ballplayers. The squad had, according to the *Shamokin News-Dispatch*, held its own in several games. Among the team stars were Lefty Mondragon, "diminutive center fielder," who reportedly tipped the scales at 117 pounds, and "a fast, hard-hitting third sacker named Sartillo." Echoing press coverage of the Travelers several years earlier, the newspaper added that Lai's nine had an advantage over opponents because they called signals in their "native tongue."[59]

Dissatisfied with supplementing his income as an entrepreneur in independent baseball, Lai headed a basketball team of ringers, usually called the Hawaiian or Aloha All-Stars, that barnstormed the East Coast. As was the case a decade earlier, professional basketball during the Great Depression seemed more lucrative when engaged in by traveling teams possessing racial, ethnic, or gender "hooks." Lai first put his basketball team on display during the winter of 1931 and 1932. In January 1932 Lai's cagers were edged by a local five in Harrisburg, 33–32. The *Harrisburg Telegraph* informed readers that "Buck Lai, the captain and flash of the Hawaiian team, was unable to play on account of illness." On February 1, 1932, the *Gettysburg Times* announced that "Buck Lai and His Aloha Stars" would arrive to play the Fleet-Wing squad. Calling Lai's team a "novelty aggregation," the publicity piece claimed that the five had won far more often than it had lost. Identifying Lai as a former major leaguer with the New York Giants, the piece purported he did not play much with his team but "directs his speedy dribblers from the bench." The *Times* promised that the "Hawaiians" would perform the first half in "hula skirts" and leis. Then, during halftime, fans would be entertained by a hula dancer and Hawaiian musicians.[60]

The Aloha All-Stars generally appeared in smaller East Coast cities, and it is hard to say how financially successful they were. When they opposed the

Wilmington Cardinals early in 1932, the game apparently enticed a "small crowd." A couple of years later, the *Yonkers Herald* admitted what probably anyone who actually saw the team knew well—Lai's squad did not consist of Hawaiians. Instead, Lai played rather well-established, white basketball hoopsters from "Western teams." Ignoring his Chinese ancestry, the daily identified Lai as the Hawaiian team manager and business agent, as well as director of entertainment. In that capacity, he booked "native performers headed by Miss Likona." After describing Lai as one of the best natural athletes Hawai'i had produced, the *Herald* also insisted that he had been tendered not one but several tryouts with the New York Giants and that "shortly after Sunday's game he will disband his basketball club and go to Miami Beach for another trial with the Giants," which was probably news to the Giants.[61]

Lai's ambitions as a sports entrepreneur inspired him to reach out to Hawai'i. Soon after he organized his basketball team late in 1931, he or his booking agent, Joseph Ward, contacted Hawai'i's American Athletic Union basketball committee. Knowing full well there was no point in promoting his squad as the Aloha All-Stars in Hawai'i, Lai proposed that his team of "Eastern All-Stars" journey to the islands to play local teams. Lai wanted a schedule of twenty games and a guarantee of $275 a game. Key members of Honolulu's sporting community considered this proposal commercially ill advised. In his *Honolulu Star-Bulletin* column, Loui Leong Hop welcomed the idea of seeing Lai's team in Hawai'i but disparaged his financial demands. Manuel Ferreira, a member of the basketball committee, agreed that Lai's request was too costly to consider further, but he had no problem with Lai's team venturing to Hawai'i "on their own hook" and accepting a portion of gate receipts for their trouble. Lai decided to remain on the mainland.[62]

Vernon Ayau's baseball ambitions were generally confined to New Jersey's Salem County, lying on the eastern side of the Delaware River across from the state of Delaware. In 1928, Ayau guarded the infield for a team representing Penn's Grove. During the early 1930s, Ayau generally drifted toward team management, although he still played some. In 1930, he headed the DuPont Smokeless Powder nine in a local industrial league. Also in 1930, the *Camden Post-Courier* noted that Ayau exhibited a "smart game" at second for Penn's Grove in a losing effort against the House of David nine. According to the Salem, New Jersey, city directory, Ayau was employed in 1930 as a bookkeeper for a firm called F. W. Layton and Sons. During the spring of 1931, the *Wilmington Every Evening* announced that "the chubby little Oriental with a familiar smiling face" was to pilot the Penn's Grove team. Claiming Ayau was then in the cigar business, the *Evening* recalled, "A corking good infielder he was, with fairly good hitting ability." Later in the year, he could be found managing the Mannington nine in the Salem County League. Moreover, Ayau's interest in sports extended beyond baseball. In the late summer of 1931, organizers in Penn's Grove decided to put together a football team to represent the town. Ayau was chosen as team secretary and booking manager. Beyond the playing field, Ayau was active in the Veterans of Foreign Wars (VFW). In September 1932, the VFW in New Jersey commemorated Verdun Day in remembrance of the long and bloody battle in France sixteen years earlier. At the ceremony held in Camden, Ayau and other World War I vets received decorations.[63]

Conclusion

Ayau's former teammate Buck Lai was a decidedly good ballplayer by almost any standard. Had he been more willing to play organized baseball outside of the Philadelphia/New York City metropolitan areas and white, he might have found a niche as a utility infielder in the major leagues. Performing some sabermetrics comparing Lai with outstanding Negro League third sackers Judy Johnson and Oliver "Ghost" Marcell," Scott Simkus concludes that Lai's performance stacks up well. Against African American teams, Lai achieved a very decent .297 batting average in 248 games. Johnson, more likely to face keen Black competition, batted .295 in 804 games, while Marcell hit .291 in 548 games. Moreover, Negro League historian John Holway told Simkus that many of the professional Black players he interviewed in the 1970s reported that Lai was one of the best they ever saw on the diamond.[64]

Aside from Lai and Ayau, other former Travelers lingered on the mainland, but to play music. George Bush continued his career as a musician on the mainland before returning to Hawai'i in 1923, conceivably helping recruit Luther Kekoa to the Ford Hawaiians. But only Lai and, to a lesser degree, Ayau remained actors on the East Coast baseball stage. In doing so, they were perhaps taking on a more transgressive project than the musicians, who, after all, were hired on the mainland to offer soothing, exoticized music to generally white audiences. With few exceptions, however, professional baseball remained resolutely white. It may not have been the big stage of major league baseball, but Buck Lai and Vernon Ayau were not supposed to do what they were doing. Asians were often racialized as passive and, if male, effeminate. However, Buck Lai, in particular, played the American pastime not only well but aggressively, while emerging as a star to independent baseball fans in the urban mid-Atlantic.[65]

6

The Travelers Back Home

Hawai'i between the Wars

Whether identified as Hawaiians, locals, members of specific ethnic groups, or haoles, island people typically embraced Hawai'i as their home. But interwar Hawai'i was pockmarked by social turbulence, despite its globalizing reputation as an "island paradise"—home to warm, tropical breezes, gracious nonwhite people, catchy tunes, and sensual hula dancers accompanied by quaintly named little guitars. Whereas Hawai'i's promoters on and off the islands characterized the territory as a racial melting pot, its colonized nonwhite people enjoyed less democracy than white mainlanders. Economically, the islands were monopolized by large-scale sugar and pineapple corporations known as the Big Five: Castle & Cooke, Alexander & Baldwin, C. Brewer & Company, American Factors, and Theo H. Davis & Company. These corporations largely controlled Hawai'i's agriculture and dominated its shipping, finance, and retail, while disproportionately influencing politics and government, largely through the Republican Party, as well as major media outlets such as the *Honolulu Star-Bulletin* and *Honolulu Advertiser*. Still, the hegemony of Hawai'i's agricultural behemoths was notably contained by the islands' colonial status. That is, even the most economically and politically privileged of those residing in Hawai'i could not claim freedom from compliance to a government headquartered thousands of miles away but possessing an intimidating military presence in the territory.[1]

While Hawai'i was no racial paradise, its racial hierarchy appeared more penetrated by class compared with that of the mainland. Possessing economic privilege somewhat whitened people, otherwise perceived on the mainland as decidedly nonwhite. Worried about haoles' minority population status on the island, the Republican Party effectively cultivated more elite Hawaiians by granting them access to political appointments and elected offices. Meanwhile, nonwhite and working-class whites in Hawai'i got lumped together as incapable of incorporation into Hawai'i's polity, let alone that of the United States. Of course, people sorted themselves or got sorted by others on the basis of race and ethnicity, fostering significant social tensions. But racial and ethnic differences were countered through the nurturing of a local culture by working- and lower-middle-class Asians, Hawaiians, and lesser privileged white ethnic groups such as the Portuguese, as well as Puerto Ricans and other Latino/as.[2]

Labor conflict shadowed post–World War I Hawai'i. A strike in 1920 caught the Hawai'i elite off guard because Nikkei strikers were joined by Filipinos, who had been recruited mainly to replace Nikkei workers moving off the plantations but also to shore up a labor force potentially depleted by draconian anti-Japanese exclusion legislation enacted by the U.S. Congress. Ethnic tensions ultimately undermined Nikkei and Filipino labor militancy, as well as the territorial government's suppression of labor leaders. Yet hoping to forestall further labor action, plantations raised wages, implemented monthly bonuses, and either began or reinforced paternalistic efforts in worker housing, sanitation, and recreation. Moreover, the plantation elite and territorial authorities were able to elicit the collaboration of people such as Protestant minister and founder of the Asahi baseball team, Takie Okumura, who sought to cultivate Nikkei cooperation with employers and territorial authorities to prove their Americanism.[3]

Generally, Hawai'i's large-scale employers asserted more unity than their multiethnic workers, enabling them to curb labor problems. Yet, in the mid-1920s, Filipinos engaged in labor actions, which provoked fierce repression. In 1924, labor activists largely unsuccessfully sought to mobilize Filipino workers on Kaua'i. Still, at Hanapēpē, on the southern part of the island, violence flared on September 4, leaving four police officers and sixteen Filipino strikers dead. The *Honolulu Star-Bulletin* declared that the Filipino strikers generally asked for it. However, a counternarrative maintained that the dead were victimized by racialized class oppression. In March 1934, Yasutaro Soga, a journalist and former labor activist, noted that Filipino strikes were instigated by abusive foremen known on the plantations as *lunas*.[4]

Rumblings of labor unrest could be detected in Hawai'i during the 1930s. Many labor activists in Hawai'i had been involved in the militant movement of maritime workers on the West Coast in the mid-1930s. Historian Moon-Kie Jung asserts that maritime workers from Hawai'i participated in the famed 1934 strike in San Francisco. Jung writes, "Attesting to their active involvement, workers from Hawai'i gained, according to one account, the reputation of being the 'toughest' on the waterfront in 'going after scabs.'" In November 1936, a maritime strike gripped the islands. In 1948, labor activists remembered "Bloody

Monday" of ten years earlier, when striking dock workers in Hilo were gassed and gunned down on August 1, 1938.[5]

Race and Class between the Wars

Racial and class bitterness intermingled when two court cases surfaced in the late 1920s and early 1930s. According to scholar Jonathan Okamura, a working-class Nisei named Myles Fukunaga was "raced to death" after he kidnapped and murdered a privileged haole child in 1928. An undoubtedly troubled soul, Fukunaga was apparently pushed over the edge when a bank threatened to throw his parents and siblings out of their Honolulu home for failure to pay their rent. The child whom Fukunaga chose to kidnap and murder was the son of the bank's vice president. Upon arrest, Fukunaga confessed to the crime, was tried quickly, and sentenced to death. Obviously, Okamura maintains, Fukunaga did the horrendous deed, but what he and Fukunaga's Nikkei and non-Nikkei supporters point out was that his trial reflected and reinforced anti-Japanese sentiment on the islands while revealing a concerted attempt to expedite Fukunaga's execution without considering an insanity defense. Race, Okamura concludes, clearly expedited Fukunaga's execution.[6]

A few years later, Hawai'i fragmented over the infamous "Massie affair." Thalia Massie, the daughter of a wealthy Washington, D.C., family and the wife of a naval officer, was living in the relatively privileged Moana neighborhood of Honolulu in 1932. One evening, she decided to go to a Waikiki nightclub without her husband. Thalia Massie subsequently told the police that during her night out she was kidnapped, beaten, and raped by five men she later identified as Benny Ahakuelo, Henry Chang, Horace Ida, Joe Kahahawai, and David Takai. Ethnically mixed and working class, the five young men were "locals" who lived in relatively impoverished Honolulu neighborhoods. While Honolulu's mainstream press lined up against the accused, their trial ended in a deadlocked jury, and they were released. But, sadly, they were not forgotten by passions inflamed by race and class. U.S. sailors beat Horace, and, worse, Thalia's husband and mother, abetted by a couple of sailors, kidnapped and murdered Joe Kahahawai.[7]

Struggling to prop up Hawai'i's image on the mainland, the islands' elites tried to keep a lid on the Massie controversy. But with the violence exacted on the accused locals, the mainland press shone a not very complimentary light on Hawai'i. Perhaps, many mainlanders were told, racial animosities diverted Hawai'i from its path toward civilization. Perhaps U.S. officials should further narrow whatever limited political autonomy the people of Hawai'i enjoyed. Indeed, some U.S. military and civilian authorities were inclined to agree, including the islands' naval commander, Admiral Yates Stirling Jr.[8]

Believing the five locals were falsely accused and Kahahawai brutally murdered by racist haoles, Hawai'i's working-class people of diverse ethnic backgrounds grew even more resentful when Thalia Massie's husband, mother, and co-conspirators received outrageously light sentences despite their confessions. Locals recognized the accused as ethnically diverse but united in their nonwhiteness and their lack of economic privilege. Perhaps the local culture did not begin with this realization, but most assuredly it was powerfully advanced by the Massie trial and its aftermath.[9]

Changing fortunes in Washington, D.C., exerted pressure on Hawai'i's elites. In 1934, Congress, inspired to protect sugar growers in the American South, passed the Jones-Costigan Act, damaging not only foreign growers but territorial growers as well. Hawai'i's corporate and political leaders, many of whom lacked enthusiasm for island statehood, expressed more interest in statehood even if it potentially extended democratic possibilities for nonwhite working- and middle-class people on the islands. However, to many mainlanders, the Massie affair thwarted Hawai'i's chances for statehood.[10]

Island Baseball between the Wars

Despite the uneasy interactions of race, ethnicity, class, and colonialism between the world wars, people in Hawai'i still played and watched baseball, and Chinese ballplayers remained relevant in the islands' sports world. Carrying many former Travelers, an all-Chinese team humbled a U.S. Cavalry nine, 42–0, in April 1919. Veteran Chinese ballplayers such as Kan Yen Chun, Lang Akana, and En Sue Pung took part in the slaughter. The latter claimed he had never seen anything like it. Yet like the Travelers in 1914, 1915 and 1916, this all-Chinese team was not entirely Chinese since Jimmy Moriyama performed as an infielder for the squad in 1919. Chinese baseball teams continued to rank at or near the top on the islands into the 1920s. Writing in 1984, journalist Bill Gee explained the supremacy of Hawai'i Chinese ballplayers of the early decades of the twentieth century by appraising them as "quick of eye, feet, and hand."[11]

Although well into his forties, En Sue Pung garnered mainland press attention. Famed sportswriter Frank Menke described the forty-six-year-old Pung as the "Ty Cobb of Honolulu," possessing an abundance of "dash and daring." Menke added that the all-Chinese had hitherto won fifteen league championships, but in the early 1920s had six players, like En Sue Pung, who were veterans of all or nearly all of those championship seasons. Menke asserted that Chinese ballplayers would not concede that "age can rob a player of his effectiveness and they hang on far into their thirties. A youthful Chinaman hasn't much of a chance to break into one of the Chinese league teams until one of the players dies or voluntarily goes into retirement."[12]

During and right after World War I, the Oahu-Service Athletic League, composed of ethnic-based and military nines, ruled Honolulu baseball. The 1919 season saw the all-Chinese, however, departing the league because team management and players felt they did not receive an appropriate portion of gate money.

League authorities responded that the all-Chinese entertained an outsize view of their talent and importance, and replaced the nine with the Asahis. The all-Chinese, however, would get their revenge by challenging the league champion Portuguese nine, to a "special series," which the all-Chinese won.[13]

The Honolulu Baseball League represented the most prestigious baseball organization on the islands during the early 1920s, carrying on the Oahu League's practice of organizing members by ethnicity and race. In the process, it apparently countered the developing multiethnic local culture, as well as the narrative advanced by powerful voices in Hawai'i and on the mainland that the islands constituted an admirable racial melting pot. During the early 1920s, two teams representing Chinese competed in the league, along with the Waikikis (Hawaiian), Braves (Portuguese), Wanderers (haole), and Asahis (Nikkei). The two Chinese nines clearly reflected Hawai'i's Chinese mastery of America's national pastime. One team was the all-Chinese, carrying several former Travelers or contemporaries of the Travelers, and the other was younger and sponsored by the All-American Chinese Association (ACA). In 1921, the all-Chinese won the league championship by beating the younger ACA, which included Buck Lai's brother, Lee. The all-Chinese nine won another league championship in 1925. Still, the ACA represented China in the Far Eastern Games, winning eleven of thirteen contests in Shanghai before losing the championship to Japan.[14]

The Honolulu baseball world shattered during the mid-1920s. Haole sportsman J. Ashman Beaven established in 1925 the Hawaii Baseball League (HBL), which would eventually hold its competitions in the cavernous Honolulu Stadium. In 1925, the Honolulu Baseball League included the all-Chinese, the ACA, the all-Hawaiians, and a Nikkei nine called the Nippons, while the HBL included a haole nine called the Wanderers, the mainly Portuguese Braves, a Filipino squad, the Asahis, and the Aloha Chinese. By 1930, Beaven's league had shoved aside the opposition. In 1931, an all-Chinese nine, as well as the all-Filipinos, all-Hawaiians, the Asahis, and an ostensibly haole nine representing the Elks Club, participated in the HBL.[15]

Primarily organized by Chinese and Japanese, youth and winter leagues reinforced racial and ethnic divisions in Hawai'i baseball. Still, baseball gathered different racial and ethnic group members together on the same squads in commercial, plantation, and school leagues, as well as the team representing the University of Hawai'i. Accordingly, while Hawai'i's elite baseball leagues had been organized along racial and ethnic lines, they still collected under the sport's "cosmopolitan canopy" culturally diverse ballplayers and fans. Some elite ballplayers such as Lang Akana and Jimmy Moriyama crossed racial and ethnic lines as the former might play for Hawaiians and the latter for the Chinese. Baseball, clearly, did not politicize the developing local culture as did the Nikkei-Filipino strike of 1920 and the Massie trial over a decade later, but it undoubtedly contributed to that culture's emergence.

Andrew Yamashiro and the Returning Travelers

After Andrew Yamashiro returned to Hawai'i in 1920, he managed his father's hotel, while keeping a hand in Nikkei baseball teams and leagues. After resuming life in Honolulu, Yamashiro could be found playing for the multiethnic Waikiki nine. In October 1920, the Waikiki nine suffered a loss to the all-Chinese. The next month, however, the outfielder became captain of the Asahis. The *Honolulu Star-Bulletin* claimed he won "plaudits from the crowd" with a "neat 'Babe' swat over the fence" for the Asahis in April 1921. Months later, Thomas Shibe, co-owner of the Philadelphia Athletics, visited Honolulu and caught a game between the Asahis and the all-Chinese. According to columnist Don Watson, Shibe admired the way Yamashiro slugged the pitches of Luck Yee Lau, likening the Nisei to Frank "Home Run" Baker. In September 1924, Yamashiro's bat helped the Asahis down a visiting Nikkei team from Fresno for the mythical championship of Japanese American baseball. A packed crowd at Honolulu's Beaven Stadium watched not only Yamashiro but also Jimmy Moriyama in action for the Asahis.[16]

During the late 1920s and early 1930s, Yamashiro's diamond presence as a player and coach informed Nikkei baseball on the islands. As his playing career waned in 1927, the *Star-Bulletin* opined that Yamashiro was "maybe old but wields a mighty bludgeon." During the late 1920s and early 1930s, Yamashiro coached and played for the Palamas in the winter Japanese League. In 1931, Yamashiro helped coach the visiting Meiji University Reserve nine, which included talented Hawai'i Japanese ballplayers Bozo Wakabayashi and Kaiser Tanaka, both of whom would carve out distinguished careers as professionals in Japan. In 1937, Yamashiro was installed as president of the Japanese Athletic Association, a position he held for nearly the rest of his too brief life. Nikkei baseball supporters on Maui acknowledged Yamashiro's contribution to the sport on the islands. In 1938, Maui's Japanese Baseball League named a trophy after him that was bestowed on a team winning two championships in a row.[17]

Yamashiro actively pursued civic affairs on the island, expressing interest in community service from the very beginning of his return to the islands. In 1930, he ran for the territorial legislature as a Democrat. Previously, Yamashiro had displayed little interest in partisan politics. But Hawaiian Democrat and friend David Trask persuaded him to attend a Democratic Party convention in Honolulu, and a converted Yamashiro agreed to run for the legislature with the help of other Hawaiian Democrats Charles Holt and John Hoomano, who served as his campaign manager. Writing for the *Honolulu Star-Bulletin*, Nisei journalist George Sakamaki profiled Yamashiro as a candidate. Sakamaki wrote that Yamashiro was grateful for the "liberal education" he received in Hawai'i and the business opportunities afforded him in Honolulu. Consequently, Yamashiro declared that he wanted to pay Hawai'i back through public service. Identifying himself as Hawaiian regardless of his Nikkei background, Yamashiro declared, "I am a son of Hawaii *nei* and I want to develop and protect our interests here." Yamashiro claimed a desire to help "rehabilitate the Hawaiian race," which many feared was "vanishing." In the process, Yamashiro positioned himself as a voice of rising Nikkei and a local who believed in "Hawaii *nei*"—Hawai'i the beautiful. His son recalled him currying voter support across racial and ethnic racial divisions by playing the ukulele and singing Hawaiian songs at Aala Park.[18]

Toward the end of the campaign, Yamashiro expressly appealed to Nikkei in his district. He told them he would be the first of his ethnic group to join the territorial legislation, and while he elicited support from other racial and ethnic groups, Yamashiro entreated Nikkei voters to display more enthusiasm for his candidacy, because "it was high time Japanese are given a voice in government." He acknowledged the pressure he faced because of his Nikkei heritage, asserting that, if elected, "I've got to do better than any other representative."[19]

Yamashiro's campaign was not free of turmoil. He claimed targeting by a Republican-inspired "whispering campaign" casting doubts on his loyalty to the United States because of his Japanese ancestry. Yamashiro responded that he was American first and Japanese second, while his birth in Hawai'i gave him more credibility than Republicans born elsewhere. Despite the controversy, Yamashiro was elected to the territorial legislature as a representative of Honolulu's fifth district. However, according to historian David Stannard, Yamashiro's election, coupled with that of another Nikkei to the territorial legislature, animated anti-Japanese animus on the islands. Many haoles called for elections on the islands in which only they were eligible to vote.[20]

Yamashiro and his Japanese supporters struggled against not only suspicious haoles but politically cautious Nikkei. As the largest ethnic group on the islands, many of Hawai'i's Japanese believed they were well advised to leave politics to others in order to avoid unwanted controversy. Issei, in particular, were politically cautious, although some Nisei, such as Steere Noda and Wilfred Tsukiyama, both also very active in Hawai'i Japanese sports, tried to steer island Nikkei away from what they regarded as the overly guarded approach of their elders. They hoped Nikkei could walk a treacherous tightrope by participating in politics without threatening haole rule. Moreover, those Hawai'i Japanese who participated in electoral politics generally supported the Republicans because the GOP was the dominant political party in the territory and they shied away from provoking GOP politicians, many of whom carped about a potential Nikkei voting bloc. However, by the 1930s, the Democrats in Hawai'i, led by Hawaiian and future mayor of Honolulu John Wilson, had made inroads among Nikkei such as Andrew Yamashiro.[21]

Yamashiro's Japanese heritage shadowed his public life. Japan had allowed overseas Nikkei to possess dual citizenship. That is, American Nikkei could claim U.S. and Japanese citizenship. Anti-Japanese nativists in America exploited the dual citizenship of Japanese Americans. Understanding this, many American

Nisei renounced their Japanese citizenship. However, in June 1932, the *Honolulu Advertiser* condemned Yamashiro for too leisurely surrendering his dual citizenship. Another prominent Nisei, Wilfred Tsukiyama served as deputy city and county attorney but lingered in dual citizenship too long to suit the *Advertiser*, which slyly editorialized that it did not doubt the patriotism of Yamashiro and Tsukiyama but held them responsible for fostering distrust of the loyalty of "orientals" living in the American empire.[22]

Reinforcing community pride among Honolulu's Nikkei, Yamashiro became the first Japanese American sitting delegate at a major party convention. Indeed, when Roosevelt won the nomination, Yamashiro took it upon himself to radiogram the occasion to Honolulu. While on the mainland, Yamashiro spoke at Buddhist and Japanese American Citizens League conferences in California. For the latter, he headed the roundtable on legal matters. A Japanese American publication based in San Francisco, *Shin Sekai*, acknowledged Yamashiro's arrival with a brief article maintaining that "the stocky Japanese is a pioneer of the second generation movement."[23]

By the early 1930s, the issue of home rule focused on the justice and efficacy of providing the people of Hawai'i with substantial governing autonomy. Yet the Massie affair had rendered the argument for island home rule harder to make on the mainland. In 1932, Yamashiro and other delegates from Hawai'i offered a home rule plank to the Democratic Party platform, but the plank was ultimately dismissed by the platform committee. Leaning Republican, the *Honolulu Star-Bulletin* editorialized within a few days of the national election that Yamashiro was embittered by the Democrats' rejection of Hawai'i home rule. Rubbing salt in the Hawai'i delegation's wounds, according to the *Star-Bulletin*, the Democrats pursued home rule for the Philippines and Puerto Rico more enthusiastically than for Hawai'i. The *Star-Bulletin* asserted that voters in Hawai'i seeking home rule would have better luck with the Republicans in power in D.C. than the Democrats.[24]

However, a few months earlier the *Star-Bulletin* ran an article in which Yamashiro expressed a philosophical perspective on what happened at the Democratic Party convention. He said that the Hawai'i home rule proposal had been caught in a crossfire between rival delegates—one side representing surging candidate Franklin D. Roosevelt and the other representing Al Smith, the party's 1928 candidate who was still seeking another shot at the White House. Yamashiro recalled that the Smith delegates to the party platform committee actually favored Hawai'i home rule but shot it down out of anger that the Hawai'i delegation had flocked to Roosevelt. In any event, Yamashiro added, the proposal may have been too long and complicated to garner much support. Putting aside any disenchantment, Yamashiro assured the press that the Hawai'i delegation met with Roosevelt's campaign manager, James Farley, who promised them that Roosevelt supported Hawai'i home rule. Professing passion for the Democratic Party ticket, Yamashiro expressed admiration for Roosevelt, who had also met with the island delegation. The Nikkei politician fully expected that the Democratic ticket would triumph, arguing that Hoover's poor handling of the Depression and cruel treatment of the Bonus Marchers stoked the fires of an eventual victory for the Democrats. While on the mainland, Yamashiro said he had spoken to various Japanese American groups and had urged members to support the Democrats. The former ballplayer further averred that mainland Nikkei were just as loyal to the United States as their counterparts in Hawai'i.[25]

A few weeks later, San Francisco's *Nichibei Shinbun* revealed seemingly more candid remarks made by Yamashiro at the Hawaii-Japanese Civic Association. Yamashiro told the association that one factor hurting the cause of Hawai'i home rule at the convention was the opposition of southern Democrats, ill-disposed to political autonomy for a territory filled with nonwhites. A second factor was that many mainland Democrats were reluctant to extend home rule to a Republican-dominated Hawai'i.[26]

Meanwhile, Yamashiro successfully campaigned for re-election. In the process, he promoted Hawai'i's statehood, claiming he had voted to overturn the territorial governor's veto of a territorial legislature bill supporting Hawai'i's admission into the United States. A provocative campaign advertisement in the *Nippu Jiji* professed Yamashiro's desire to prevent "capitalists [from] exploiting the common masses." Speaking in Hawaiian and English at one rally, Yamashiro defended his party from Republican accusations that southern Democrats had opposed Hawaiian home rule for fear of "Orientals." Contradicting remarks cited by the *Nichibei Shinbun*, Yamashiro said he had spoken to several southern Democrats at the party convention and found them open-minded.[27]

Admiral Yates Stirling Jr. was the naval commandant of Hawai'i in the early 1930s. Condemning territorial authorities as too weak in handling the Massie case, Stirling threatened martial law to control Hawai'i's nonwhite population. The admiral was also quoted as questioning local Asians' loyalty to America. In response, Yamashiro called Stirling a "pain in the neck." He declared, "The most astounding thing to me is that the admiral, who has been stationed at the naval base probably less than two years, thinks he knows it all. . . . He is without a background to be any authority on conditions among the citizens of oriental ancestry." Yamashiro described himself and, by implication, other Asians on the islands as patriotic Americans who would gladly bear arms for the United States against Japan if necessary. Yamashiro even insisted that Nikkei on the islands would submit to unnecessarily self-segregating themselves if called on to do so by the U.S. government. Japanese scholar Hiromi Monobe writes tellingly that Yamashiro assumed the mantle of a spokesperson for not just the Nikkei but all people of Hawai'i by asserting that "we know we are capable of self-government": "The . . . group that Stirling most explicitly attacked was the local Japanese. But, by repeatedly using the word 'we,' Yamashiro strove to mobilize and unify the entire island population, regardless of race, ethnicity, social class, or political ideology, in an attempt to organize a fight against a mutual 'enemy': a grave threat to Hawai'i's self-governance from the continental United States. It was his vision of racial cooperation in the islands that enabled him to devise such a strategy, which drew on and raised people's pride as local residents and attracted many sympathizers from various segments of the society of Hawai'i." In 1933, Yamashiro met Stirling, who shook the legislator's hand while exclaiming, perhaps in jest, "So this is the 'Pain in the Neck.'" Significantly, when serving on the island, future World War II hero George Patton assembled a list of Hawai'i Nikkei who might face incarceration if hostilities between the United States and Japan erupted, and Yamashiro was on that list.[28]

As a nonwhite ethnic minority member and a Democrat in a legislature dominated by Republicans, Yamashiro did not get a great deal done. In the spring of 1932, he aroused some controversy when he proposed that a bill exempting the YMCA and YWCA from taxes be extended to non-Christian organizations such as the Young Men's Buddhist Association. Moreover, he supported legislative efforts to, in Monobe's words, "support and promote the rights of the Hawaiian minority as indigenous inhabitants of the islands." Yet after his many political battles, Yamashiro quit the legislature in 1934 only to campaign as a Democrat for Honolulu's Board of Supervisors. Seattle's *Japanese American Courier* observed that Yamashiro disappointed some voters when he decided not to run again for the territorial legislature, but added that, if elected, Yamashiro would become the first Japanese American elected to the Honolulu Board of Supervisors. Along the way, labor unions and the Nikkei *Jitsugyo-No-Hawaii* promoted his campaign. The latter told readers early in October that it opposed "racial bloc voting" but thought that Yamashiro deserved the votes of Japanese as "a friend of the common people." Unfortunately, an insufficient number of "common people" agreed and Yamashiro lost the election. After returning to Hawai'i in 1935, Buck Lai observed that few back in the Travelers' days would recognize the portly Yamashiro as the slim outfielder "Yim." Moreover, Yamashiro "has become quite an upright citizen of the community and has transferred his interest from the diamond to politics."[29]

By 1940, Yamashiro had become a Republican. Claiming a weariness of the Democratic Party's internal politics, he emerged as president pro tempore of the GOP's 24th precinct club in Honolulu. Yamashiro confided to the press that he had no intention of running for office as a Republican but would do everything possible to support the GOP, including serving as a delegate to the party's convention in Hawai'i in 1940. Perhaps, like many Americans of color, he was turned off by the sway of white southern Democrats in the party. Perhaps, as a businessperson, he felt that the GOP was more protective of his interests. And, perhaps, as war clouds hovered over the Pacific, he was convinced that aligning his political affiliation with the islands' predominantly Republican leadership made sense. As it turned out, Yamashiro would not live long enough to see wartime Hawai'i. He died in 1941 after a lengthy bout with stomach cancer—a struggle that took him to Japan for "special treatment." The *Nippu Jiji* reported that 600 people attended his funeral in Honolulu at the Hongwanji Temple on Fort Street. Longtime friend Wilfred Tsukiyama served as master of ceremonies.[30]

After his return to Hawai'i late in 1924, Alfred Yap seemingly prioritized work and politics over baseball, although he did play in the Honolulu Baseball League in 1925 for the all-Chinese. A proud veteran, Yap enrolled in the Kau-Tom American Legion post. In 1932, Yap joined Yamashiro in running for the territorial legislature as a Democrat. At a rally in which both spoke, they declared themselves in favor of lowering taxes. Somewhat more courageously, Yap asserted support for the territorial legislature getting out in front of the prohibition controversy by supporting the sale of alcohol in Hawai'i. A week later, Yap backed the Democratic presidential ticket headed by Roosevelt. He argued that Democratic presidents had been good for the country. For example, he praised Woodrow Wilson's support for the Federal Reserve System and women's suffrage—the latter of which the late president had been lukewarm at best. Unlike Yamashiro, Yap lost. According to Chock Lun of the *Honolulu Star-Bulletin*, Yap's failure stemmed from his attempt to win election in a district of Honolulu heavily populated by GOP voters. In 1936, he ran for Honolulu's Board of Supervisors but quit the race without giving a reason.[31]

Fred Markham decided on a different, less public path for himself. Sometime after the 1924 baseball season on the East Coast, Markham left for Hawai'i. In 1925, he was one of the best hitters in the Honolulu Baseball League while playing for the all-Hawaiians. At that time, Loui Leong Hop declared that Markham's performance constituted an "eye opener" for Honolulu baseball fans. Later in the 1920s, he caught in Honolulu's Bankers League for a multiethnic nine called the Treasurers. The *Honolulu Star-Bulletin* conceded that Markham was not as "spry" as he once was and, apparently, had lost much of his "batting eye," but "used uncanny judgement in working his pitcher." Yet while Markham did not take up electoral politics, he did, however, join the territorial government as a chief clerk.[32]

The Stay-at-Home Travelers

Among the stay-at-home Travelers, En Sue Pung resembled Markham in generally steering clear of politics. The press admired his ability to play the game at a fairly high level as he reached forty and beyond. After he slugged a homer against a U.S. marine nine for the all-Chinese in 1919, the *Honolulu Star-Bulletin* marveled that Pung had been "playing for twenty years and [was] still going strong." By the end of the 1920s, Pung withdrew significantly from active ball playing, but he decidedly kept his head in the game. In 1930, he was identified as president of the Chinese Barefoot Baseball League. Later in the year, he headed a team of Chinese ballplayers from Hawai'i—a team that represented China in the Far Eastern games.[33]

Pung's large and athletic family attracted press attention from the eastern side of the Pacific between the world wars. Appearing early in 1927, a mainland wire story reported on the "swimming Pungs." It declared that the Chinese father and Hawaiian mother had produced a family of ten children, all expert in competitive swimming. Moreover, the Pungs challenged any similarly sized family to a swimming contest. Indeed, Charley En Sue Pung Jr. was a world-class swimmer. In the spring of 1924, Pung Jr. headed to the mainland to try out for the Olympics. However, despite his island birth, which automatically accorded him U.S. citizenship, he was waylaid at Angel Island. The *Honolulu Star-Bulletin* editorialized that the younger Pung had been victimized by the racism sustaining the Chinese Exclusion Act. The *Star-Bulletin*, nonetheless, pulled its punches and failed to fault the U.S. government's bigoted immigration practices, focusing more on a reported recent outbreak of Chinese immigrants smuggled into America. Despite the brief controversy surrounding his citizenship, Pung Jr. made the U.S. team in 1924. Sadly, in 1926, the teenaged former Olympic swimmer died much too soon after competing in a Honolulu swim meet.[34]

En Sue Pung worked as a district supervisor for the Mutual Telephone Company, while living in the racially diverse Kakaako area of Honolulu. His ball-playing nephews, Afo and Hans Pung, worked for the same company as clerks. Pung's attachment to baseball remained great. When a plaque honoring baseball pioneer and subsequent resident of Hawai'i Alexander Cartwright was unveiled, Pung, as well as former Travelers Andrew Yamashiro and Bill Inman, were invited to attend. In 1940, Pung joined Henry Kuali on the Chinese Baseball League's advisory board. According to author Betty Dunn, the Pung family was living on the crowded waterfront of Honolulu when Jacki Liwai met son Barney Pung, a leading Hawaiian swimmer. The Hawaiian Liwai, emerging as an excellent amateur golfer, found her reputation tainted among Honolulu's country club elite as her relationship with Barney Pung evolved into a romance and then marriage. Consequently, she lost entrée to the elite Waialae Country Club. In 1938, En Sue Pung's talented wife died. Born Hana Makainahulu, she was reputedly a first cousin of King Lunalilo, who reigned briefly over Hawai'i from 1873 to 1874. Hana Pung's obituary described her as a respected authority and conveyor of Hawaiian musical traditions as a hula instructor and composer. When En Sue Pung died in 1944, his obituary extolled him as one of the greatest baseball players in Hawai'i history.[35]

Lang Akana also had one foot in Hawai'i baseball circles and another in civic affairs. In the process, the biracial former Traveler seemingly identified himself as more Hawaiian than Chinese. In 1919, though, Akana covered the outfield for the all-Chinese. The next year, he captained the multiethnic Waikiki baseball team. In the fall of 1921, he took a racially mixed island nine to Japan, where it did well by winning nine of eleven games against generally college squads. Beginning in the early 1920s, Akana played for as well as managed the all-Hawaiian nine, supposedly representing indigenous people in Honolulu's elite baseball competition. In 1928, a Black team billed as the Cleveland Giants arrived in Honolulu to take on local nines. In one game, Akana's Hawai'i nine edged the Giants, 2–1, while he emerged as the hitting star for the victors. Meanwhile, Loui Leong Hop admired Akana's managerial skills, calling the head of the all-Hawaiians a "mastermind of the national pastime."[36]

Beyond baseball, Akana worked as an accountant and secretary in Hawai'i's public education system, while participating in civic affairs on the islands. Politically, Akana was a loyal Republican, serving in 1930 as vice chair of the O'ahu County Republican committee. And like Yamashiro, Akana became embroiled in the controversy surrounding the Massie affair. After Joe Kahahawai was murdered, civil unrest in Honolulu prompted the organization of a five-person committee aimed at tamping down violence. Both Akana and Yamashiro were on this committee. Several months later, Akana introduced a resolution at a Hawaiian Civic Club meeting protesting congressional efforts to circumscribe the rights of Hawaiian residents—efforts prompted by the Massie trial. Meanwhile, he headed the Board of Industrial Schools, which meant he was Hawai'i's chief parole officer. In 1935, he was appointed executive secretary of the Hawaiian Homes Commission. Established by the U.S. Congress in the early 1920s, the Hawaiian Homes Commission was mandated to "enable native Hawaiians to return to their lands in order to fully support self-sufficiency for native Hawaiians and the self-determination of native Hawaiians in the administration of this Act, and the preservation of the values, traditions, and culture of native Hawaiians." While perhaps well intentioned, the Hawaiian Homes Commission has been condemned by Hawaiian scholars and activists for ultimately advancing the land ambitions of sugar and pineapple plantations and a spurious notion of Hawaiian identity. Critics of the commission claim that the bill assumed people possessing 50 percent or more indigenous ancestry were eligible for homesteading support because they were "incompetent" and needed help. But those people's presumed incompetence meant they could not claim fee simple title to the land. Moreover, those possessing less than 50 percent indigenous ancestry, regardless of class, were abandoned to the whims of the market, where those who monopolized the land already possessed powerful advantages.[37]

Akana's appointment elicited praise and disapproval. The *Honolulu Star-Bulletin* extolled Akana as a leader in both sports and civic life while expressing confidence in his ability to fashion Hawaiian homesteaders into "tillers of the soil." One Democrat, however, complained that Akana should not have been appointed because he was an "old line Republican,"—that, after all, FDR and the Democrats were in charge, and many qualified Democrats in Hawai'i deserved the appointment over Akana. The commission's Hawaiian chair Curtis Iaukea responded, "To hell with political parties and partisan politics" and supported Akana. In 1940, however, Akana was ousted from the commission after being vaguely accused of "inefficiency." Akana tried his hand at electoral politics as well in 1940. He ran for and lost the Republican nomination for Honolulu's city and county auditor in 1940.[38]

Albert Akana shared Lang Akana's commitment to playing baseball well into his thirties, as well as his commitment to public service and the Republican Party. During the early 1920s, he played with the all-Chinese. He also competed in the Honolulu Commercial League, made up of squads representing some of the more powerful firms on the islands. In one game, he was in the lineup for Alexander & Baldwin against a team representing Mutual Telephone, which fielded En Sue Pung. Working as a clerk in C. Brewer's Land Department after a stint in the territorial records office, Akana got elected as a Republican to the lower house of the territorial legislature in 1926. As a legislator, Akana chaired the Honolulu County and Municipal Affairs Committee, described by the *Honolulu Star-Bulletin* as the second most important committee in the lower house. In 1931, Akana introduced a resolution calling on Congress to permit Hawai'i to establish a state government. His resolution passed the house, 24–2. Subsequently, he boasted that while many politicians talked about Hawai'i home rule, he actually introduced a resolution favoring statehood—a resolution vetoed by the territorial governor, Lawrence M. Judd, because, Akana complained, Judd feared for his job. Akana added that even though his critics lamented he was easily manipulated by "the big people" in Hawai'i, those "big people" did not want statehood. In 1932, Akana ran for re-election, but, unlike the Democrat Yamashiro, lost his bid.[39]

The Moriyama brothers blended baseball with civic affairs. While both were deeply involved in Nikkei baseball, they also performed on multiethnic nines. In 1918, Jimmy joined former Travelers En Sue Pung, Fred Swan, Bill Inman, Kan Yen Chun, and Luck Yee Lau on the Waikiki Athletic Club nine, and both Jimmy and Clement competed in a military league during the last year of World War I, representing the Hawaiian First Regiment. In 1920, Jimmy could still be found at second base for the all-Chinese. Called a "stalwart little Nipponese" by a *Honolulu Advertiser* reporter, Jimmy joined a team of Hawai'i all-stars headed by Lang Akana. This nine journeyed to Japan in 1922. Four years later, he captained an all-Oahu team competing in an inter-island baseball tournament. Former Traveler Fred Swan managed the nine, while Kan Yen Chun caught and Lang Akana roamed the outfield.[40]

For much of the 1920s, Jimmy played for the Asahis. He also managed the team, although his tenure was embroiled in controversy. During the spring of 1927, unsettled relationships surfaced between Asahi players, supporters, and team management. In an effort to soothe matters, the players chose Jimmy Moriyama as manager and Andy Yamashiro as captain. In the early 1930s, Jimmy's reign as manager of the Asahis ran into trouble. Moriyama claimed that as team manager he had worked out an informal agreement with the recently deceased owner to inherit the Asahis' franchise upon the latter's death. This in and of itself might have raised a few red flags, but then it was publicized that Moriyama sold the team without the players' permission, which, according to journalist Wallace Hirai, would have been illegal. Moriyama, however, denied that he had sold the Asahis, but the bad feelings lingered. After a brief respite from running baseball teams, Moriyama guided the Aiea nine of the Rural Oahu Japanese League to a title in the late 1930s, prompting columnist Andrew Mitsukado to praise him for possessing one of the smartest baseball minds on the islands.[41]

Jimmy Moriyama cared about matters beyond the baseball diamond. He participated in the efforts of the Japanese Civic Association to encourage Nikkei citizens to vote. And, in 1928, Moriyama unsuccessfully ran as a Republican for the territorial legislature. During the campaign he encountered racist opposition from a Democratic spokesperson who pronounced Moriyama a "Jap," unqualified for electoral success but qualified for removal to Japan. According to the *Japanese American*, Moriyama was the first Japanese American to run for public office—an inaccurate observation, according to Hawai'i Nikkei journalist George Sakamaki, who pointed out that a Japanese from Kaua'i had unsuccessfully sought elected office in 1922. Still, Moriyama was the first Hawai'i Japanese to seek elected office in Honolulu. He remained a GOP activist for a while, attending a territorial party convention with brother Clement and Albert Akana in 1930. Meanwhile, he worked for the federal government in the early 1920s as a prohibition agent and later served as deputy auditor for the city and county of Honolulu—a position from which he was fired after a Democrat was elected his boss.[42]

Clement got into legal hot water while working as a customs officer in the mid-1920s. He was accused of taking bribes as part of a drug smuggling scheme. A trial found him not guilty, but he was not reinstated to his former job. Fortunately, he had joined his brother Jimmy in starting an auto painting company in Honolulu. Clement served as the company's auditor and Jimmy was vice president. Subsequently, he worked as an auditor for the city of Honolulu. In 1938, Clement campaigned for and lost the Republican nomination for the fifth district of the Honolulu state legislature. In promoting his candidacy, Moriyama stressed his World War I military service, although he saw no action beyond the islands. He did recall that he and his brother were the only Japanese accepted at the Hawaiian Infantry Officer's Training Camp held at Schofield. In 1940, he campaigned again for the fifth district nomination, proclaiming, in the process, his strong conviction that island Nikkei would express loyalty to the United States in case of war with Japan.[43]

Conclusion

Former Travelers sought to keep their memories alive in Hawai'i between the wars. A reunion for the team was organized by Alfred Yap and Lang Akana in 1927. Many of the former Travelers attended, and Albert Akana, Lang Akana, Fred Markham, Kan Yen Chun, and Sam Hop delivered speeches. An empty seat was set up in honor of Apau Kau, hailed by all in attendance as the greatest pitcher nurtured on the islands. Some years later, former Travelers joined other onetime island baseball luminaries to greet the reappearance in Honolulu of Wilbur Rogan, who had starred for the 25th regiment nine nearly two decades earlier when it battled for Honolulu baseball supremacy with Chinese and ethnically mixed Traveler teams. Since then, he had become one of the great pitchers on the mainland, although largely unrecognized by the white baseball establishment. In 1934, he was over forty but came to Hawai'i as a member of the Philadelphia Giants in early March. On March 11, "Rogan Day" was declared in Honolulu's baseball world. A group of old-timers, including several former Travelers, batted against Rogan in a special exhibition, and nearly all struck out. Conceivably, once-formidable batters like Andy Yamashiro and Henry Kuali were not looking too hard for base hits against the respected guest hurler, but when Rogan was done with the old-timers he then shut down a highly respected and younger Chinese nine for five innings in a game in which the Black nine won, 11–3.[44]

Hawai'i's baseball world would again be strongly reminded of the Travelers in 1935, when another visitor from the 1910s resurfaced in Honolulu. Buck Lai, called Buck Lai Tin in Hawai'i, returned to his home to assemble a team of all-star Hawai'i ballplayers to tour the mainland. Yet beyond the baseball diamond, Hawai'i, while romanticized in American popular culture by such icons as Bing Crosby, was coping with potentially explosive class, racial, ethnic, and political tensions. And throughout the American empire, people like Buck Lai were coping with a Great Depression that did not seem to want to go away.

7

Buck Lai's Journeys, 1935–1937

Called Buck Lai Tin on the islands, the former Traveler returned to Hawai'i intending to round up some of the best ballplayers in the colony to barnstorm the mainland. For three seasons, Lai's team toured the continental United States playing independent and semiprofessional teams. Unlike the Travelers, this band of ballplayers, named the Tourists by the press on the islands, too rarely won, and the crowds they played for in the heartland of Depression-ridden America were seldom large. Still, this team, like the Travelers, was often passionately and erroneously promoted in many of the towns and cities it visited.

It is understandable why Lai might want to return to Hawai'i to catch up with old friends and relatives, but less understandable as to why he might want to stay on the road, away from his wife and children and the possibility of steady employment during a depression. His aging mother still lived in Honolulu, as well as his brothers and sisters and a plethora of nephews and nieces. Aside from reconnecting with family, Lai explained to the press that he aspired to inject spirit into the game of baseball and thought a talented team of islanders might do the trick. Still, Lai entertained the ambition of becoming a sports, particularly baseball, entrepreneur—to join the ranks of Nat Strong, Eddie Gottlieb, and Abe Saperstein. And, perhaps, given the nature of the Great Depression, he worried that he could not depend on a job working for others. For a few years at least, Lai's ambitions aligned with those of Hawai'i's political, commercial, and press elites to project to the mainland a retrofitted image of the islands' comforting exoticism.

The 1935 Tour

Early in January 1935, Honolulu newspaper readers learned of Lai's imminent arrival. Loui Leong Hop observed that the former Traveler had corresponded with nephew Frank Lai, who worked at a Honolulu music store. Lai told his nephew that he had been inspired by the news that an all-Chinese nine had won the Hawaii Baseball League (HBL) pennant. Lai said that the all-Chinese achievement got him to consider running a Hawai'i Chinese nine that would barnstorm the mainland. Hop was convinced that Lai intended to consult the heads of the all-Chinese team in a hunt for talent, but the sportswriter did not believe the veteran ballplayer would actually journey to the States with an all-Chinese squad. Rather, he would need to recruit ballplayers from other ethnic groups in order to guarantee the nine's credibility on mainland ball fields. Hop also speculated that Lai must have acquired some assurances of decent paydays by East Coast promoters. Otherwise, he would not have bothered to come back to Hawai'i to organize another iteration of the Travelers.[1]

Around the same time, Nikkei newspapers acknowledged Lai's homecoming. The *Nippu Jiji* honored him as "the greatest Mandarin baseballer to be raised here" and an "idol to Chinese fans." Echoing Hop, the Japanese publication surmised that Lai planned on organizing a generally all-Chinese squad. The *Hawaii Hochi* claimed that Lai was coming with uniforms bearing the "Hawaiian coat-of-arms." It added that in a letter to Luck Yee Lau, Lai revealed that Nat Strong would handle the team's bookings. However, the noted promoter died around the same time the *Hawaii Hochi* published this piece. A few weeks later, the *Hawaii Hochi* informed readers that Nikkei ballplayers were reluctant to join Lai's traveling squad. They were more enthusiastic about staying home to play the Dai Nippons, the pioneering professional team from Japan that was expected to visit Hawai'i before journeying to the U.S. mainland and would eventually gain notoriety as the Tokyo Giants.[2]

When Lai disembarked in Honolulu, he was celebrated as a beloved prodigal son returning home. His boat was greeted by a "special tug," and he was personally decorated with fifty leis. At the time, Lai told Loui Leong Hop that he was nervous about his rusty Chinese, fearing he would not be able to communicate with his mother. He marveled at how modern Honolulu had become, wagering, however, that his old neighborhood had not changed all that much. Meanwhile, En Sue Pung joined the conversation, amazed at how well Buck Lai looked at forty. Moreover, a Buck Lai Tin League had been launched. Organized by the All-American Chinese Association, the Buck Lai Tin League was, according to the *Honolulu Star-Bulletin*, designed to persuade Lai to recruit as many Chinese players as possible. The press further readied Honolulu for Lai's venture. The *Honolulu Advertiser*'s William Peet reminded readers of Lai's past, adding that he had married a "white girl" and was deemed "a real American citizen and stands well in his community."[3]

The celebration of Lai's return endured in Honolulu. He was feted at Sin Yun Wo's restaurant in Honolulu. According to columnist William Peet, onetime Travelers such as Kan Yen Chun, En Sue Pung, and Luck Yee Lau had arranged a dinner honoring Lai. The *Honolulu Advertiser* reported that the event occasioned fireworks and oratory. Lang Akana served as master of ceremonies, while many well-known locals and Hawaiians such as Duke Kahanamoku attended. Lai conferred with the territorial governor, Joseph Poindexter, who promised he would do whatever was needed to assist Lai's venture. Poindexter told the ballplayer that a journey of Hawai'i ballplayers to the mainland would effectively publicize the islands. Given the bad press occasioned by the Massie trial, political leaders like Poindexter were eager to cultivate in mainlanders' minds Hawai'i's fitness for tourism, investment, and perhaps even statehood.[4]

The *Honolulu Star-Bulletin* promoted the impending excursion of island ballplayers. Columnist Don Watson extolled Lai, even hailing his ability to tell stories and to inspire budding island ballplayers. He added that big leaguers passing through Hawai'i were always complimentary to Buck Lai Tin. Moreover, Loui Leong Hop surrendered his column to Lai's memories in baseball on more than a few occasions. Lai told tales of the Travelers and his past career in baseball, while claiming to have discussed baseball with its celebrities, such as Ty Cobb and Casey Stengel. For example, Lai approvingly explored Cobb's approach to the game as asserting "aggressive rights," which meant "taking all the rules allowed and then some."[5]

Echoing the *Honolulu Star-Bulletin*'s enthusiasm, Wallace Hirai, a sportswriter for the *Nippu Jiii*, called Lai Tin "one of the [Honolulu's] genuine sons, having been born and raised here during his young manhood." Meanwhile, Yasutaro Soga, Hirai's boss and editor of the *Nippu Jiii*, mused over the generally welcoming reception accorded Lai by "Haole newspapers," such as the *Star-Bulletin* and the *Advertiser*. An Issei and prominent leader among Hawai'i Japanese, Soga too naively insisted that the good press Lai enjoyed on the mainland was "an indication of that in sports, there is no such thing as racial differences. Americans admire athletes, if they are outstanding, regardless of race." Yet Soga lamented that none of Honolulu's haole journalists gushing about Lai Tin knew him when he cavorted as a young man on the city's baseball grounds or could appreciate him as much as the city's multicultural locals. Soga, who came to Honolulu in 1899, especially remembered Lai when he played shortstop for the Chinese Athletic Union team in 1915. He recalled the sizzling ground balls Lai whacked through the infield, as well as his dazzling glove work. Lai Tin, according to Soga, was venerated with "kid worship" transcending ethnic lines.[6]

Lai hoped to find funding for a bus that would transport his players across the mainland. For this, he eyed island supporters who perhaps looked upon his venture as an effective means of recouping, as well as building on, the good graces of mainlanders, even those perhaps put off by the Massie scandal. A benefit game was scheduled on March 31 at Honolulu Stadium to give Lai one last look at the available talent pool and hopefully draw enough people to get Lai his bus. As a bonus, a five-inning old timers' game was scheduled for March 31 as well. Many veteran ballplayers with and against whom Lai played on the islands were expected to appear. En Sue Pung said he would be there, and he anticipated that former Travelers such as Kan Yen Chun, Lang Akana, Andy Yamashiro, Fred Markham, and the Moriyama brothers would take the field. Pung reportedly said, "A man who has played baseball loves the sport no matter what his age and the old timers, I am sure, will go to the game like nobody's business."[7]

The Honolulu sporting press did not dial back on supporting Lai's enterprise as the departure date for his team drew closer. In the *Honolulu Advertiser*, William Peet asserted that Lai would muster a team in which the people of Hawai'i could take pride. He wrote, "Buck is a hustler and knows what he is doing all the time." The *Advertiser* maintained that Lai would patiently assemble his squad and scour the Japanese and commercial leagues. Percy Koizumi advised that Lai anticipated playing games in New York City's Polo Grounds and Brooklyn's Ebbets Field, expecting that performing in these cathedrals of the American pastime would inspire his players to excel.[8]

But Hawai'i's racial and ethnic dynamics tenaciously stuck to Lai's efforts to assemble a team. In the *Nippu Jiii*, Wallace Hirai declared that Lai had found himself in hot water with both Chinese and Japanese baseball fans. On the one hand, some Chinese baseball lovers complained that Lai would not lead an all-Chinese team to the mainland. On the other hand, Japanese fans, widely considered the popular backbone of the HBL, were not uniformly content with Lai's ethnic background and feared he was biased toward ballplayers of Chinese ancestry. Hirai did not buy into either of these objections. He contended that for years Lai had represented all of Hawai'i very well on the mainland and deserved encouragement from all island baseball fans. At the same time, the *Nippu Jiii* also reported that Lai contemplated taking a few outstanding Nisei ballplayers along with him. However, they were mainstays on the HBL's Asahi team and franchise owner Wilfred Tsukiyama expressed dismay over losing them.[9]

The *Hawaii Hochi* clearly backed Lai. One of the articles it published to ease Nikkei doubts about Lai quoted Ted Shaw extensively. A former Negro Leaguer who made a home in Hawai'i, while playing and coaching considerably in Honolulu, Shaw described himself as "Buck Lai's biggest booster," urging Nikkei ballplayers to join Lai's traveling squad. However, they should know that barnstorming is tough, Shaw insisted, as both he and Lai well knew. Shaw then warned that Lai wanted physically strong ballplayers capable of taking on the rigors of traveling extensively while enjoying relatively little rest.[10]

Aware of tensions belying the islands' reputation for racial and ethnic harmony, Lai promised, according to the *Hawaii Hochi*, to carry at least three Japanese Americans on his team. He would have to, he confided, because he did not think there were enough talented Chinese Americans available to fill his roster. The *Hawaii Hochi* generously countered that Lai was unfair to Hawai'i's

Chinese ballplayers by comparing them with their supremely skilled predecessors of two decades earlier. The newspaper's Percy Koizumi, furthermore, liberally promoted the impending benefit game.[11]

The *Honolulu Advertiser* worried about fan support for Lai's project. The *Advertiser*'s Red McQueen doubted Lai could raise the $3,000 necessary to purchase the team bus, although the columnist probably did not help matters a week earlier when he ridiculed a speech by prominent Chinese Hawaiian businessperson P. Y. Chong on behalf of Lai's fund-raising efforts. Chong's command of English, McQueen believed, was an appropriate target of derision. The columnist further condemned Honolulu business interests, regardless of ethnicity, for not really understanding the wealth of publicity Lai's team would bring to Honolulu and the commercial importance of "Hawaii U.S.A.," which would be emblazoned on the squads' uniforms. Clearly, some may not have appreciated the financial potential of Lai's venture, but the messaging of "Hawaii U.S.A." should have been clear to all who sought to advance Hawai'i's fortunes within the American empire.[12]

The March 31 game itself proved anticlimactic as one squad of prospects humbled the other, 13–4. Buck Lai shone as one of the rare highlights, making some good plays at third base. Two thousand were in attendance, according to columnist Andrew Mitsukado, while Loui Leong Hop estimated that 2,600 watched the game, most of whom were youngsters. A parade and old timers' game were probably more interesting for Honolulu baseball fans. In the old timers' game, as the two teams displayed their waning skills for six innings. One nine was managed by Bill Inman; the other by En Sue Pung, who impressed the crowd by making a nifty catch of a low line drive in the outfield. Among the hitting stars were Lang Akana, declared "a colorful showman" in the *Honolulu Star-Bulletin* account, and, while out of shape, Andy Yamashiro. The *Star-Bulletin* confided that the apparently overweight Yamashiro was "affectionately known as 'Balloon Tire'" and would probably wake up sore owing to all the base running he did. Kan Yen Chun and Henry Kuali put in appearances as well. In any event, Inman's squad came out on top, 9–4.[13]

In early April, Lai's team was nearly organized even though, according to the *Hawaii Hochi*, he had trouble mustering the roster that he wanted. Some players reportedly either had to or wanted to stay on the islands. In addition, Hawai'i's American Athletic Union, raising the specter of tainted amateurism, claimed Lai could not use ballplayers from the University of Hawai'i and then expect them to continue to represent the university athletically. Yet among those on the multiethnic roster were ballplayers of Hawaiian, Chinese, and Japanese ancestry, including John Kerr, a powerful hitter and excellent pitcher of Hawaiian and Chinese descent. Acknowledging doubts about his choices, Lai expressed confidence in his aggregation. Lai told Loui Leong Hop that he believed his team was stronger than the 1912 Travelers—a competent nine but not nearly as dominant as subsequent Traveler squads. According to the *Honolulu Advertiser*, he promised the team would perform well and effectively promote Hawai'i. The *Advertiser* conceded that some island baseball followers were disappointed in the team's makeup, but declared that the general consensus was that it would represent Hawai'i adequately. Moreover, according to Red McQueen's column, the Hawaiian Tourist Bureau helped finance the tour with $2,500, which Lai used to purchase a team bus.[14]

The mainland press set the stage for the Hawai'i ballplayers' arrival. As early as February, the *Brooklyn Daily Eagle* speculated that Nat Strong and Max Rosner stood behind the trek. *Eagle* sportswriter James Murphy wrote that African American teams had rebelled against Strong and Rosner, threatening to boycott Dexter Park if the two failed to give them a percentage of the Dexter Park gate in addition to a guarantee. Given how much the Bushwicks played Black nines, this posed a threat that Strong and Rosner could not easily ignore. According to Murphy, Strong had urged Lai to return to Hawai'i and organize a team that might fill Dexter Park during the summer of 1935 in place of visiting Black nines. After Strong's death, however, Rosner gave in to pressure by Black baseball entrepreneurs Gus Greenlee and Alex Pompez. Consequently, he offered Black teams a percentage of the gate instead of the flat fee that Strong and Rosner had previously tendered. Thus, Lai's team was not all that much needed in Dexter Park, although it did play the Bushwicks in some games.[15]

The Hawaii barnstormers' first game on the mainland occurred in San José, then a largely agricultural city some fifty miles south of San Francisco and home to a sports-loving Nikkei community. There, they opposed one of the best Japanese American nines on the Coast, the San José Asahis, who commanded a great deal of respect in Bay Area semipro circles and, in the process, constructed their own ballpark in San José's Japantown. The ballpark had a capacity of 10,000 and was often borrowed by white teams. The *San Jose Mercury*'s Henry Hickman commended Russ Hinaga, the Asahis' biggest star and team manager, for arranging the visit of Lai's team to the small city. Hickman also boosted Lai's image, heralding him as "the greatest all around athlete ever developed on the islands"—an athlete who had mastered not only baseball but football, basketball, and swimming as well. Further promoting the game, columnist Hickman cited San Francisco Seals' manager Lefty O'Doul's prediction that the islanders would win 80 percent of their games on the mainland.[16]

The Asahis, playing their first game of the season, proved overly generous hosts, committing nine errors. Consequently, the Nikkei nine lost, 13–4. A Bay Area Japanese American newspaper, the *New World Daily News*, acknowledged the Asahis' drubbing at the hands of the Hawaiians. It praised John Kerr's pitching while also pointing out that outfielder Francis Goo went five for five, clubbing a triple and a double along with three singles. Kerr subsequently expressed pride in the victory over the Asahis, informing *Honolulu Star-Bulletin* readers that the San José contingent had previously defeated a touring team of Japanese professionals, the Dai Nippon.[17]

Kerr, indeed, expressed optimism about the excursion to the mainland. He asserted that O'Doul was impressed with Lai's contingent and voiced a desire to bring them to the "Orient." Indeed, O'Doul had been building a reputation as a baseball ambassador to Asia, particularly Japan—a reputation that would grow over the years. But O'Doul's regard for people of Asian ancestry was not extended to Black ballplayers wishing to join the Seals after World War II. As for Lai, Kerr said he and his teammates were learning much from the old third sacker. He noted that Lai's "strategy" differed from island coaches. The latter preferred to use the sacrifice bunt to put runners in scoring position, but Lai preferred the "hit and run" to advance runners, expressing a distaste for "wasting an out."[18]

Kerr reported that after leaving San José, the team journeyed to Stockton. Before the game in that small central California city, the Chinese Civic Club paraded the visitors around town. After the game, a Stockton resident named Alex Lai, probably not immediately related to Buck, tendered the team a chop suey dinner. Meanwhile, the barnstormers were beaten by the Stockton Native Sons, 7–4. The *Stockton Independent* found the visitors' performance uninspired. Playing before a small crowd, Lai's nine failed to muster much offense. They then drove to Nevada, where the ballplayers saw an American desert for the first time.[19]

Lai's team did not linger on the West Coast; instead, they headed eastward swiftly. Writing from Salt Lake City, Kerr informed the *Honolulu Star-Bulletin* that the ballplayers advertised Hawai'i's virtues effectively and that they all appreciated the bus Lai purchased with the Tourist Bureau's money. Corresponding as well from Salt Lake City, Lai also claimed delight with the team bus. According to the *Honolulu Star-Bulletin*, he called the blue-and-white-trimmed bus "nifty looking." The words "All-Hawaii Team" were emblazoned on the bus's front as well as the sides, according to Lai. In addition, "Aloha" was painted on the front. Lai boasted that the bus clearly attracted helpful exposure for the islands and got a nice ten miles per gallon. While in Denver, Lai sent a letter to the *Honolulu Advertiser*'s sports department. He wrote that his nine had just played a game before 1,200 on a cold evening in the mile-high city. He asserted that the barnstormers won the game, earning good press in the process. However, the *Advertiser*'s William Peet groused about the attendance of only 1,200. He hoped Lai's contingent would return to Denver, lure more fans, and generate more publicity for the islands.[20]

As Lai's contingent motored across the Great Plains, William Peet predicted rough going for the nine. In the East, he wrote, teams had been practicing longer than those in the West. Moreover, because of daylight saving time on the mainland, the barnstormers would encounter unfamiliar twilight games, played before sundown. To be sure, victories did not get any easier as Lai and his team approached the Mississippi River, journeying into Kansas and Missouri in late May. They were scheduled to meet the legendary Kansas City Monarchs in Emporia, Kansas. The *Emporia Gazette*, clearly racializing the opposing teams, promised that baseball fans would see something unique if they bothered to watch the Monarchs meet the "Chinese All-Stars." Subsequently, Kerr told the *Honolulu Star-Bulletin* about how the Monarchs swept the islanders in a doubleheader before a crowd of 2,500. To Kerr, the Monarchs were a team that would do well in the major leagues. He especially admired the pitching of Chet Brewer, who, he stressed, combined talent with brains to shut down opposing batters. On May 30, the *Hawaii Hochi* published correspondence from infielder Richard Yamada. In the wake of losing under lights to the Kansas City Monarchs, Yamada reported that he and at least some of his teammates were already tired of night games, which they normally did not have to worry about in Hawai'i. Consequently, Yamada lamented, the team lacked "pepper."[21]

In June, Lai's squad drove to Chicago. The *Chicago Tribune* publicized the nine from Hawai'i as the "Chinese All-Stars," while speculating that "Oriental baseball fans in Chicago will stage a celebration" when the Mills nine takes on an "all-star Chinese team from Honolulu" in a doubleheader. The *Tribune* promised that the Chinese consul, as well as other members of the consulate, would attend the game and would even throw out the first ball. The *Tribune* then advanced the fabricated story that while in Hawai'i, Babe Ruth and the American league All-Stars played Lai's team. The slugger was so impressed that he persuaded Lai to take the squad on a tour of the United States.[22]

In June, Lai's aggregation arrived in New York City. On June 8, the *New York Evening Post* called the visitors a "scrappy club of young college men from the land of hula-hula." A couple of days later the *Brooklyn Daily Eagle* averred that the former Bushwick standout had brought his "Oriental Nine" to New York City to play a doubleheader at Dexter Park. Consequently, the Bushwicks swept the doubleheader against the "Chinese All-Stars." A week later, the visitors did just as poorly against the Parkways at Brooklyn's Erasmus Field, although pitcher John Kerr held the home team down in the first of two losing games. The *Brooklyn Times Union* declared a moral victory for the visitors, maintaining "the Hawaiians had reason to sing and strum on their guitars even in defeat." Still, the daily added, Lai's team could use more pitchers like Kerr. The *Chicago Defender* reported on June 22 that the New York Cubans beat "Buck Lai's strong Hawaiians," 12–1, at Dychmann Oval in Upper Manhattan. John Kerr later dismissed the "Cuban Negro team" as not all that good—that the Cubans took advantage of his team's dreadful off day. Kerr also worried that folks back home in Hawai'i would misunderstand why defeat stalked their baseball representatives in New York City. In particular, he feared that people might think he and his teammates were breaking training rules to take full advantage of the city's offerings. Kerr insisted that the "strict" Lai would not let that happen. Rather, the team's inability to field consistently and adjust to the East Coast heat constituted the real culprits.[23]

Writing from Philadelphia, John Kerr told the *Honolulu Star-Bulletin* that the team visited Buck Lai's home in nearby Audubon. There, they ate a tasty dinner prepared by Isabelle Lai and were led by their manager into the "Dungeon Room," which housed Buck Lai's numerous awards. An awed Kerr counted sixty-four medals and twenty trophies. The guests also pored over several scrapbooks, including a nearly filled one containing clippings of Buck Lai Jr.'s high school athletic exploits. In June and July, Lai's squad appeared in his old stomping grounds of Delaware County, where he had played independent ball. The impending arrival of Lai's contingent prompted the *Chester Times* to point out baseball's growing popularity in Hawai'i. It insisted, "Every kid in the land of melody has tossed away his guitar and grabbed a baseball bat." On June 19, the *Chester Times* announced that local fans were eager to see "Buck Lai's Hawaii All-Stars," and planned on honoring Lai with a Buck Lai Day. The *Times* pronounced Lai a favorite among Delaware County baseball lovers who remembered his diamond exploits of several years earlier. The daily warned fans that Lai would not be playing, but the ballplayers from Hawai'i possessed top-notch talent. Unable to quiet its promotional fervor, the *Times*'s piece confided, "If you hear the rumble of the Rhumba down at Sixty and Yarnell streets this evening go into your dance and hie your carcass to that vicinity to get a load of the most colorful attraction in semi-pro baseball—the Hawaiians." Lai's squad performed adequately in Chester. John Kerr pitched the barnstormers to a victory over Chester, 2–1. Not only was Lai honored, but the game, according to the *Times*, sparkled as "the fastest and best played ball game of the year." On July 4, Chester beat the visitors, 6–3. The *Chester Times* heralded the game's "sensational fielding and lively maneuvers."[24]

Meanwhile, John Kerr attracted mainland baseball scouts. Lai corresponded to Loui Leong Hop that he was negotiating with the Philadelphia Phillies on Kerr's behalf and hoped as well to entice the National League club into considering infielder Walter Rodrigues. However, while the athletically versatile Kerr was attracted to the idea of playing either professional baseball or football on the mainland, he also suffered from a bout of homesickness for the islands. The *Hawaii Hochi*'s Percy Koizumi saw the Phillies' interest in Kerr as probably a publicity stunt. In any event, Koizumi believed that even if there was no substance to reports that Kerr was headed to the Quaker City, the publicity surrounding the athlete at least prominently promoted Hawai'i. At the same time, the *Advertiser*'s William Peet expressed reservations about the excursion. The ballplayers from Hawai'i were losing more often than they won, Peet complained, although conceding that generally they performed respectably and advertised the islands.[25]

In July and parts of August, Lai's squad spent a great deal of time in upstate New York, with excursions into adjoining states, as well as back to New York City. New Jersey's *Patterson News* appeared somewhat impressed with the visitors, describing them as "strange but good." On July 22, the *Schenectady Gazette* announced the arrival of the "All-Hawaiian" team, stressing that the visitors brought a "touch of the Orient" to the region. Another stop in upstate New York was Syracuse, where the barnstormers encountered the Negro League Detroit Clowns in a doubleheader at the city's Municipal Stadium. The *Syracuse Herald* declared that the visitors were composed of "Japs, Chinese, and Hawaiians." Kerr subsequently reported that while in Syracuse, Lai promoted the team and Hawai'i on a local radio show. Kerr declared, "We may not be winning all our ball games for Hawaii but we are giving Hawaii a lot of publicity." He admitted, however, that trips through the East Coast drained the players of needed energy.[26]

Sometime that summer, Buck Lai's son joined the team. Buck Lai Jr. previously excelled as an athlete at Audubon High School in New Jersey. In football, "Bucky Lai," as he was called by the school's 1935 yearbook, was named to the All-South New Jersey's second team. The *Camden Courier-Post* praised him as a "brilliant halfback star" and "undoubtedly . . . the sweetest pass receiver" in Audubon High School's history. When it came to baseball, the teenager proved a swift outfielder and decent hitter. In mid-July 1935, John Kerr informed *Star-Bulletin* readers that Lai Jr. exhibited "great promise" as a ballplayer. Interestingly, when Buck Lai Jr. was a child, his future as an athlete seemed in doubt. A Bridgeport newspaper in 1920 was quoted extensively by the *Pacific Commercial Advertiser* in an article displaying the child in a Buster Brown outfit and carrying a little bat. Buck Lai reportedly brought his son to Bridgeport American practices three times a week, and while the players and manager, Ed Walsh, were ostensibly fond of the young fellow, they worried about their safety whenever he displayed "his weird pitching form" with a hard ball in his hand. Walsh advised chess as a better sport for Lai Jr. than baseball. While the article's author allowed that the child was only five years old and not expected to throw a baseball well, Lai Jr. was actually just two. Six years later, the *Honolulu Advertiser* published a photograph of Buck Lai and his son in the snow. The accompanying article cited Fred Markham, who testified that young Buck revealed promise in baseball and boxing.[27]

In late August, Lai's team made its last mainland appearances of the year in Delaware County. On August 25, "Buck Lai's Hawaiians" defeated the Chester nine before a reportedly small crowd of 800. Hawaiian Al Nalua pitched for the nine "from the land of wicky-wacky," according to the *Chester Times*. Aside from Nalua, the *Times* was impressed with Richard Yamada, "the astonishing second sacker." The next day the team demonstrated power, according to the *Chester Times*, in beating a nine from Lenni, Pennsylvania. The fielding sparkled, and the daily noted that teenager Buck Lai Jr. appeared in center field. Perhaps the victories in Chester County compelled Buck Lai to write to the *Honolulu Star-Bulletin* that his team was learning how to "fight" as they reinforced positive images of the islands.[28]

On September 27, Lai's team pulled out of San Francisco for Honolulu on the SS *Malolo*. The 1935 tour did not produce much revenue and certainly not many victories. A few weeks earlier, Loui Leong Hop's column conceded that the ballplayers were coming home without bulging wallets, but they had experienced much of value inside and outside of mainland ballparks. Moreover, they were led by a man who treated them fairly—like a good "daddy." Another potential positive to come out of the journey was that professional franchises truly took a shine to John Kerr. A William Peet column in the *Honolulu Advertiser* warned Kerr to take care, however. Peet disclosed that the only Hawaiian pitcher to make it to the big leagues, Johnny Williams, had counseled Kerr to "come home" with the rest of Lai's ballplayers. Kerr might be enticed by offers from organized baseball, but Williams knew from experience that Hawaiians trying to make it to the big leagues would encounter grief along the way. Still, in late November, the *Sporting News* announced the Phillies' inking of Kerr. According to a wire story, the Phillies planned on using Kerr as a pitcher.[29]

On October 3, 1935, the Honolulu press reported that Lai and ten of his stars had arrived back in Honolulu, greeted by Kan Yen Chun, among others. While his team's performance was at best mediocre, Lai insisted that many of his players had improved over the tour even though they lacked the "fight" of the Traveler squads. Initially, Lai admitted displeasure with his team's play. They committed too many errors, struck out with men on the bases, and, worst of all to an old-school ballplayer, missed signals from the bench. Nonetheless, according to Loui Leong Hop's column, Lai's contingent broke even financially after journeying through twenty-four states and visiting Canada. The barnstormers might have made more money had they not suffered several rainouts. The team did well financially in cities such as New York, Philadelphia, and Montreal, but not so well in New England, where inclement weather canceled many games. Interviewed by the *Honolulu Advertiser*'s Red McQueen, Lai boasted his tour had shone a positive light on Hawai'i.[30]

John Kerr admitted that the barnstormers could not claim a profit. However, he echoed Lai by arguing that he and his teammates had learned a great deal about baseball while on the mainland. He told Loui Leong Hop that getting a chance to watch big league ballplayers in action was an important educational experience, as was paying attention to Lai. In particular, Kerr learned how to take better care of his pitching arm by listening to the veteran third sacker. Kerr claimed that island ballplayers outshone most of the white semipro teams they encountered but experienced more difficulties when facing the "colored outfits." Meanwhile, infielder Richard Yamada griped that the trip seemed too much of a "whirl" for him, although he expressed no regrets about going.[31]

Even after his return to the mainland, Lai boosted Hawai'i. Don Watson cited a Philadelphia newspaper column quoting Lai, who celebrated life in Hawai'i first by extolling football on the islands. Perhaps inspired by his son's success as a high school gridder, Lai enthused that football teams from Hawai'i performed well against mainland elevens. Moreover, he urged top mainland college teams to prioritize journeying to the islands at the end of their regular seasons rather than the Rose Bowl in Southern California. Then he oozed exoticism like a travelogue or a Bing Crosby song: "The very name of Hawaii conjures up a vista of palm-fringed shores of coral and washed by the bluest of summer seas, soft, crooning voices in the moonlight, tinkling guitars, flaming poinsettias, glowing hibiscus and bougainvillea, winter bathing and surf-board riding at Waikiki, dusky maidens in grass skirts dancing in the moonlight, a land of romance and song."[31]

The 1936 Journey

Early in 1936, the *Honolulu Star Bulletin* announced the scheduled return to Hawai'i of the "versatile Chinese athlete," who planned on organizing another "All Hawaii" nine to "invade the mainland this summer." Loui Leong Hop assured readers that another trip made sense in that the "Tourists" had done all right financially in 1935, adding that Lai was considering excursions into Cuba and Mexico. According to an overly sanguine *Honolulu Star-Bulletin*, Lai had already recruited many of Hawai'i's better ballplayers. The *Star-Bulletin* pointed out that Lai was convinced he could assemble a better team than the one he managed in 1935, expecting to accompany fifteen players on a four-and-a-half-month tour.[32]

Around the same time, Hawai'i's sports fans tracked Johnny Kerr's fortunes with mainland professional baseball. Despite his apparent signing with the Phillies, the San Francisco Seals of the Pacific Coast League (PCL) surfaced as his primary choice, according to Don Watson. For many mainland baseball fans, choosing the National League franchise would have been a no-brainer. After all, the Seals were minor leaguers, albeit the PCL was widely deemed the best of the minor leagues at the time. However, Kerr perceived the East Coast as an expensive jaunt, especially since he hoped to bring his family along. Moreover, Lefty O'Doul, the Seals' famous manager, liked Kerr's chances with his ball club. As it turned out, according to Loui Leong Hop, Kerr got a tentative release from the Phillies, and he and Portuguese islander Allen Andrade tried out for the Bay Area nine.[33]

After several weeks of spring training and exhibition games for the Seals, Kerr wrote home to the islands that he and Andrade performed respectably for O'Doul. However, he feared that Andrade, while the fastest player in camp, would be viewed by the Seals as too small and light weight to withstand the rigors of PCL ball. Andrade, too, wrote home, confident that Kerr would make the Seals. Ultimately, the Seals decided to cut both. Andrade was farmed out to a lower-division minor league team in Muskogee, Oklahoma. After getting sent down, Andrade wrote home that he wished he could have joined Lai's team on its second mainland journey, but his contractual responsibilities to the Seals kept him in Muskogee. The Seals offered to give the Hawaiian and Chinese Kerr a taste of lower-level minor league ball as well, but apparently returning to the islands seemed more enticing than a summer in Oklahoma. So, Kerr turned the Seals down.[34]

Honolulu's sports' press corps generally offered tepid support of the second venture of Lai's squad across the Pacific. The *Star-Bulletin*'s Don Watson wrote, "Last year's trip was very successful as far as getting publicity for the islands is concerned, although we would not go so far as to give the baseball tour as the reason for Honolulu hotels being crowded this tourist season." Watson confessed that while the 1935 trek did not make much money, it did not lose much either. Moreover, Lai was at least ahead of last year's schedule in that he already had a "truck" that could carry his team across the mainland. At the same time, Watson revealed that Lai's squad manifested enough drawing power in 1935 to entice invitations for return engagements in many cities and counties on the mainland. The *Hawaii Hochi*'s Percy Koizumi, however, doubted that Lai could assemble a decent team. The HBL and its players resisted cooperating in a time-consuming, financially dubious venture. Lai, meanwhile, arranged a schedule that he was convinced was an improvement over the prior year. Yet he could only hope that the team would get a better break regarding the weather, reminding the press that his outfit experienced over thirty rainouts in 1935.[35]

After two months on the islands, Lai departed with his squad for the mainland on May 12. The ballplayers Lai took with him constituted an ethnically diverse contingent of what must have been a disappointing six ballplayers: Nikkei Kenichi Enomoto, Hawaiians Al Nalua and Bill Whaley, haole James Graham, Portuguese Richard Moniz, and Chinese Ship Lo. The team was expected to pick up Hawaiian pitcher Bill Vickery in San Francisco and another Hawaiian on the mainland, Walter Rodrigues. Perhaps thinking of Kerr and Andrade, an overly optimistic Lai claimed that the San Francisco Seals would send along three or four prospects. The *Honolulu Star-Bulletin* complained that Lai's team looked anything but strong as it embarked for the mainland. Lai responded that he was not worried and that if he could not pick up another good infielder on the mainland, he would handle third himself.[36]

Lai's nine was scheduled to play in Fresno for the first game of the 1936 tour. In that California central valley town, the barnstormers were supposed to face the Fresno Japanese Baseball Club, headed by Kenichi Zenimura. Promoting the game, the *Fresno Bee* touted Lai as a veteran of many baseball wars while playing on the East Coast. The *Bee* also maintained that Zenimura's club would give the visitors all they could handle. However, since Lai's departure was delayed, Zenimura scrubbed the game with Lai's squad and chose to play a Chinese American nine from Oakland instead.[37]

Lai designated pitcher and outfielder James "Hank" Graham as the team correspondent to the *Honolulu Star-Bulletin*. The haole Graham previously starred for the University of Hawai'i in baseball and later stood out in the HBL. Perhaps Graham's skills and Lai's desperation for talent eased the latter's opposition to recruiting haoles. On May 30, the daily published Graham's musings about the team encounters in California. Graham wrote that the barnstormers landed first in Wilmington, a port town southwest of Los Angeles. The ballplayers had a short stay in Los Angeles, spending the day exploring the city. Graham told readers what many visitors to Los Angeles would tell the folks back home for years: "You can ride at least two hours and never seem to leave the city limits." The ballplayers then voyaged to San Francisco, where Lai's team lingered only a little longer than they did in Los Angeles. While the islanders dawdled in the Bay Area, they observed the construction of two major bridges linking San Francisco to the north and east—the Golden Gate and Bay Bridges. Graham proclaimed, "Those bridges will be the wonder of the western world."[38]

Upon arrival in the Bay Area, Lai was met with a telegram informing him that his team, missing the date in Fresno, was scheduled for its first game in Olympia, Washington, 975 miles north of San Francisco. Fortunately, awaiting the ballplayers was "old Betsy," the bus that had transported them across the United States in 1935. When the barnstormers boarded the bus, they found it completely overhauled and repainted. The interior was decorated with leis and other images associated with the islands. Graham enthused that the "fame and name of Hawaii will be spread all over the country by our bus."[39]

Predictably, Lai's squad did not remain on the Pacific Coast for long. In late May, Helena, Montana's baseball fans were inundated with publicity about "Buck Lai's Hawaiian All-Stars" coming to town. In its announcement of the visitors' game against the East Helena nine, the *Helena Independent* printed a piece hailing the "Great Oriental Squad [as] One of Game's Great Attractions." None too subtly, readers were told about "the greatest attraction to ever invade the United States." Refusing to confine himself to any particular "nationality," Lai assembled a team consisting, according to the *Helena Independent*, of Chinese and Japanese ballplayers who would supply plenty of defensive and "running thrills expected of them by the fans." But while these players were known for their "deceptive speed and agility," they lacked power because they lacked size. Thus, Lai added some Hawaiians to furnish the team with more punch. As for haole Graham, the *Independent* failed to shoehorn him into the discussion.[40]

Lai's squad easily handled East Helena, 13–2. According to the *Helena Independent*, "the Islanders played a snappy and interesting game.... Buck Lai's boys were all they advertised to be and possibly more.... They were... active little fellows and their actions showed they thoroughly understand the game of baseball and could play it pretty well." On the other hand, the locals appeared "listless" in losing to the "little Brown boys." Meanwhile, the "Tourists" had stopped in Missoula in western Montana, where they beat a team representing University Store, 7–5. Lai, according to the *Missoula Missoulian*, displayed brilliance at third base.[41]

Within a week, the barnstormers journeyed to the Midwest. While in Chicago, they were described by the *Chicago Tribune* as the "All-Star Chinese," despite the squad having just a few ballplayers of Chinese ancestry. By early June, Lai's aggregation had made its way into Ohio. The team was scheduled for a game in Lorain, a town located along Lake Erie. The local press fed area baseball fans the dubious tale that "the Hawaiians... boast of what Honolulu sportswriters agree is the most powerful team that has ever represented the Hawaiian Islands." A newspaper from nearby Elyria, Ohio, reported that the "Buck Lai Hawaiian All-Stars" would appear in the first night game in Lorain's history. The *Elyria Chronicle Telegram* published a photograph of Kenichi Enomoto. The photo's caption heralded Enomoto as "the smartest catcher produced in a decade in Hawaii." As it turned out, the game in Lorain was canceled because the truck carrying the portable lights that would illuminate the festivities got into an accident.[42]

By late June, Lai's ballplayers had reached the East Coast, where they remained for several weeks. On June 21, "Buck Lai's Invaders" split a doubleheader with the Bushwicks, with Lai playing both games. In the second game, won by the visitors, the Bushwicks put future New York Yankee Marius Russo on the mound. A nonplussed Lai batted two for four and scored a run. Also in the lineup was Buck Lai Jr., who played in the outfield and got one hit in four at bats. Both father and son earned plaudits for their fielding. Some days later, the Bay Parkways beat Lai's aggregation in a game praised by the *Brooklyn Daily Eagle*. Owned by Max Rosner's brother Joe, the Bay Parkways played at Brooklyn's Erasmus Field, where an over-the-hill Babe Ruth swung a bat for the Bay Parkways in October 1935. On June 28, 1936, Lai Sr. got two hits in five at bats, while the son was collared with no hits in five at bats. Still, the *Brooklyn Times-Union* claimed that Lai Jr. thrilled fans as a center fielder.[43]

By late August Lai's squad had slowly journeyed back to the Pacific Coast. In the urban Midwest in late August, the "Chinese-Hawaiian All-Stars," as the *Chicago Tribune* dubbed Lai's squad this time, lost a doubleheader to the Spencer Coal nine before 2,500 at the latter's home field. Within a week, the Hawai'i ballplayers were in South Bend, Indiana, where they easily fell to the prestigious, all-Black Chicago American Giants. The barnstormers subsequently picked up games in the Southwest. In Pampa, a town in the Texas panhandle, the local newspaper boosted an upcoming matchup between the islanders and a local team by hailing Lai as a "Hawaiian boy who made good." In announcing Lai's starting lineup, the daily advised readers that if they could not pronounce the players' names, L. B. Autry could help out since he had spent "several years in the islands and learned to chatter a little in the native tongue."[44]

In early October, the first players home offered mixed messages about their experiences. Some told the Honolulu press that the team did a bit better financially than in 1935, adding that Lai wanted to front another barnstorming team from Hawai'i in 1937. A gloomier Al Nalua revealed that the team had lost money in 1936, as well as too many games. Still, he too insisted that Buck Lai was ready for another such venture in 1937. Hank Graham, meanwhile, decided to stay on the mainland after the trip ended. The *Honolulu Star-Bulletin* reported that he was playing for a winter league team in the Bay Area called the San Leandro All-Stars, which included several major leaguers such as future Hall of Famer Ernie Lombardi.[45]

The 1937 Journey

Unlike in 1935 and 1936, Buck Lai failed to show up in Hawai'i to marshal a traveling team for 1937. Perhaps the time and cost of a third trip to the islands proved too exorbitant for him while the Great Depression was still eating away at American pocketbooks. Or perhaps he understood that Hawai'i's baseball world was not that invested in a venture that diluted the talent pool for the HBL. Instead, Lai apparently lured some Hawai'i-based players to the mainland while picking up various, and often white, mainlanders to fill in the rest of the roster spots.

In early April 1937, a wire story announced the upcoming tour of the mainland by "Buck Lai's Hawaiian All-Stars." Mainland promoter Tom Baird proclaimed that cities and towns throughout the continental United States should welcome a talented and colorful team composed of "Hawaiians, Chinese, and Japs." Unrestrained by the truth, Baird declared that Lai played one year in the Southern Association and one year for the New York Giants, and had managed the New York Bushwicks. Co-owner of the Kansas City Monarchs and reputedly a onetime member of the Ku Klux Klan, Baird promised, moreover, that the barnstormers would wear hula skirts for part of the game and dance the hula for interested fans. Lai, added Baird, was recruiting Alabama Pitts, then known as a skilled ballplayer and former Sing Sing convict, to don a Hawai'i uniform. Pitts apparently never played for Lai but tried his hand at minor league and "outlaw" league baseball in the South en route to a life cut short by a fatal stab wound in a barroom brawl in 1941.[46]

Lai's contingent took on few, if any, publicized games west of the Rockies in 1937. But in mid-May, newspapers in Lubbock, Texas, and Ada, Oklahoma, proclaimed the coming of the barnstormers. The *Lubbock Morning Star* averred that a local promoter received a letter from Buck Lai, insisting that his team had played thirteen games in California, winning ten of them and losing three by close margins. The barnstormers, the Lubbock daily declared, were making their first visit to the region and would arrive in "their large, expensive motor bus provided by the Hawaiian government." The *Ada Evening News* published a photograph of Buck Lai and two other ballplayers dressed in hula skirts. The photo's caption read, "They're baseball players—and hula dancers." The Oklahoma daily asserted that the visitors actually preferred playing in hula skirts, while advising fans of the difficulties of pronouncing the names of the barnstorming ballplayers.[47]

The Southwest proved inhospitable to the barnstormers. Before reaching Ada, Lai's contingent committed eight errors, five in the first inning, in a loss to the Pampa Oilers. The *Pampa Daily News* generously observed that Lai's fielders also made some spectacular plays and probably were inexperienced in playing under the lights. Lai's team failed to show up in Lubbock, and an organization called the Lubbock Baseball Association filed a suit against "Buck Lai and his traveling

Hawaiian baseball club." Lai reportedly had phoned the litigants from Pueblo, Colorado, claiming he and his squad would not make it to the Texas town. Moreover, according to the *Lubbock Avalanche-Journal*, the ballplayers had failed to keep their dates in Douglas, Arizona, and Carlsbad, New Mexico. The *Avalanche-Journal* added, "How the team got 'sidetracked' in Colorado was not explained to the satisfaction of the local organization." The legal action against Lai apparently went nowhere.[48]

The next month, Lai's squad motored into Clearfield, Pennsylvania. A local newspaper publicized the approaching game by announcing the arrival of "Buck Lai's Famous Hawaiians." As an added attraction, Lai had brought along a major ringer in Jackie Mitchell, a female pitcher relatively well known in East Coast barnstorming circles. Indeed, Mitchell gained fame for striking out Babe Ruth and Lou Gehrig in an exhibition game in 1931. While some doubted that the strikeouts actually happened or believed that Ruth and Gehrig let themselves be struck out, Mitchell's command of off-speed pitches was real enough and could have troubled big league sluggers. And despite Mitchell's appearance on Lai's roster, Pennsylvania's *Franklin News-Herald* racialized the visitors as the "dark-hued crew." Lai's use of mainlanders such as Jackie Mitchell may have complicated the perceptions baseball fans entertained about the barnstormers from Hawai'i. Confusing matters further was that Russ Hoff, a youthful white pitcher from Ohio, also suited up for Lai.[49]

The Milton Bradley Toy Company, headquartered in Springfield, Massachusetts, hosted Lai's team in July 1937. The *Springfield Republican* dubbed the visitors a "Chinese-Japanese Hawaiian club, managed by an ex-New York Giant man." Fronting the "aggregation of foreign stars," Lai needed no introduction to local fans, the *Republican* insisted. The daily, moreover, noted the appearance of Buck Lai Jr. on the team's roster. It reported that Buck Lai, although in his early forties, was the fastest man on the team. But that "reputation goes up in smoke . . . once his son . . . starts to race around the outfield."[50]

Lai's team returned to Pennsylvania by August. The ballplayers found themselves close to the New York border in Sayre, Pennsylvania, where the "Hawaiian-Chinese-Japanese All-Stars," according to the *Sayre Evening Times*, topped the Sayre Systems Shop before 2,000 under the lights. The *Evening Times* described the victors as "all young fellows [who] showed plenty of pep in the field," and praised Buck Lai Jr.'s fine catch in the outfield. In Warren, Pennsylvania, Lai's team easily fell to the Warren Independents, 14–4, in early August. The visitors performed well at the outset, according to the local newspaper. However, "lackadaisical play" stymied the nine in the later innings. Still, Buck Lai Jr. proved the visitors' best player, with three hits in four at bats, including two doubles.[51]

In August, Lai's aggregation took on at least a couple of Black nines. While in the vicinity of Chicago, the barnstormers played the East Chicago Giants at Graselli Park. Before the game, the *Hammond Times* stressed that the visiting ballplayers were more comfortable wearing hula skirts than official uniforms, adding that "feminine fans" might entertain novel ideas about skirts after watching the visitors performing the hula. To Chicago fans who wondered why a team from Hawai'i was in their midst, the *Hammond Times* explained that Lai organized the club to inject "new spirit" into the game. In any event, the "grass skirted" nine wound up beating the Giants, 9–5. Lai Jr. slapped a hit and scored a run. At the very end of August, Lai's nine took on the Homestead Grays, the famed Negro League team featuring Josh Gibson. Before playing a game in Rochester, New York, the *Rochester Democrat and Chronicle* promised local baseball fans "a novel event" given the nonwhite but distinctive racial identities of the opponents. Further boosting the game, the daily asserted that Hawaiian Al Nalua had conquered many PCL teams in the past—intelligence that would have surprised many on the West Coast. As it turned out, islander pitching held Gibson to no hits but could not hold down many of his teammates, as the Grays easily won, 12–0.[52]

The end of the 1937 tour seemingly went as unnoticed in Hawai'i as the tour itself. Lai was back home on the East Coast when his mother celebrated her eighty-first birthday. The event was commemorated with a dinner at Yee Hop's chop suey restaurant. The celebrators ate birthday cake and golden peaches and listened to speeches by territorial senators David Trask and David Akana and music by the guest of honor's son-in-law on violin and her granddaughter on harp. According to the *Star-Bulletin*, Lai Lum Shee wore "a beautiful black mandarin jacket" for the occasion along with a red carnation lei and necklace of golden peaches.[53]

Conclusion

With the words "Hawaii U.S.A." embellished on the front of their uniforms, Buck Lai's traveling team represented an intricate effort on the part of powerful segments of island society to strengthen ties between Hawai'i and the U.S. mainland. While the barnstormers did not seem to blatantly advocate Hawai'i statehood, their uniforms spoke volumes. This may explain why the *Honolulu Star-Bulletin* provided some coverage of Lai's team and the *Honolulu Advertiser* more rarely mentioned the barnstormers. Significantly, while the former favored statehood, the latter, largely out of fear of growing Nikkei political power as represented by Yamashiro, did not. Still, Lai's squad was not promoted on the mainland as just another American baseball team. Like the Travelers, they were exoticized to attract curious press coverage and paying customers but also normalized as much as possible as regular American men playing a regular American sport. Unfortunately for the barnstormers, they were not as good as the Travelers, and they came to the mainland during the Great Depression—a time when the need for diversion was ample but the ability to pay for it limited.

Even though Buck Lai's contingent could not re-create the magic of the Travelers promotionally or financially, Hawai'i did not give up on using baseball and other sports to boost the islands' image on the mainland. A decade after the Tourists trekked to the mainland, other nines from Hawai'i were dispatched eastward. Like the Travelers and Lai's barnstormers, these teams were wrapped up in a project to consolidate goodwill among mainlanders in order to foster tourism and investment through exoticizing and normalizing ballplayers from Hawai'i. Unlike the older barnstorming teams, the post–World War II movements of Hawai'i-based nines more stridently supported Hawai'i statehood—an idea, as explored more in the next chapter, that stirred controversy on the mainland and the islands. Reflecting the relatively large, baseball-loving Nikkei population on the islands, the core of these teams was composed of the ball-playing descendants of Andy Yamashiro and the Moriyama brothers.[54]

In the meantime, Buck Lai generally faded from the sporting consciousness in Hawai'i as he remained on the East Coast. Further, few islanders even noticed the achievements of Buck Lai Jr. as he effectively negotiated racial borderlands on the mainland. Yet Hawai'i's multiethnic followers of sports kept busy and not just because they might have cheered proudly for golfer Jacki Liwai Pung, prizefighter Bobo Olsen, ballplayer Wally Yonamine, and gridders Herman Wedemeyer and Charlie Ane, as well as a bevy of world-class swimmers. Beyond the field, arena, and pool, they were also finding their islands rocked by political and social turmoil during and after World War II.[55]

8

Playing in the Twilight

American popular culture often persuasively represented Hawai'i in the mid-twentieth century as a timeless paradise despite the Massie affair, reports of labor conflict, and the bombing of Pearl Harbor. It was hard to listen to Bing Crosby and radio-television personality Arthur Godfrey singing about the enchantment of the islands and imagine communities of people struggling with racism, labor exploitation, and political conflict. Yet this fashionable narrative constructed a Hawai'i that contested the realities of political and social clashes on the islands. Up until World War II, the Big Five's hegemony and American colonial backing were assailed but largely unscathed by labor and a smattering of liberals and leftists, but that would change with an emergent union movement on the islands crossing racial and ethnic barriers by the 1940s. Still, racial and ethnic tensions flared. Suspicions of Hawaiian Nikkei grew as friction between the United States and Japan heightened. Yet as Japanese bombs dropped on Pearl Harbor, Nikkei made up the largest ethnic group on the islands. Compared with Nikkei on the mainland, those on the islands were less isolated geographically and occupationally. There were no Japantowns or Little Tokyos as one might find on the West Coast. Hawai'i's Nikkei resided in neighborhoods throughout Hawai'i, and while some continued to perform plantation labor, they also engaged in a variety of jobs in the public and private sectors. They were Republicans and Democrats, business owners and trade unionists, high school cheerleaders and high school athletic stars. Accordingly, while World War II clearly aggravated racial and ethnic tensions on the islands, and some leaders of the Hawaiian Nikkei community were incarcerated without a trial, most

Japanese on the islands remained in their homes and schools, and in their jobs. The wholesale internment of West Coast Japanese Americans was not their fate, partly because Hawai'i Nikkei were considered vital to Hawai'i's economy and partly because many non-Nikkei on the islands expressed hostility to the removal of 60,000 people—their neighbors, auto mechanics, and favorite athletes—from Hawai'i.[1]

The local culture persisted through the war, while buffeted by a stifled fear of a Japanese takeover of Hawai'i and limited by the U.S. military's imposition of martial law. In a sense, baseball reflected and reinforced the local culture's resilience as locals of diverse racial and ethnic backgrounds, including Nikkei, played with and against each other as well as military personnel from the mainland. Social fault lines clearly existed but were at least contained on the baseball diamond, which served as something of a cosmopolitan canopy.[2]

More important for Hawai'i's future, the local culture fostered an ultimately effective challenge to the Big Five and their allies thriving largely in the territory's Republican Party and most influential newspapers—the *Star-Bulletin* and *Advertiser*. Toward the end of the war and afterward, the militant International Longshoremen's and Warehouse Union (ILWU) not only organized multiethnic dockworkers but had moved inland to the plantations. Organized labor on the islands gained receptive allies among many of the territory's Democrats. However, an unproblematic alliance between labor and Hawai'i's Democratic Party was thwarted by some Democrats' fear that the ILWU was too infested by communists, as well as Nikkei and Filipino/as. But cooperation between center-left Democrats and organized labor on the islands held together well enough to destabilize Big Five hegemony in the late 1940s and 1950s.[3]

Returning vets also played a role. Daniel Inouye was no political firebrand. He served as a lieutenant in the all-Nikkei 442nd regiment during the war. While fighting in Europe, he was severely wounded and lost his right arm. Receiving a Bronze Star, Purple Heart, and eventually the Medal of Honor, Inouye earned a promotion to captain and left the service in 1947. However, like many other people of color serving during World War II, Inouye was impatient with political marginalization. In the 1950s, he joined the more centrist faction of the Democratic Party, which hoped to wrest political control of Hawai'i from the Big Five and their largely Republican allies, while marginalizing left-wingers within the party and the labor movement.[4]

Weakened by labor struggles and the growing power of the Democratic Party, Big Five hegemony encountered further blows from the Cold War and tourism. The U.S. government sought to maintain a robust military presence on the islands. Thus, postwar Hawai'i's economy continued its wartime shift toward sustaining that presence. Moreover, thanks to technological advances in commercial flight, the islands became more accessible to people with limited time and somewhat limited income. Thus, Hawai'i's policy makers, who favored building hotels to growing sugar and pineapple, proved more in touch with what was happening in mid-twentieth-century America. And centrist Democrats, like Inouye and their leader, haole John Burns, understood where the economic winds were blowing better than their Republican opponents. In 1954, the Democrats swept the territorial legislature with the help of Hawai'i Japanese, who made up 40 percent of Hawai'i's electorate.[5]

The issue of Hawai'i's statehood proved surprisingly divisive on the islands, while tepidly greeted on the mainland. Although those for and against statehood crossed social and political lines, Nikkei and island Democrats seemed most consistently partial to the idea of Hawai'i entering the union as either the forty-ninth or the fiftieth state. On the mainland, conservative Republicans and Democrats, the latter mostly from the South, warned that Hawai'i came with a price tag that white, anticommunist Americans should not have to pay. In other words, Hawai'i seemed to them too nonwhite and particularly too Nikkei, while dangerously unenthusiastic about anticommunism. The reality, as we would learn, was more complex. Like many mainlanders, some people in Hawai'i were suspicious of the loyalty of Hawai'i Japanese, and some worried about the influence of the Left on island politics. In 1958, a poll indicated that outside of the Nikkei, Hawai'i's ethnic groups disapproved of statehood. This was especially the case among Hawaiians, who saw statehood as just one more step toward the total loss of their sovereignty. Nonetheless, when the issue came up for an official vote, statehood received voter approval by a large margin.[6]

In 1959, Hawai'i acquired statehood. Alaska's entry into the union as the forty-ninth state helped clear the way for Hawai'i. Congress was more willing to admit a largely nonwhite state since it had previously admitted a very white state, although a significant presence of indigenous persons in Alaska complicated matters. The Cold War also played a role as policy makers in DC considered a denial of Hawai'i statehood as damaging to the American image in Asia and the Pacific Rim. Nonetheless, Hawai'i statehood produced a congressional delegation composed largely of people of Asian and Hawaiian ancestry. Daniel Inouye arrived as a house member and then a U.S. senator for five decades.[7]

The "Democratic 'Revolution'" liberated locals from dependence on the Big Five and haole political hegemony. At the same time, it expanded the islands' dependence on tourism and military spending. Many critics of this process have declared that statehood replaced colonialism with neocolonialism—a more indirect form of colonialism. The big losers in all this were not just elite haoles but Hawaiians who witnessed the loss of land to economic development and U.S. military expansion. The Hawaiian sovereignty movement erupted as a consequence and persists in pricking the collective conscience of all people living on the islands, while exposing the cracks in Hawai'i's "melting pot."[8]

Baseball, Politics, and the Former Travelers in Wartime and Postwar Hawai'i

When Buck Lai arrived in Hawai'i in 1935 to assemble a traveling team, the Honolulu-based Hawaii Baseball League (HBL) dominated baseball on the islands, although commercial and ethnic-based leagues operated by Chinese and Japanese also attracted supporters and press attention. The HBL continued to feed off racial and ethnic diversity with teams representing Nikkei, Chinese, Filipino/as, Hawaiians, Portuguese, and haoles. At the same time, it did a decent job of keeping a lid on racial and ethnic tensions on the baseball diamond, probably because many of the players donned uniforms for multiethnic commercial and school nines as well. World War II changed Hawai'i baseball. The HBL included military teams that featured major and minor league ballplayers, including the great Joe DiMaggio. Hoping to limit anti-Nikkei animosity, the Asahis were transformed into the Athletics and the team was run by future governor John Burns, while the HBL dispersed some prominent Nikkei players to other teams such as the Braves, a traditionally Portuguese Hawaiian squad.[9]

After the war, the importance of military teams receded, and the Athletics once again became known as the Asahis. The ethnic foundation of the HBL continued for a while but countered the growing Cold War embrace of the melting pot and cultural consensus. That is, organizing teams on the basis of race or ethnicity appeared unfashionable and unnecessary—even un-American. Nevertheless, race and ethnicity still shadowed island baseball. Demonstrating cultural citizenship in the American empire, Nikkei, adopting the term "Americans of Japanese ancestry" (AJA), forged AJA teams and leagues throughout the islands.[10]

Indeed, Nikkei ballplayers formed the backbone of nines traveling to the postwar mainland. In 1948, the Hawaii All-Star team journeyed eastward, playing eighty games and winning forty-five of them, while appearing at major league ball fields such as Yankee Stadium, Shibe Park, and Forbes Field. Promoting Hawai'i statehood through representations of the exotic and the familiar clearly motivated the journey. Team manager George Rodriquez maintained, "Everywhere we went . . . the boys played Hawaiian music and presented their opponents with leis." Future Japanese major leaguer Jyun Hirota was one of the nine's stars, but other stellar Nikkei performers played alongside him, as well as the clever Filipino lefty pitcher Crispin Mancao. In 1955, the largely Nikkei Rural Red Sox, a powerhouse in the HBL, competed in a baseball tournament in Milwaukee. Hailed as "the first global World Series" by *Sports Illustrated*, the tournament included various teams from around the globe as well as the continental United States. While island supporters of the Rural Red Sox perhaps hoped the nine would appear as symbols of Hawai'i's desire for statehood, the *Sports Illustrated* coverage concentrated on the team's foreignness, although the kind of foreignness was unclear: "The Japanese were met at the airport by Japanese American girls who later made up a special cheering section. The Hawaiians were greeted with hula dancers and leis." In praising the Rural Red Sox performance at the tournament won by the mainland representative, *Sports Illustrated* called the nine "plucky little Hawaii."[11]

Early in the 1960s, organized baseball finally sought roots on the islands. A minor league team competing in the Pacific Coast League (PCL) started to play at Honolulu Stadium. Affiliated with several big league franchises over the years, such as the Los Angeles Angels and the Pittsburgh Pirates, the Hawaii Islanders lasted until 1987, when subpar attendance pushed the franchise eastward to Colorado Springs. Meanwhile, the Islanders' existence sidelined the HBL further, although AJA and other ethnic-based and multiethnic leagues for adults and youths were embraced.[12]

Among the former Travelers, Lang Akana was the most visible in Hawai'i from the 1940s into the 1960s. Still running the Hawaiian team in the HBL during the early 1940s, he encountered recruitment problems. Indeed, according to the *Honolulu Advertiser*'s Andrew Mitsukado, the HBL aided Akana in putting a nine on the field in 1942 by allowing him to recruit nonindigenous ballplayers, but he was not allowed to steal from other "race" teams, like the Chinese or the Asahis. Mitsukado supported Akana as head of the Hawaiian franchise and declared himself mystified that Hawaiians would not embrace baseball. After all, he pointed out, many of the great island ballplayers in the past possessed indigenous ancestry. Meanwhile, Hawaiians concerned about promoting baseball should, Mitsukado advised, establish a farm league to train younger ballplayers for HBL competition. The Chinese had done it, he declared, with significant success. The next year, the *Hawaii Hochi* commiserated with Akana's misfortune with injuries plaguing his pitching staff but urged him to keep "plugging." When the Navy service team quit the HBL, Akana kept plugging by attempting to pick up "colored pitcher" Sunny Jeffries, but the Tigers, the putative Chinese nine, got him instead.[13]

Despite his travails as head of the Hawaiian franchise, Akana was chosen president of the HBL during World War II. Before his promotion, he served as league vice president, a position that another former Traveler, Bill Inman, assumed when Akana became president. Akana remained as the Hawaiians' franchise owner until 1949, when he transferred the team's reigns to one of the more interesting Hawaiians of the twentieth century—Alice Kamokilla Campbell. An outspoken critic of Hawai'i statehood, Kamokilla Campbell combined a reverence for Hawaiian sovereignty, resentment of U.S. colonialism, and a barely disguised disdain for Asian settlers. Despite his Chinese ancestry, Akana expressed confidence in Kamokilla Campbell, extolling her commitment to the Hawaiian people. Subsequently, Kamokilla Campbell returned the franchise to Akana after the 1949 season. In 1950, the *Honolulu Record*, a press voice of the burgeoning, multiethnic post–World War II island labor movement, criticized Akana's tenure presiding over the HBL. Two teams, representing Filipinos and Puerto Ricans, had been dropped from the league in 1950. The *Record* described these nines as competent and "colorful." However, Akana's Hawaiian team, which finished last, remained in the league. The *Record* suspected a double standard was at work. Akana responded that the league simply could not afford to carry so many squads. What he did not say was that obviously the league president's club would remain in the HBL.[14]

Akana's commitment to public service endured. In 1942, a somewhat mystified *Honolulu Star-Bulletin* reported that Democrats in Honolulu had considered nominating the Republican Akana for the city and county auditor position, but they ultimately backed off. By the 1950s, Akana was deputy city and county coroner of Honolulu, as well as deputy sheriff of Honolulu County serving under sheriff Duke Kahanamoku. According to author David Davis, many Honoluluans believed that Akana and another former athlete of Hawaiian descent, Leon Sterling, ran the sheriff's department while the revered Kahanamoku emerged more as a figurehead. Indeed, when Kahanamoku left for Hollywood to appear in a movie, Akana took over as sheriff. His tenure in the sheriff's department provoked occasional controversy. In 1958, the *Honolulu Record* wondered why Akana and the sheriff's department did not publicize how many haoles had been imprisoned, while casting a light on the numbers representing other nonwhite ethnic groups.[15]

While possessing Chinese ancestry, Akana cherished his Hawaiian roots in his last years, while not forgetting about baseball. Akana participated in the Hawaiian Order of Kamehameha, eventually becoming "supreme head" of that organization from 1953 to 1958. As such, in 1954, he was quoted in the *Honolulu Advertiser* as proclaiming that "without Hawaiians, there's no more aloha spirit." Described by journalist Sanford Zalberg as a "man of great enthusiasm and drive at the age of 65," Akana fretted that "Hawaiians are beginning to turn into haoles now." By the early 1960s, the PCL Hawaii Islanders arrived to take up residence in Honolulu Stadium. Lang Akana surfaced as one of the franchise's directors. Sadly, he did not enjoy his new position very long as a stroke fatally felled him in mid-April 1961 at the age of seventy-two. The locally well-known Reverend Abraham Akaka eulogized him as "one of our great Hawaiians."[16]

Jimmy Moriyama did not get to enjoy much of the postwar era. In 1946, the *Honolulu Advertiser*'s Bill Pacheco devoted a column to him. Remembering his Traveler days, Moriyama seemingly found humor in the promotion of he and Clement as the "Chin" brothers. In 1950, Jimmy Moriyama died of a heart attack while on the way to a doctor. The *Honolulu Advertiser*'s Charles E. Hogue eulogized him as "an ardent ambassador of interracial amity." Hogue claimed that Moriyama took pride in Hawai'i and America. He loved to travel and meet people from around the world, according to Hogue, and he believed that sports helped unify Americans. At the time of his death, he owned a Honolulu gas station and sold cars. Described in his 1970 obituary as a "salesman," Clement died at seventy-six. The *Honolulu Star-Bulletin* remembered him as one of the toughest pitchers in early Hawai'i baseball, and his brother as one of the best island second sackers.[17]

Alfred Yap asserted a vital, if troubling, concern with civic affairs on the islands. A Democratic Party activist, Yap served as chair of the party's Finance Committee in Honolulu during World War II. And while he continued to try, the former Traveler could not get elected to public office. Yap seemingly represented the conservative wing of Hawai'i's Democratic Party, which was fragmented over ideology and personality. Responding to the rise of postwar labor militancy, some liberal and left-wing Democrats allied themselves with union activists, many of whom were communists or prioritized workers' rights over surrendering to McCarthyism—Democrats that provoked Yap's hostility. In 1947, he succeeded the controversial left-wing activist and trade union supporter John Reinecke as fourth precinct chair of the party in Honolulu in a skirmish roiling Hawai'i's Democrats. Reinecke, a haole who came to Hawai'i in the 1920s to teach at the University of Hawai'i, and his Nikkei wife, Aiko, emerged as not only critics of the plantation oligarchy but activists seeking to forge an alliance between Democrats and the increasingly militant post–World War II labor movement. This activism got him in trouble with conservatives like Yap, but also eventually cost Reinecke and his wife their teaching jobs when McCarthyism briefly held sway on the islands in the early 1950s. During the spring of 1948, Yap and other more conservative Democrats opposed the Reineckes' further party involvement. Subsequently, John Reinecke, in a letter to the *Honolulu Star-Bulletin*'s editor, derided Yap as a do-nothing fourth precinct chair.[18]

Unlike many Hawaiians who objected to statehood in the name of indigenous sovereignty, Yap apparently opposed statehood significantly because he feared that the labor Left and the Nikkei had gotten too powerful in the territory after World War II. However, he hoped to contest statehood without incurring public wrath, which meant that he used various pseudonyms in professing his antistatehood beliefs in letters to Honolulu newspapers. In 1948, he maintained that, if given a choice between the dominance of the Big Five and Hawai'i's Japanese population, he would prefer the former. In 1950, he wrote to U.S. senator Hugh Butler, tasked with looking into the matter of statehood, that if the Senate admitted Hawai'i it would show its preference for "Japs" over Blacks, who could not vote in the South. By 1951, Yap's cover had apparently been blown. People knew that the "Jonathan Lee" who was critical of Hawaiian statehood was actually Yap. Accordingly, Butler asked the FBI to protect Yap.[19]

Perhaps Yap, like many Chinese throughout the world, deeply opposed Japan's aggression against China before and during World War II, but unlike many ethnic Chinese in America, he could not learn to disassociate Nikkei in America from Japan's imperialism. Indeed, one wonders what Yap's former Nikkei teammates such as Yamashiro and Jimmy Moriyama would have thought as Yap expressed his disapproval of the postwar movie *Go for Broke*, depicting the heroism of the Japanese American 442nd regiment in Europe. While this movie has been rightly criticized for focusing on a white officer, played by Van Johnson, as the hero, *Go for Broke* expressed too much sympathy to Nikkei for Yap, who in 1951 further condemned it as financed by "Hollywood Jews." Meanwhile, the Rural Red Sox emerged as a power in the HBL. Representing the less urban Waipahu region of Oahu, the Red Sox were not exclusively Nikkei but nearly so. Moreover, they played with a design of the Rising Sun on their sleeves, arousing Yap into viewing the Red Sox as a symbol of Nikkei conquest of the islands. Catching wind of Yap's diatribes, John Stennis, a staunch white supremacist senator from Mississippi, bemoaned the possibility of Hawai'i statehood in 1951.[20]

Previously, Yap had been hired as a consultant to the committee headed by Butler, a conservative, anticommunist senator from Nebraska. After visiting the islands in Hawai'i, Butler declared that he opposed statehood because of what he perceived as the treasonous infiltration of Hawai'i's politics by left-leaning labor leaders and Democratic Party activists. When Butler's opposition became public, it was widely believed that Yap had a hand in shaping the senator's opinion. However, Butler protested that his opposition to Hawai'i becoming a state reflected his own beliefs and not necessarily Yap's. Yap, in any event, cozied up to the anticommunist fervor assailing post–World War II America. In April 1950, the *Honolulu Star-Bulletin* displayed a photograph of Yap shaking hands with Frank S. Tavenner Jr., counsel for the House Un-American Activities Committee, then investigating communist influence in Hawai'i. For Yap, however, fears of a Nikkei takeover seemingly trumped anticommunism. In 1953, he warned Olin Johnston, another white southern Democrat, that Honolulu was "the only city on American soil where you can be arrested by a Jap policeman, booked by a Jap clerk, prosecuted by a Jap prosecutor, judged, fined, and be sentenced by a Jap judge." Yap died in 1961, a few years after Hawai'i became a state. At that time, he was a real estate broker.[21]

Unlike Yap, Foster Robinson supported Hawai'i statehood after World War II. Identified as a Maui political figure and superintendent of the Kula sanatorium, he visited the mainland in 1950, plugging Hawai'i as a new state. Robinson told the press that Californians, in particular, supported statehood. The former pitcher lingered on the mainland for a couple of months, throwing public luaus to garner backing of Hawai'i statehood. Politically, Robinson served on the Maui county board of supervisors as a Republican in the early 1950s and sought election as county chair but was defeated by his Democrat opponent. In 1954, he resigned as a county supervisor. Afterward, he became Maui County's subland agent. In 1959, he retired to tend to cattle raising but remained active in the GOP. In 1971, the former pitcher died.[22]

The Changing Postwar American Empire

The U.S. mainland to which Buck Lai returned for good after the 1937 baseball season was still struggling with the Great Depression. FDR's New Deal had given people hope, but recovery would wait until the country mobilized for World War II in the several months before Pearl Harbor was attacked. The war did more than end the Great Depression; it helped usher in important, albeit piecemeal, efforts to advance racial democracy and eventually elevate Hawai'i to statehood. Hovering over these efforts was what Swedish social scientist Gunner Myrdal called "The American Dilemma." Recruited by the Carnegie Foundation before the war to investigate race relations in the United States, Myrdal and a team of sociologists conducted fieldwork in the South. Primarily focused on Black-white relations, the research culminated in a book, *An American Dilemma: The Negro Problem and Modern Democracy* (1944). A main takeaway from the book was that if America deserved to lead the forces of freedom, equality, and democracy against totalitarianism, it would be well served to get its house in order and actually expand the benefits of freedom, equality, and democracy to millions of nonwhite citizens.[23]

Realizing that war was not just about guns and bombs, American policy makers fretted over the bad optics of a nation seeking support from people of color in the United States and around the world while sustaining Jim Crow and race-based immigration restriction and colonization. Thus, even before the war began, FDR submitted to pressure by Black civil rights activists, such as A. Philip Randolph, and issued an executive order setting up the Fair Employment Practices Committee, aimed at eliminating racial and ethnic bias in hiring by firms doing business with the U.S. government. Moreover, after America entered the war, Congress revisited the Chinese Exclusion Act. Chinese Americans had long sought an end to the law as did most racial liberals. However, a decisive factor was the need to elicit military support from China, which the United States hoped would effectively counter the Japanese in Asia. That is, the U.S. government worried that Chinese confidence in America would flag if the American government continued to bar Chinese immigrants and deny naturalization rights to those in the United States. Even so, the Magnuson Act of 1943 proved only cautiously generous, admitting a mere 105 Chinese immigrants a year, although significantly it did grant naturalization rights to Chinese immigrants living in the United States.[24]

Other Asian ethnic groups would have to wait until war's end to achieve immigration quotas and naturalization rights. Yet many Asian and nonwhite veterans, like Daniel Inouye, found that the war had politicized them. They were less likely to accept second- and third-class citizenship after fighting the forces of totalitarianism and militarism. Indeed, their loved ones were also affected. In Southern California, a contingent of Chinese American female bowlers protested the racial discrimination of the sport's national organizations, claiming that if their husbands and brothers were good enough to fight for Uncle Sam, their wives and sisters were surely good enough to bowl in any tournament.[25]

For racial reformers, the Cold War did little to diminish the importance of the American Dilemma. After all, communist propaganda urged nonwhite people around the world to understand that American capitalist-inspired imperialism stoked their exploitation and oppression. If for no other reason than to render that propaganda less persuasive, many American policy makers sought to chip away at institutional racism in the United States, as well as ultimately chip away at the American empire by promoting Hawai'i statehood. Yet racial reform was not just about winning the Cold War. Policy makers were pressured by civil rights activists and their own consciences.[26]

The politics of racial reform and the melting pot were embraced by large swaths of Cold War America, while certainly shaping the world of American sports. The integration of major league baseball by Jackie Robinson, Larry Doby, and other African American and African Latino ballplayers not only changed the face of organized baseball but ultimately led, for better or worse, to the demise of the Negro Leagues and other racial-ethnic-based baseball organizations such as those once prominent in Hawai'i. More than that, racial discrimination was assailed in other sports. In 1946, African Americans such as Marion Motley and Kenny Washington integrated big league professional football. The next year, a Hawai'i Japanese named Wally Yonamine joined the San Francisco 49ers of the then All-American Football Conference. The 1948 U.S. Olympic squad included a diverse contingent of athletes of color. Korean American Sammy Lee and Filipino American Vicki Manalo Draves won Olympic gold medals in diving. A number of other Asian and Pacific Islanders took home medals in swimming. Don Barksdale, a Black American basketball star from UCLA, played on a gold-medal-winning team coached by Kentucky's Adolph Rupp, a longtime supporter of Jim Crow. Moreover, in tennis, a working-class Mexican American from East Los Angeles, Richard "Pancho" Gonzalez," won the U.S. Open in the late 1940s.[27]

The intrusion of racial reform in American sports interweaved with changes in legislation and various court cases in the ten years after the end of the war. In California, Buck Lai's marriage to Isabelle Reynolds would have been illegal owing to the state's antimiscegenation law as of 1945. In 1948, however, the state's supreme court struck down that law in its decision in *Perez v. Sharpe*. California's courts also struck down racial covenants that protected racial and ethnic discrimination in terms of housing and an alien land law that for years had forbidden Japanese and other Asian immigrants from owning farmland in California. On a national level, President Harry Truman issued an executive order in 1948 to racially integrate the armed forces. And four years later, Congress ceased the barring of immigrants from citizenship on account of their race, as well as allowing a small yearly quota of immigrants from Japan to enter the United States.[28]

Racial reform walked a tightrope in Cold War America. Its supporters channeled their arguments along the lines of rendering the American Dream more tangible to people of color—that people of color wanted to vote, rise up the economic ladder as far as their skills could take them, and consume as much as possible whatever American manufacturers of commodities and culture offered. Arguments that racial discrimination and economic inequality were tied together and systemically ingrained in American society stirred too much controversy and evoked cries of communism as often discovered by labor leaders in Hawai'i, as well as nonwhite activists on the mainland such as Paul Robeson and Bayard Rustin.[29]

Cold War racial reform benefited all racial minorities in one way or another in the United States, but Asian American historians have effectively asserted that it perhaps aided people of Asian ancestry living in the U.S. empire the most, however superficially. American policy makers deemed Asia, especially after the Chinese revolution, a key battleground in the Cold War. This was one reason the McCarran-Walter Act (1952) raised the bar on Japanese immigration. The United States wanted to count on Japan's permanent goodwill in its effort to contain and perhaps roll back Chinese communist influence in the region, and so halting Japanese immigration and excluding Nikkei immigrants from attaining U.S. citizenship was hardly a useful way to ensure Japan's friendship. Moreover, historian Madeline Hsu has argued that by lowering immigration barriers for Asian immigrants and refugees possessing significant human capital in terms of marketable educational and employment backgrounds, the United States demonstrated its generosity to Asians, who might otherwise dawdle on the sidelines of the Cold War if they did not lean toward communism. Further, it would help shape Asian Americans as people of color who have successfully cast aside the burdens of race and ethnicity, thus delegitimizing militant protests and propping up the veracity of the American Dream.[30]

The U.S. State Department sponsored treks of nonwhite American athletes as well as other celebrities to Asia. Americans of Asian ancestry sent to Asia to create a better narrative of the United States included Chinese Americans such as artist Dong Kingman and writer Jade Snow Wong, Korean American Sammy Lee, who won an Olympic gold medal in diving, and perhaps the best Asian American community basketball team, the all–Chinese American San Francisco Saints. The message seemingly conveyed by these American "ambassadors" was that the United States had truly caught up with its melting pot image, but the problem, most glaring when it came to the Saints, was that if racial barriers were collapsing in America, why not send to Asia a racially and ethnically polyglot squad that included Asian Americans? The answer was that such teams, at least on the mainland, rarely existed.[31]

Thus, the Cold War may have punctured more holes in the racial barriers facing Asian Americans; it may have helped, historian Ellen Wu writes, to forge the stereotype of Asian Americans as a "model minority" to buttress the argument at home and abroad that in the United States, democracy and capitalism corresponded. Yet those barriers remained. For example, Sammy Lee won four Olympic gold medals, served for years in the military, and was a loyal, anticommunist member of the Republican Party. Nonetheless, when he left the service to enter private practice and tutor diving, he and his family could not find a home in Orange Country. Facing racial discrimination, Lee decided to call on the services of a Republican acquaintance, Vice President Richard Nixon. Nixon made some inquiries, and Lee eventually got his home. Around the same time and on the opposite coast, Buck Lai Jr. seemingly made his way into the melting pot. In the process, his experiences represent the twisted history of racialization in America, for while it seemed easy for the public to forget his Chinese heritage, it proved harder to forget the Blackness of bi- and multiracial people of African ancestry such as the great catcher Roy Campanella.[32]

Buck Lai Jr.

After World War II, William T. Buck Lai Jr. enjoyed a distinguished career as a coach and administrator, rendering him into both a beneficiary of and an admittedly minor contributor to the postwar sports boom in the United States. A decade earlier, he departed high school as a versatile athlete, excelling in football, basketball, and baseball, for Ursinus University in Collegeville, Pennsylvania, northwest of Philadelphia. Lai stayed there for only a year before moving on to Long Island University (LIU), where he played varsity baseball as a first baseman and outfielder. He also suited up as a forward on the frosh basketball team. When Lai Jr. enrolled at LIU, it was roughly a decade old. Despite its name, LIU began in the heart of Brooklyn in 1926, eventually establishing a campus on Long Island itself in the early 1950s. Lai was a steady performer for LIU's nine, coached by the legendary Clair Bee, who also led the Blackbird basketball team to national prominence and directed the athletics department. Meanwhile, he met his future wife, Mary, who would serve the university for decades as financial director after World War II. In June 1941, Lai graduated from LIU.[33]

Lai also played independent baseball as a young man in the south New Jersey/Philadelphia area. In August 1939, Lai was in right field and got a key hit for the Lloyd Athletic Club nine when it beat the Philadelphia Black Meteors. Playing out of Chester, the Lloyd nine often competed against several top-notch African American teams. In 1941, the younger Lai held down center field for an independent team out of Camden County called the Collingwood All-Stars—a team that was managed by the older Lai. Midway through the month, he got two hits in a losing game against the Brooklyn Royal Giants. The next week, Lai managed two hits against the New York Black Yankees in a winning effort.[34]

In 1947, the *Brooklyn Daily Eagle* announced Lai's return to LIU to coach frosh basketball and varsity baseball after service in World War II as a navy pilot. The daily described the son as "sturdier and stockier" than his "lithe and nimble" father. During the war, Lai performed well with and against former major leaguers while playing ball for Pensacola Naval Air Station, attracting the interest of the New York Yankees. However, the *Daily Eagle* asserted that Lai preferred postgraduate work rather than head to the pros after his military service ended.[35]

Buck Lai Jr. gained recognition as one of Clair Bee's basketball assistants in the late 1940s and early 1950s. Ace Bushnell, in the *Brooklyn Daily Eagle*, dubbed him one of Bee's "capable, young assistant coaches." A part of Lai's duties seemed to entail that of the primary public relations person for the basketball program, speaking at press conferences and luncheons. Lai revered Clair Bee as a mentor. But historians Randy Roberts and James Olson call Bee "a study in contradictions." He was, indeed, scholarly, a well-published author of fiction and nonfiction, and a fervent advocate of the virtues of clean living and discipline. Coaching football and baseball at one time at LIU, in addition to basketball, Bee embraced the ethos of victory at any cost. One of his former players reportedly said, "Breathing and winning had the same importance to Clair Bee." *Sport* magazine's Milton Gross contended in 1951, "There are those unkind to describe LIU as Clair Bee University. Others regard the university as a state of mind perpetuated by Bee and his astounding basketball team."[36]

LIU's basketball team not only had a very good 1950–1951 season, but, to Clair Bee's credit, was racially integrated by the standards of the time. During the season, the University of Arizona five visited Madison Square Garden to play LIU. An Arizona politician and University of Arizona booster attended the game, sitting much too close to the LIU bench. After calling the LIU players a "bunch of Harlem Globetrotters," he got into a fracas with an angry Clair Bee. The abusive fan was escorted from the arena, and the University of Arizona team manager was dispatched to the LIU locker room, where he reportedly apologized to Lai. Consequently, LIU considered canceling a rematch with the University of Arizona in Tucson, fearing their prospective hosts embraced Jim Crow too ardently. LIU, indeed, could not find accommodations in Tucson for the whole team, Eventually, Buck Lai worked something out with a friend who owned a motel in Tucson so that the LIU hoopsters, regardless of race, could sleep in one place. LIU, accordingly, wound up playing the University of Arizona. Nerves were still raw as the home team edged the visitors. Buck Lai voiced contempt for the referees, claiming his team suffered through the "worst officiating ever." Abe Chanin, columnist for the *Arizona Daily Star*, countered that Lai, as LIU's "Faculty Athletic Manager," sat in the press box, where he should have kept his mouth shut. Instead, he broke an "unwritten rule" by constantly berating the referees.[37]

Later in 1951, college basketball was rocked by a point-shaving scandal that engulfed several institutions on the East Coast, netting, in the process, LIU hoopsters. Since the late 1930s, college basketball had become big business. Venues such as New York's fabled Madison Square Garden drew thousands to games featuring the best teams in the nation, in addition to very interested professional gamblers. And college basketball developed into an even bigger business during the postwar sports boom. Clair Bee took responsibility for what happened to LIU's basketball program. He conceded, "I was a 'win-em-all' coach who helped to create the emotional climate that led to the worst scandal in the history of sports." He confessed to internalizing "misplaced priorities." College basketball had become just too profitable: "We were playing basketball for money and some boys followed the college's example." The consequences of the scandal proved devastating for LIU's basketball program, at least in the short run. The school's administration, unlike administrations of other colleges implicated in the scandal, shut down its basketball program. Bee was slotted into a nonathletic administrative post at LIU, and Lai was promoted to athletic director in February 1952. Meanwhile, he remained at the helm of the school's baseball team.[38]

As LIU's key figure in intercollegiate athletics, Lai Jr. enticed press coverage from New York City newspapers. In 1955, the *Brooklyn Eagle*'s Harold Burr presumably failed to interview Lai Jr. or paid much attention if he had. Burr maintained that the LIU athletic director was born in Hawai'i and migrated with his parents to Audubon, New Jersey, as a small child. Ignoring that Hawai'i-born residents were U.S. citizens, Burr's column assured readers that Lai "has been thoroughly Americanized and bears the good old baptismal name of Bill." In the mid-1950s, Lai spearheaded a project called Operation Rebound, aimed at reviving LIU's intercollegiate basketball program. While Lai hoped to resurrect basketball at his alma mater, he also hoped to shun the "limelight" and the temptations of Madison Square Garden. Taking on the job of head basketball coach in addition to his other duties in the athletics department, Lai led fives that won their share of games. In 1959, the *Bridgeport Post* noted that LIU was coached by "veteran Bill Lai who is known for his superb teams at the New York school."[39]

In May 1961, Lai resigned as LIU's basketball coach. After six years, Lai's teams had achieved a record of forty-four victories and thirty-nine defeats. Yet as athletic director, he hardly ignored intercollegiate basketball. In 1963, the *New York Times* announced that Lai was overseeing the transformation of the old Paramount Theater in Long Island into a gym for the basketball team. At this time, Lai promised that LIU's basketball teams would not seek the elite status they enjoyed prior to the scandals.[40]

Lai proved a winning head coach of LIU's baseball team. When Lai took over LIU's baseball program in the late 1940s, it had been exiled from the baseball campus for seven years because of a lack of proper facilities in downtown Brooklyn. A grassroots movement of students both passionate about baseball and skilled enough at playing it convinced Lai that LIU could engage in intercollegiate baseball again. According to LIU's 1952 yearbook, fifty-five potential recruits showed up for the tryouts. Eventually, Lai pared the squad down to eighteen. The team practiced at the "sadly lacking facilities" of nearby Red Hook Stadium. Nonetheless, despite the apathy toward intercollegiate baseball manifested by the student body in general, the "Laimen" performed well. Indeed, *New York Daily News* columnist Jimmy Powers heralded Lai's baseball coaching in 1950 as the Bluebirds claimed a surprisingly strong season. Powers, moreover, fondly remembered watching Buck Lai Sr. as a youth living near Dexter Park. Four years later, Powers praised Lai Jr. as "one of the best college coaches around." Indeed, during the 1950s, Lai Jr.'s team won three straight New York City titles.

And, to Lai's credit, he recruited female Ilene Somkan as team manager. As such, she became the first woman to win a varsity letter at LIU. Bert Clemens, a columnist for the *Boston Daily*, testified that she did more than lug bats and other equipment around by demonstrating keen baseball knowledge and winning the respect of Lai and the male players.[41]

According to columnist Bernie Beglane, Lai emerged as a college baseball innovator for making his players wear fiber caps while batting in 1955. A year earlier LIU batters had just worn shells. Lai told the press, "If they think enough to use [fiber caps] in the majors, then the college kid should be protected too." A decade later, Beglane reported that Lai wanted to establish a summer college league in the New York metropolitan area, and he hoped that the big leagues would help financially. Looking at the large bundles of cash that major league franchises were throwing at young, unproven ballplayers out of high school at the time, Lai reasoned, "When you see the amount of money that is wasted on big bonuses, this would be a good investment. Even if the league produced just one major leaguer a year, it's a good return for $30,000.[42]

In the late 1960s, Lai, his wife, Mary, and their two children finally visited Hawai'i. The *Honolulu Star-Bulletin* contended that this was the first time the son of the great Honolulu-raised athlete had stepped on Hawai'i's shores. Family members and friends of his father greeted the mainlanders. He probably welcomed the vacation as he and the LIU campus were caught up in the student movement embroiling colleges and universities in the late 1960s and early 1970s. In the spring of 1968, Lai had been promoted to acting provost of LIU. In late April, fifteen members of the Student Organization for Black Unity barricaded themselves in his office. They objected to the proposed sale of LIU's Brooklyn campus to the City College of New York (CCNY). And they demanded more Black history courses and faculty members, higher wages for nonfaculty employees, and office space for their organization. LIU eventually agreed to all the demands save for selling the Brooklyn campus land to CCNY. Lai subsequently continued as athletics director, physical educator, and coach at LIU's CW Post campus, the U.S. Merchant Academy, and the New York Institute of Technology into the 1980s.[43]

Beyond the university, Lai fervently supported youth baseball and basketball. In June 1950, the *Brooklyn Daily Eagle* sponsored a youth sandlot baseball team and announced that Lai would help coach the nine. At that time, *Eagle* columnist Jimmy Murphy described Lai's father as "a famous Chinese infielder." Five years later, Harold Burr said that Lai helped organize a nine known as the Brooklyn Rookies Program, which, in turn, was an outgrowth of a baseball-based project called Brooklyn Against the World. Fifteen of the borough's most outstanding high school ballplayers were chosen to play a full summer schedule. Among the standouts on Lai's teams were Billy Loes, who would have some good seasons pitching for the Brooklyn Dodgers, and the future great New York Yankee southpaw Whitey Ford.[44]

Lai also worked as a scout and instructor part time for the Brooklyn Dodgers, the National League's most dominant team of the early Cold War era. One of his jobs for the Dodgers was to coach a youth team called the Brooklyn Dodgers Stars of Tomorrow. In August 1952, Lai's contingent opposed the Manhattan-based Junior City All-Stars. In 1953, the Dodgers conducted a school in Florida for sandlot organizers. Dodger stars Pee Wee Reese and Carl Erskine were on hand along with Lai and Dodger administrator Fresco Thompson. In February 1956, Lai joined Dodger manager Walt Alston in running a baseball school for the U.S. Air Force personnel in Montgomery, Alabama. After the Dodger organization fled westward in 1958, Lai maintained his involvement in youth baseball. In the summer of 1960, he assisted major league notable Tommy Holmes in managing a New York City nine in the city's Sandlot Classic. Meanwhile, according to Mary Lai, her husband, unlike many locals, did not blame Walter O'Malley for moving the franchise to Los Angeles. He believed that the City of New York, as represented by controversial urban developer Robert Moses, had largely compelled the move—a view generally supported by historian Jerald Podair.[45]

Buck Lai Jr. wrote and illustrated popular instructional books on baseball and basketball in the 1950s. Fresco Thompson, a well-known figure in the Dodgers' front office, wrote the foreword to his baseball book. Thompson hailed Lai's work with the Dodgers, noting that the author's expertise grew out of about twenty years of baseball experience. The *Brooklyn Daily Eagle* promoted the book, calling Lai a "talented athlete, teacher, and artist." Dick Young, renowned *New York Daily News* columnist, praised Lai's book, extolling not only the writing but also the illustrations. Al Cartwright, a sports editor for the *Wilmington News Journal*, declared that Lai's book was "the best piece on baseball fundamentals to ever reach the layman." The *Cleveland Plain Dealer* commended Lai's book, describing it as aimed at both young ballplayers and their coaches The *Plain Dealer* added that it stressed the kind of fundamental skills taught by the Dodgers at their then famous Vero Beach, Florida, training camp. The book about basketball urged coaches and players to emphasize fundamentals. Lai's take on youth basketball was that coaches should admonish pre-teenage hoopsters to foster cooperation and competition in equal parts. Winning was good, Lai maintained, but youth coaches should not stress it too much.[46]

Buck Lai Jr. worried about Little League baseball emergence as a sacred institution in American suburbs in the 1950s. Indeed, his PhD dissertation for Columbia University focused on Little League baseball. In it, he criticized the hierarchical manner in which Little League was organized. In particular, he frowned on the farm system, reserved for less talented players. Lai complained, according to columnist John W. Fox, that the organization unfairly stigmatized farm leaguers as "minor leaguers." Significantly, Little League would eventually rebrand the farm leagues as minor leagues without removing the stigma that the players were inferior to the major leaguers. Around the same time, columnist Earl

Ruby cited Buck Lai Jr. as a critic of Little League baseball's increasingly well-promoted and profitable World Series. According to Lai Jr., advancement toward the World Series consumed too much time for the young competitors and their families, as well as exerting excessive financial and competitive pressure on them. Recognizing that the Little League World Series invited teams from all over the world, the LIU athletic director conceded it helped spread international goodwill through baseball.[47]

Interestingly, Buck Lai Jr.'s biracial ancestry was generally ignored in the press. Perhaps biracialism was too complicated for a cold war culture tied to the narrative of America as a melting pot. Still, in May 1950, the *Brooklyn Daily Eagle* observed that Lai threw out the first ball when a Chinese American youth team played a game in Brooklyn. Columnist Jimmy Murphy identified the LIU coach as "an oriental whose dad . . . originally came here as a member of the Hawaiian University nine."[48]

Buck Lai Jr. received many honors in his retirement. In 2001, he joined LIU's sports Hall of Fame. In 2005, LIU named him to the university Hall of Fame. When he died in 2003 at the age of eighty-five, Lai, along with his wife, Mary, was praised by the chair of LIU's Board of Trustees and the university president: "Together, they helped build the University as we know it today. His influence is deeply engrained in the very fabric of the institution. His spirit will live on through the many lives he touched."[49]

Buck Lai

After his jaunts with the Hawai'i barnstormers, Buck Lai Sr. returned to permanently live on the East Coast, although in 1938 he wrote people in Hawai'i that he wished to journey back to the islands and become a plantation recreation director. Loui Leong Hop suggested that a recreationally minded plantation company should hire Lai, who at the time was still working for the Philadelphia Railroad. Lai, however, did not remain with the railroad. Perhaps the Depression ended his employment, and his long absences running the barnstorming ball team from Hawai'i probably did not help. In any event, the U.S. Census Manuscripts tell us that in 1940 he worked for the Workmen's Progress Administration's Recreation Project. Living with him in Audubon was not only his wife but also a nineteen-year-old daughter, Alice, and a sister-in-law, Irene. In 1942, he registered for the World War II draft, although he was well over forty years old. His registration card reveals he worked for the Cramp Ship Corporation, headquartered in Philadelphia.[50]

Buck Lai Sr. tried to revive his mid-Atlantic independent baseball wanderings upon his permanent return to New Jersey. In the spring of 1938, Lai swung a bat for the Bushwicks and for a team called the All-Phillies. Late in May 1938, the *Camden Evening Courier* ran a photo story on Lai Sr. and Lai Jr. Both were playing for Audubon of the Camden County League. Lai Sr. also taught baseball to young people. Jack Coombs, a former Philadelphia Athletic hurler and later a longtime coach at Duke University, ran a baseball school in Camden in July1938. Lai was hired to teach the infield to would-be ballplayers. The *Camden Courier-Post* later reported in 1938 that the New Deal's Works Progress Administration (WPA) had recruited Lai as a youth baseball instructor in the area. The WPA was designed to hire people in a variety of occupational areas, including the arts. Its employment of Lai suggests that he was having problems finding steady work in the last years of the Great Depression. A few weeks later, Lai conducted a WPA baseball school in Salem. In 1939, the *Chester Times* notified readers that Lai was umpiring local baseball games and scouting for both the New York Yankees and New York Giants. Another New Jersey daily reported early in 1939 that Lai had applied to the Brooklyn Dodgers for a stint as the team's batting practice pitcher—a job he apparently did not get. Meanwhile, another iteration of the Aloha All-Stars basketball team barnstormed under his leadership in the winter of 1938–1939.[51]

Lai found a niche teaching baseball and other sports to youths. Early in 1939, he conducted athletic activities for the YMCA in the Camden area. He also organized a baseball league for boys in Camden County. In October 1939, the *Camden Courier-Post* notified readers that Camden County's Oaklyn Boys' Club had recruited him as athletic director. Lai's enthusiasm for youth sports would remain an important part of his life and was clearly a legacy he passed on to his son.[52]

Lai also turned to managing a semipro team out of the Camden area, known as the Collingswood All-Stars or the Camden All-Stars. In June 1941, the *Camden Morning-Post* described Lai as comanager of the nine scheduled to meet the House of David team. The Camden County nine, according to the *Delaware County Times* in September, had beaten the Philadelphia Stars, Black Yankees, House of David, and Cuban Stars. Meanwhile, Lai appeared with other Bushwick "old timers" at a celebration of the eleventh anniversary of night baseball at Dexter Park in late July 1941 and was reportedly scouting for the Philadelphia Athletics.[53]

Willing to sign Latin American ballplayers if they did not seem to possess African ancestry, Clark Griffith, owner of the American League's Washington Senators, unveiled his latest find in 1945—Manuel Hidalgo, a Cuban who also reputedly had some Chinese ancestry. Hidalgo's signing inspired the press to evoke the memory of Buck Lai often inaccurately. For example, the *Sporting News* reminded readers that Hidalgo "would not be the first Chinese to reach the majors as Buck Lai, a utility infielder, broke into a few games with the New York Giants some 20 years ago." The *Brooklyn Daily Eagle*'s Harold Burr recalled Lai's career with a little more specificity as a result of the Hidalgo signing. Burr wrote that Pearl Buck would do better than he at writing a column about Lai since she knew a million Chinese, while the columnist knew only his "laundryman" and

Buck Lai, whom he called "a son of a dragon." Pearl Buck was well known for her orientalist, yet sympathetic, novels about life in China—novels that garnered global support for the Chinese as they confronted militaristic Japan. Linking Lai as well to Charlie Chan, the orientalist creation of novelist Earl Derr Biggers, Burr asserted that, like the fictional detective, Lai was a Honolulu native. Born "Tin Lai," the ballplayer took "the good American name of Bill" when he settled down with an "Irish girl" and played for Bridgeport, Burr added. While with Bridgeport, Burr claimed, Lai ridiculed those on his team who denied a Chinese American's claim to cultural citizenship in the United States. Lai supposedly insisted, "I am more American than half you guys." Burr conceded Lai had a point in that Bridgeport possessed a "Mexican, an Italian, a Cuban, German, and Irishman" on its roster. Referencing a relatively well-known Chinese magician, Burr praised Lai's talents as a ballplayer. "Buck Lai," he wrote, "could do almost as many things with a baseball as Ching Ling Foo with a bowl of goldfish. He was a magician in his own right in a pepper game and a big league fielder." However, Burr cited Lai's hitting as the reason why he failed to make the big leagues, while extolling him as a "good semi-pro and a good gate attraction."[54]

The baseball world of Delaware County and surrounding communities remembered Buck Lai as he headed into his sixties. In 1951, the *Trenton Evening Times* noted that Lai coached the Audubon Little League All-Star team, adding that his "baseball capabilities [were] well known to Trenton baseball enthusiasts." He also served as commissioner of the Audubon Little League. In the early 1950s, he helped coach the RTC nine, which competed in the Camden County League and represented a shipbuilding company. One of his pitchers was Ray Narleski, who would achieve some success as a big leaguer for the Cleveland Indians. In 1953, the *Flatbush Times*'s columnist Lawrence Lowe referred to Lai as one of the fastest ballplayers ever, as well as a good fielder. The next year, the *Philadelphia Inquirer* introduced readers to Buck Lai in its "Your Neighbor" section. The *Inquirer* recalled Lai as "the little man who was one of the big names in the 'Golden Age' of semi-professional baseball." The daily observed that Lai worked for the RTC Shipbuilding Company in Camden and still coached the company team. In 1951 and 1952 his nine had copped the Camden County Championship. The *Inquirer* also reported that his daughter Alice had just given birth to a child named William Lai Park. Sadly, Alice would die much too young in 1967 at the age of forty-six. Called an "outstanding" former Chester player, Lai was named to the city's Old Timers' Hall of Fame in 1961.[55]

In September 1964, two northeastern sportswriters recalled Lai. Columnist Bill Lee wrote in the *Hartford Courant* about watching Lai and Yim create a "sensation" in the late 1910s. He insisted they were more "Hawaiian-Chinese" than "full-blooded" Chinese. And while his memory of Yim was vague, Lee reminisced that Lai possessed "the speed and the grace of an antelope." A few weeks later, columnist Bill Duncan of the *Camden Courier-Post* illuminated the baseball career of a neighbor of many of his readers. He reported the hitherto undisclosed and probably erroneous intelligence that Lai had turned down a contract offer from Art Fletcher, a manager of the Philadelphia Phillies in the mid-1920s, because he was making more money working for the Pennsylvania Railroad Company and playing semipro ball. Duncan further revealed Lai's memories of playing against elite African American players such as Satchel Paige and Josh Gibson. Lai declared that a young Paige was relatively easy to hit because all he had then was a straight fastball; however, as he got older, Paige would subsequently command an array of baffling pitches. As for Gibson, Lai heralded the Black catcher as the most powerful hitter he had ever witnessed, and he had seen Ruth. Describing Lai as a Hawaiian and not Chinese, Duncan noted that Lai worked as an expediter for the Cramp Shipyard Company in Philadelphia. "All in all, it's been a great life," Lai swore to Duncan.[56]

In November 1977, a correspondent to the *New York Daily News* recalled attending his first Bushwick game back in the 1920s. The only player that the correspondent remembered was Buck Lai, presumably because of his dynamic approach to the game. By this time, Lai's health was failing. A *Honolulu Advertiser* columnist, Dick Fishback, observed that Buck Lai Tin was entering the hospital. He urged well-wishers to send their thoughts of comfort to his Audubon home. Buck Lai died in 1978 at the age of eighty-three. An obituary published in the *Honolulu Star-Bulletin* remembered him as a "former Isle sports star." Many years later, Mary Lai remembered her father-in-law as a kind and gentle man.[57]

By the 1940s, Lai's former teammate Vernon Ayau had drifted away from active involvement in baseball. But he was hardly a recluse. In 1940, he served as treasurer and quartermaster of Penns Grove's VFW. Three years later, Ayau was an election official in his adopted town. He also threw himself headlong into the war effort, with unfortunate passion. In the *Camden Morning Post* in late 1942, columnist Elm McCormick wrote, "Ayau who came to this land as part of the Chinese All-Stars won't sell anything made by 'Japs,' whom the former shortstop denigrated as 'Little Beasts.'" In 1959, the *Millville Daily* reported that Ayau had attended Chief Bender's funeral. It also noted he was working at Frankford Arsenal, a U.S. Army ammunitions plant in northeast Philadelphia, and frequently saw Buck Lai. Meanwhile, the Chinese American had married a white woman named Esther Dolbow, a daughter of working-class native-born parents. The shortstop died in 1976.[58]

Conclusion

By the time Lai and Ayau died, they and the other Travelers were largely forgotten, even in Hawai'i. More pointedly neglected on the islands and, of course, the mainland was that the Travelers briefly subverted the racial conventions of the time—conventions that mandated the perception of Asian and Pacific

Islanders as, at best, timeless relics fated to be overrun by modern Western civilization. Yet there they were, passionately and skillfully cavorting on baseball's "green cathedrals"—knee deep in what Mark Twain famously described as "the very symbol, the outward and visible expression of the drive, and push, and rush and struggle of the raging, tearing, booming" modernizing world. That world, as Twain well knew, was ruled by white men, and the racial conventions they cultivated and reinforced have proved more enduring than the memories of Buck Lai tearing around the base paths, Vernon Ayau snagging hot grounders, and Apau Kau mowing down batters.

Conclusion

While the stories we tell about baseball history have become more admirably inclusive over the past few decades, they still seem to marginalize, if not exclude, the experiences of Hawai'i's Travelers, both on and off the field. That they were generally Asian or Hawaiian in descent and did not accommodate the way race was (and is) supposed to work in baseball and, indeed, America undoubtedly abetted their marginalization. Still, to be sure, none of the Travelers were Hall of Famers, although author Scott Simkus makes an interesting case that Buck Lai was perhaps the equal of Judy Johnson and Oliver Marcell, other third sackers whose feats playing for Black nines eventually propelled them into the Hall of Fame. The Travelers were, nevertheless, very good, capable of holding their own against some of the top white semipro and Black professional nines of the period.

The Travelers contested a racialized and colonized hierarchy in what scholar Moon-Kie Jung has called the U.S. empire-state. Baseball, despite the evident talent of African American, indigenous, and Latino ballplayers to anyone who paid attention at the time, was widely perceived in the early twentieth-century United States as a white American's game. Even the children of southern and eastern European immigrants were often exiled to the game's "cheap seats." As for occupied colonies of Hawai'i and the Philippines, their indigenous people could be taught baseball as a way to civilize and Americanize them to the limits imposed by race, but few of the colonizers expected to see the nonwhite people of Hawai'i and the Philippines actually excelling at the sport. Still, especially in the case of Hawai'i, Asian and Hawaiian ballplayers on the islands proved capable of surpassing haoles between the foul lines. And out of the ethnic and multiethnic nines that had proliferated on the islands during the first decade of the twentieth century, the Travelers emerged to conquer most of the nines they faced on the mainland.[1]

Yet the Travelers also traversed the racial and ethnic terrain of the United States as a nation-state—a terrain that offered varying degrees of inclusion into and exclusion from American peoplehood. To those who watched them play on mainland ball fields, the Travelers were not just colonized Hawaiians; they were also seen as Chinese, albeit often inaccurately. That is, they were viewed as members of a racial group, condemned in the United States in the late nineteenth and early twentieth centuries to exclusion, exploitation, derision, and intermittent acts of vigilante violence. To justify all this, people of Chinese ancestry found themselves racialized in a variety of frequently contradictory ways—such has been the manner in which race works over time, according to Omi and Winant. But one important line of racialized attack was to impute to Chinese males supposedly inherent feminine qualities. In other words, Chinese males lacked the manliness to excel in a sport such as baseball and to gain entrée to American peoplehood. Yet young men of Chinese descent showed up on American ball fields in 1912 and 1913 competing effectively against not only all-white nines but racialized and gendered perceptions of the American national pastime. And even if we acknowledge that from 1914 through 1916, Chinese made up only a minority of Travelers, clearly no one who saw them with an open mind could doubt the competitiveness, let alone the skills, of Lai Tin, Apau Kau, En Sue Pung, and Vernon Ayau.[2]

Significantly, Nikkei, Hawaiian, and even haole Travelers were folded into a Chinese identity, reminding us that how the barnstormers from Hawai'i were represented and how they represented themselves down through the years defy fixed notions of Asian and Pacific Islander peoples. Whether based in Hawai'i or on the mainland, promoters seemingly colluded in advertising the Travelers as Chinese. They portrayed the ballplayers as students of the fictitious Chinese University of Hawaii, which provoked puzzlement in Hawai'i's print media and amusement among the players themselves, who seemingly enjoyed spinning tales to the mainland press of their fabricated student experiences. Indeed, even when the story that the Travelers represented a nonexistent university was ignored by the mainland press, they were still publicized as Chinese, which apparently prompted no protest from Nikkei, Hawaiian, or haole ballplayers.

The racialization—indeed, the doubling down on the racialization—of the Travelers as Chinese remains something of a mystery. Perhaps promoters deemed that marketing the Travelers as Chinese exoticized the multiethnic, multiracial team more effectively than just presenting to mainland baseball fans a contingent of at least competent island ballplayers possessing a myriad of racial and ethnic backgrounds. Indeed, Guy Green had tried to promote such a team on the mainland in 1913 but came nowhere near the success of the Travelers. Japanese and Hawaiians, meanwhile, had already laid claim to competence in America's national pastime. But stigmatized as unworldly and feminized Celestials, Chinese males were widely looked upon as unlikely, even ridiculous, baseball prospects. To market a barnstorming team as Chinese might have made sense in order to arouse the curious—those anticipating a good laugh or two at the baseball park. As for haoles such as Bill Inman and Roy Doty, by the early 1900s it was not unheard of for white boxers to perform "Yellowface" in order to get people to their bouts, just as white stage performers did when they played Asian roles. One might think that by the second or third tour of the mainland, baseball fans, especially of the independent ball played in the urban mid-Atlantic region, would know better—that Andy Yamashiro, Buck Lai, Fred Markham, and Bill Inman were not all Asian, let alone Chinese. But it is not clear how many of them knew or, for that matter, even cared.[3]

From the standpoint of their supporters in Hawai'i, the Travelers represented more than baseball. Many business leaders of the Honolulu Chinese community helped fund the 1912 journey, hoping that the Travelers would foster on the mainland a more enlightened view of people of Chinese ancestry. There was a class bias behind this objective in that Honolulu Chinese business leaders sought to undercut the widely held opinion "in the states" that Chinese mattered little except for doing laundry and other forms of cheap, servile labor. Rather, Honolulu Chinese business leaders wanted mainlanders to see on their ball fields relatively educated, modern, reputable young men who, because they were born in Hawai'i, were not immigrants but U.S. citizens—to see that the Chinese Exclusion Act deprived America of worthwhile people. Not unusual for elite members of a racialized minority, Honolulu Chinese community leaders may have been at least initially complicit in promoting the ballplayers as university students given the United States' official willingness to exempt students from the Chinese Exclusion Act.[4]

Beyond Honolulu's Chinatown, Hawai'i's haole oligarchy saw the barnstormers as assets in reaching out to potential mainland tourists, investors, consumers, and, if white and well heeled, residents. Globalizing capitalism shadowed the Travelers' treks. In Hawai'i, capitalism assumed the guise of dependency on mainland goodwill. Accordingly, haole commercial interests helped finance the Travelers' journeys eastward just as they helped finance Duke Kahanamoku's trip to the mainland in 1912 to gain a spot on the U.S. Olympic team. The Pacific crossings of athletes such as Kahanamoku and the Travelers can be viewed as a part of larger movements of Hawai'i musicians and dancers to the mainland. These movements, although they allowed participants social spaces in which to assert their agency, were largely blessed by the haole elite in the name of island capitalism.[5]

The financial backers of island Asians and Hawaiians displaying their athletic skills on the mainland engaged in a delicate balancing act. On the one hand, they evaded a frontal assault on white supremacy and American colonialism even if individual members of the haole elite and mainland promoters were relatively free of racism. On the other, they wanted these athletes to hold their own against mainland competition and, in the case of Kahanamoku, demonstrate island athletic supremacy. However, every time the Travelers beat a white nine, which they did regularly (especially from 1913 to 1915), and every time Kahanamoku stroked to first place, white supremacy and its justification for colonialism seemingly took hits, however light years away from fatal.

The challenge was met by trying to adjust the terms of white supremacy while upholding the beneficence of American colonialism. Perhaps it was time to backtrack a bit from the inflated conclusions drawn from St. Louis's 1904 "Anthropology Days." Perhaps with the help of white mentors, athletes of color could harness and improve on their innate skill while gaining sufficient discipline to compete with and even defeat whites. The Travelers' victories over whites could be explained, then, with the white-dominated racial hierarchy suffering little damage and the righteousness of American colonialism suffering none at all. The young men had acquired their love of baseball thanks to Uncle Sam. Perceived as racially incapable of directly challenging white males physically, the Travelers, according to much of the popular press, used their cunning to gain an edge on opponents. As deviousness constituted part of the orientalist vocabulary, the Travelers' deployment of it did not need to detract from white athletic supremacy. Even if it did, and even if the Travelers were conceded the possession of athletic skills such as speed and coordination, they still could be looked upon as products of white colonial engineering while leaving the myth of white manhood's claim on physical strength, toughness, and endurance intact.

At a time when memories of the Philippine-American War lingered and Mexican defiance of U.S. imperialism stirred controversy in the United States, the Travelers, much to the delight of their island promoters, fed a narrative of them as polite young men determined to entertain mainlanders with their ukuleles, guitars, and songs. Often, however, the mainlanders were confused by their inability to place the ballplayers into orientalist or primitivist boxes. They spoke English well, wore middle-class American clothing, and evinced familiarity with American culture from ragtime to Ty Cobb. They could appear to mainlanders as simultaneously exotic and familiar.

Running the Empire's Base Paths

Lai Tin was a key member of the Travelers. He not only excelled as a third sacker and base runner but also often proved an adept hitter. Further, he emerged as team leader in 1915 and 1916. A self-proclaimed devoted son of Hawai'i, Lai Tin ostensibly retreated from heading to the mainland in 1914 with the Travelers in order to stay at home in Honolulu. When offered a chance to try out for the Chicago White Sox in the spring of 1915, he failed to appear at the American League team's spring training camp in Paso Robles, California. Perhaps he feared cultural isolation on the mainland, preferring the company of friends, teammates, and family in Hawai'i.

Romance kept Lai Tin on the mainland after the 1916 tour. He had fallen in love with a white Brooklyn woman, Isabelle Reynolds. Their subsequent marriage was a bold move at the time as they displayed cultural dexterity. Interracial marriage was not an all-or-nothing matter in the United States at the time. Animus toward it varied depending on where such unions occurred and who was getting married. Lai Tin's marriage to a white woman would not have been allowed in California. In that state, as well as in much of the Far West, unions between Asians and whites were banned, as were those between Blacks, mulattoes, or Indians and whites. Fortunately for Lai Tin and Isabelle Reynolds, Asians and whites could legally marry in the state of New York, where antimiscegenation laws had never existed. This does not mean their marriage was socially approved. The controversy stirred by Nikkei actor Sessue Hayakawa's portrayal of a character lusting after a white woman in a silent movie, *The Cheat*, in the mid-1910s surfaced as one example of Americans' general censure of mixed-race romance. The subsequent antimiscegenation movie code issued in 1930 surfaced as another. Moreover, while unions between white males and nonwhite females garnered some tolerance, such was rarely the case for marriages between nonwhite males and white females.[6]

Once Lai made up his mind to stay in the Philadelphia area, a coterie of former Travelers gathered around him. Alfred Yap had previously decided to stay on the East Coast to attend Lehigh University and play college and independent baseball in central Pennsylvania and in Philadelphia. After the Travelers' 1916 tour, the multiethnic circle of Lai, Japanese Andrew Yamashiro, Hawaiian Fred Markham, and two other Chinese, Vernon Ayau and Apau Kau, developed, with Luck Yee Lau briefly joining later in 1920. Lai, Markham, Ayau, and Yamashiro (performing as "Yim") played frequently with one another in and around Philadelphia as well as for the famed independent outfit the Brooklyn Bushwicks.

While for Lai it was love that kept him on the mainland, the ballplayers from Hawai'i were lured to the mid-Atlantic region by other matters. Opportunities to advance their education at one of the many fine postsecondary schools in the area enticed at least Yap, Markham, and Yamashiro. Apau Kau found a job at a prominent Philadelphia department store selling ukuleles and instructing mainland patrons in how to play them. Moreover, multiple independent nines in the area displayed a willingness to recruit the former Travelers, thus evoking the possibility that, under the right circumstances, America's national pastime in the early twentieth century could shine as a cosmopolitan canopy.[7]

Economics played a role in providing nonwhite Hawai'i-born ballplayers with opportunities to make at least a partial living in baseball. The more financially shaky minor league and independent franchises might reasonably hire a ballplayer of Asian ancestry in order to market him as an exotic novelty. After all, American popular culture through movies, plays, music, and books was rendering Orientalism and primitivism into financial gold. Perhaps a minor league or semipro team might hope to do the same. The more commercially stable major league teams could better afford racial exclusiveness. Yet even they circled around Buck Lai as a colorful gate attraction before scurrying away.

Lai and the other former Travelers staying on the East Coast were very good ballplayers capable of helping an independent team looking for victories and gate money. The sporting press in and around Philadelphia and New York City frequently praised the performances of Ayau, Yamashiro, Markham, Yap, and Apau Kau against often keen opposition, while Lai arose as a minor celebrity through independent baseball. But while it should not totally surprise us that independent players, managers, and owners were willing to tolerate nonwhites on their teams, those nonwhites would have to be identified as something other than Black. Ballplayers of indigenous, Latino, or Asian ancestry could occasionally penetrate the racial barriers of the professional and semiprofessional teams. African Americans could not. Nonetheless, indigenous, Latinos, or Asians required enough skill to help white ballplayers win the victor's share of the gate. At the same time, given that semipro teams did not do much traveling together, white ballplayers expected only to share the field and the dugout with nonwhites and then everyone would go on their way. Minor league teams, however, presented more of a challenge to interracial harmony. The minor league Bridgeport Americans took road trips together to various East Coast towns and cities. Thus, white ballplayers were compelled to, in a sense, live with Lai. This makes Lai's ability to negotiate the contours of racial politics in early twentieth-century baseball seem remarkable. But the cases of Ayau and Yamashiro, the first two Asian American minor leaguers, suggest a limit to what nonwhite ballplayers could do to escape racism. Indeed, Ayau's short minor league career in the Pacific Northwest played out under the shadow of anti-Chinese violence.

Of the Travelers who lingered on the East Coast after World War I, only Lai and Ayau remained there for the rest of their lives. Tragically, Apau Kau did not have much choice in the matter. But Yamashiro, Markham, Yap, and Luck Yee Lau returned to the islands. Conceivably, their returns were, in part, motivated by race and xenophobia—the insults, the glowering stares, the frequently well-intended condescension. Conceivably, winter snow had lost its charm for them. And conceivably they just wanted to reunite with their families and friends on the islands.

As they trickled back to their homes in Honolulu, they reunited with many of the former Travelers who decided that the mainland was not for them, even briefly. Generally, the former Travelers, whether they had spent time on the mainland or not, maintained their passion for baseball. They played on ethnic-based and ethnically mixed teams. They coached and managed various nines in and around Honolulu. Indeed, Lang Akana owned a franchise and presided over Hawai'i's most elite baseball organization—the Hawaii Baseball League. Yet many of the former Travelers were not content to consign themselves to the ball field; instead, they engaged in civic affairs on the islands by serving in local and territorial governments in a variety of elected and appointed capacities. They were embroiled in territorial controversies. In Alfred Yap's case, at least one former Traveler seemingly courted controversy, although under a pseudonym.

That they could do all this reflected in large measure the way Hawai'i was settled and governed. As opposed to the settler colonialism of the mainland, most settlers in Hawai'i mainly came from Asia and so they faced a different, more onerous configuration of race and class than white settlers in places like Kansas and California. While fewer in number, haole settlers monopolized land and political power on the islands, and these dominant haoles often disparaged even elite Hawaiians engaging in civic affairs, while resisting Asians assuming positions of authority on the island. Yet there simply were not enough whites to legislate, audit, and police on the islands. And those lesser privileged whites who did seem plentiful traced their ancestries to places like Portugal and Spain, which rendered them insufficiently white in the minds of many racial nativists on the mainland and Hawai'i. Thus, often the kind of people in terms of race and ethnicity who got themselves elected or appointed to public office in Hawai'i would have had their political ambitions easily brushed aside on the mainland, where plentiful numbers of whites could take up seats in city councils and state legislatures.

Several former Travelers ran for office in Hawai'i, but all of them lost except for Albert Akana, who captained the 1912 squad, and Andrew Yamashiro, who won an election to the territorial legislature. Significantly, Yamashiro's victory represented a threat to the islands' haole elite. Nikkei, like Yamashiro, represented a particular menace to haole rule given their numerical potential for political power, their participation in controversial labor strikes in the early decades of the twentieth century, and the fear of the Japanese "Yellow Peril" infesting both the mainland and the islands. Although Yamashiro was not a radical, his election to the territorial legislature aggravated already existent racial anxieties in Hawai'i. These anxieties were further heightened by the Massie case.

Meanwhile on the mainland, Buck Lai was offered well-publicized opportunities to make baseball history as the first Asian American major leaguer. Fretting over the economic and personnel impact of World War I, the 1918 Philadelphia Phillies took a look at Lai to lure curious fans and plug some holes in the infield. Poor hitting ostensibly doomed Lai's chances with the National League team, and the Phillies sent him to relatively nearby Bridgeport, where they could bring him up to the "show" if needed. Although Lai performed well and was popular in the Connecticut industrial city, the Phillies kept their distance. Ten years later, the New York Giants, then a fabled franchise in baseball, found themselves locked in a rivalry for dominance in New York City with the Ruth-led Yankees and, to a lesser extent, the Brooklyn Dodgers. Led by John McGraw, the Giants hoped that Buck Lai's presence on the Giants' roster would entice spectators and publicity, as well as help strengthen the infield.

Lai's generally ignored experiences with the New York Giants remain perplexing. To be sure, however frustrating it must have been to Lai and baseball fans of Asian ancestry then and now to see how close he got to the major leagues only to be thwarted, it must have been even more frustrating to Black ballplayers who might have wondered why they could not get the same opportunity as Lai. Race worked differently for Lai and the great Black players like Judy Johnson. The notion of Asian Americans as "perpetual foreigners" could occasionally give them a foot in the door as exotic curiosities, but they also had to deal with what scholar Clair Jean Kim has called "civic ostracism" entailing political and cultural marginalization.[8]

It is possible that the Giants had no intention of adding Lai to their roster. Just having him in their training camp offered McGraw enough publicity to draw at least some attention away from the World Champion Yankees and their burly slugging duet of Ruth and Gehrig. Lai, however, seemingly believed that the Giants were not exploiting him, that McGraw was worthy of respect. At the same time, Lai pushed back on the franchise's and organized baseball's belief that he should gratefully submit to the Giants farming him out to the minor leagues. To the best of his ability, Lai played professional baseball on his own terms.

Amid the Great Depression, Buck Lai bestirred himself to do something that he had not done since the 1910s—leave his home for a prolonged period of time. By the time Lai returned to Hawai'i to organize a team to barnstorm mainland America, he had already gotten a taste of sports management and entrepreneurship. The Great Depression had conceivably created economic insecurity in the Lai household, and Lai took the risky road of going into business for himself. He, accordingly, managed in the spring of 1930 a mostly Filipino team known as the Orientals. By making this move, Lai emerged as a pioneering Asian American entrepreneur. And while Issei Kenichi Zenimura fronted barnstorming nines out of the West Coast, those teams were composed of Nikkei. Lai, however, headed a team composed of ballplayers possessing ethnic identities distinctive from his own. But by branding his team as "Orientals," he was clearing a path for spectators to view his management of the team as not all that troublesome—as one "Oriental" managing other "Orientals." Clearly, the brand helped him market his team, like the Travelers, as both exotic and familiar.[9]

Lai's efforts to lead a professional basketball team in the early 1930s seem riskier. While not known for his basketball prowess, Lai had performed competently in a brief stint as a professional hoopster in the early 1920s. Ten years later, Lai hoped to cash in on his relative fame in East Coast sports circles by fronting a contingent of professional basketball players on barnstorming tours of the mid-Atlantic region. The team, like many traveling aggregations of professional basketball, sold exoticism. It identified with Hawai'i by showcasing the players in hula skirts in newspaper photographs and by performing a halftime show with supposedly Hawaiian music and hula dancers. However, the players were generally seasoned white professionals and were not likely to take on-court direction from a relative neophyte like Coach Lai. Still, one can imagine that Lai booked and publicized games and tended to team finances. A nonwhite coach of a professional team with white players was rare, in any event. Although in professional football Native American Jim Thorpe and African American Fritz Pollard coached predominantly white squads in the early 1920s, no person of Asian ancestry had shouldered the challenge facing Lai in the early and mid-1930s. Nonetheless, by branding his squad as Hawaiian, Lai possibly eased the racial anxieties of potential spectators.

That Lai led barnstormers of the U.S. mainland from 1935 to 1937 suggests that he still hoped to nurture a career as a sports entrepreneur. This time, however, he would steer a team of baseball players, most of whom were nonwhite and raised on the islands. After nearly two decades of absence, he returned to Honolulu early in 1935 to organize a reputable barnstorming contingent. Various stories circulated regarding his return. Lai proclaimed himself homesick and desirous of seeing his aging mother and his family and friends. He also told the press that he believed that a team resembling the aggressive Travelers would enliven baseball, which had grown too dependent on waiting around for someone to hit a homer. During Lai's team's journeys, the press published a story that Babe Ruth himself advised the Chinese American to lead a team from Hawai'i after the Bambino visited the islands and saw island ballplayers in action. One of the more interesting reports came from a Brooklyn sportswriter who insisted that the owners of the Brooklyn Bushwicks encouraged Lai to bring a team from Hawai'i to the mainland and ultimately to the Bushwicks' own Dexter Park. The reason, according to this sportswriter, was that Bushwick ownership wanted to exert pressure on Black teams that were making financial demands on Holman and Rosner. If these teams did not want to play the Bushwicks at Dexter Park, Lai's nine would take their place.

Honolulu greeted Lai warmly when he arrived to assemble his team in 1935, although some involved in the Hawaii Baseball League worried that Lai would steal away some of the best local players. Family and friends, including former Travelers, gathered to welcome the prodigal son, who had traveled thousands of miles away from Isabelle and his children. Moreover, Hawai'i's power brokers seemed pleased at the prospect of a baseball team promoting the islands on the mainland. After all, the Massie case had severely pierced the romantic image of an island paradise so assiduously advocated by the islands' political and economic elite. Lai's baseball team might help Hawai'i recover some lost ground in terms of positive publicity. And for a growing segment of Hawai'i's power brokers, more was at stake than just attracting mainland consumers, tourists, and home seekers. This segment sought to push Hawai'i statehood, largely to remove the threat of U.S.-initiated tariffs against sugar and ease the movement of investments from the mainland to the islands. By displaying Asians and Hawaiians at home with America's national pastime while still surrounding them with an exotic sheen, Lai was deemed useful in promoting the islands to a perhaps skeptical mainland still mired in the Great Depression.

Lai obviously hoped his nine would echo the triumphs of the Travelers twenty years earlier. The latter had promoted the islands effectively while winning a majority of games—and from 1913 to 1915, winning a vast majority of games. Lai's contingent may have fostered good publicity for Hawai'i, but his team was not very good. Island backers lost interest, and the Hawaii Baseball League resisted Lai's efforts to enlist the talents of some of its players. In 1937, Lai did not even bother to show up in Honolulu to recruit a nine. Instead, he stayed on the mainland and sought to organize a barnstorming team composed of ballplayers who were advertised as being from Hawai'i but, in most cases, probably were not. Indeed, he even recruited renowned white, female pitcher Jackie Mitchell to broaden exposure for his team, members of which were obligated to play at least a few innings in hula skirts.

A Chinese American as a sports entrepreneur did not seem to resonate in Depression-ridden America, but Lai maintained his passion for baseball. No person of Asian ancestry did more for baseball than Buck Lai in the mid-twentieth century. He scouted for major league teams and coached semipro and youth teams. Lai even served as president of the Audubon, New Jersey, Little League. Yet among those persons of Asian ancestry who did a lot for baseball was his son, Buck Lai Jr.

At a time when mixed-race people remained problematic in American society, Buck Lai Jr. seemingly escaped efforts to problematize or exoticize him. The press might occasionally mention his "Chinese" or "Hawaiian" father, but Buck Lai Jr. could have seemingly been the prototype for what noted sociologist Robert Park had in mind as the goal of his Race Relations Cycle. According to Park, immigrants and their offspring experience four stages in race relations: contact, conflict or competition, accommodation, and assimilation. Thus, while Lai Sr. had made his way through the first three stages with some difficulty, the son had come out of the fourth stage with barely any traces of a racial or ethnic identity. That Buck Lai Jr. looked and generally acted like a middle-class white male rather than what was widely perceived as Chinese or Hawaiian made it easier to ignore his biracial background. Yet one should remember that while Buck Lai Jr. rose to distinction as a coach and educator, interracial marriage was still illegal in many states, such as California, and Asian immigration and naturalization restriction remained legal until the early 1950s. Accordingly, there are at least a couple of ways to look at Lai Jr.'s biracialism. We can wish he would have done more to assert his nonwhite, Asian identity, or we can admire his willingness to acknowledge that identity to the extent that he did.[10]

The Last Out

Over one hundred years ago, young men from Honolulu to Brooklyn played outside the confines of organized baseball. They did not make much money doing it, if they made any money at all. But independent teams and their supporters—representing diverse racial and ethnic groups, as well as women, religious organizations, businesses, neighborhoods, and labor unions—congregated on baseball diamonds within sight of Honolulu palm trees and New York City skyscrapers.

On one side of the American empire during the early twentieth century, thousands might show up to watch the all-Chinese take on the Asahis, while on the other side thousands might show up to watch the Brooklyn Bushwicks take on the African American Hillsdale nine.

Representing an alternative to the hierarchy nurtured by organized baseball, independent baseball had Nat Strong and his imitators promoting a mid-Atlantic oligarchy that would determine which teams played where, against whom, and how much money would be at stake. Along the way, Jim Crow reigned in independent baseball, mitigated somewhat in the North by the prevalence of games pitting Black against white or, in the Bushwicks' case, nearly white teams. And except for occasional female traveling teams and individual female ballplayers such as Jackie Mitchell, independent baseball, like organized baseball, sequestered women to the bleachers.

But in some ways the presence of independent baseball rendered the sport more inclusive than it is today. Ball fields pervaded the American empire, especially its urban landscapes, inviting the skills and passion of culturally diverse, but almost exclusively, young and not so young men and their supporters. The independent baseball player often shared his love of the game with his concerns for his work and family. Rarely did he possess major league promise, but, like Buck Lai, he could be very talented. He was ordinary not in the sense of plain or boring but in the sense that Raymond Williams advanced when he declared that culture is ordinary—that is, it belongs not just to the wealthy and powerful but to all. Today, when many of us think of baseball we conjure up images of multimillionaire baseball players and even wealthier owners thanks to all the money the rest of us fork over for tickets, food, and memorabilia. To be sure, attending ball games at Yankee Stadium in New York and Oracle Park in San Francisco can be joyful, but watching family members, coworkers, friends, and neighbors spearing line drives and stealing second at a neighborhood ball field can be joyful too.[11]

Buck Lai and many of his Traveler teammates emerged out of working-class and lower-middle-class backgrounds to face barriers constructed out of racial nativism and colonialism. Yet they insisted on asserting their agency as best they could. At a time when "We the People" did not typically mean people like them, they declared their cultural citizenship in various ways. Through baseball they sought to establish a few rows on the third base side of an American identity, while not surrendering their right to be different from other Americans—to be Chinese, Japanese, or Hawaiian.

In retrospect, some of the choices they made appear hard, and in some cases questionable. The Nikkei and Hawaiian ballplayers might have angered family and friends for teaming up with Chinese ballplayers, but some of that anger may have been justified when those family members and friends learned that the players had to surrender their surnames and wear uniforms adorned with the words "Chinese." Alfred Yap's opposition to Hawai'i statehood may puzzle us. There were and remain legitimate reasons to question Hawai'i statehood given how the United States dragged the islands into its empire, suppressing indigenous sovereignty. However, Yap seemed more intent on expressing his hostility to the influence of Nikkei and the labor Left on island life than voicing opposition to American colonialism.

Unlike Alfred Yap and other former Traveler teammates, Buck Lai generally kept his politics to himself. That his mother was ineligible for U.S. citizenship simply because of her race and nativity probably bothered him, but he said nothing public about it. Yet he claimed agency by marrying a woman he was not supposed to marry and helping her raise children who were not supposed to exist in the United States. He claimed agency by refusing to assume occupations stereotyped as oriental. He earned much of his living by playing baseball for several years. He was not a major league star but a glove and a bat for hire, journeying from his home in Honolulu to one mid-Atlantic ball field after another, swiftly running the base paths of empire, trying to keep a step or two ahead of racism's traveling eye.

Acknowledgments

I began research for this book while reading *Baseball: The People's Game*, by Harold Seymour and Dorothy Jane Mills. There, I ran across a reference to the Chinese University of Hawaii baseball team. As I was teaching Asian American Studies at the time, as well as writing about Asian and Pacific Islander sporting experiences, this reference piqued my interest. It is fitting, then, that I acknowledge the inspiration of Seymour and Mills and the growing number of academic and nonacademic sport historians who have sought to broaden our perspectives of sport history beyond the Babe into generally marginalized communities. More particularly, I want to acknowledge the advice of anonymous readers of this manuscript and my editor, Jasper Chang. Mary Lai, Andrew Yamashiro Jr., and Chris Pung helped me with insights about three of the major characters of this book. And my family has always provided me with all the necessary love and support to do my work.

Notes

Introduction

1 Steven Riess, *Touching Base: Professional Baseball and American Culture in the Progressive Era* (Westport, CT: Greenwood Press, 1980), 194.
2 Joel S. Franks, *The Barnstorming Hawaiian Travelers: A Multiethnic Team Tours the Mainland, 1912–1916* (Jefferson, NC: McFarland, 2012).
3 Franks, *Barnstorming*, 196–222; Franks, *Asian American Basketball: A Century of Sport, Community and Culture* (Jefferson, NC: McFarland, 2016), 169–170.
4 Franks, *Asian American Basketball*, 180–181.
5 Franks, *Asian American Basketball*, 163–165; Franks, *Asian Pacific Americans and Baseball: A History* (Jefferson, NC: McFarland, 2008), 82–83.

Chapter 1 Defying Assumptions

1 Patricia Nelson Limerick, *Legacy of Conquest: The Unbroken Past of the American West* (New York: W. W. Norton, 1987); Richard White, *"It's Your Misfortune and None of My Own": A New History of the American West* (Norman: University of Oklahoma Press, 1993).
2 Franks, *Barnstorming*.
3 Robert S. Wiebe, *Self-Rule: A Cultural History of American Democracy* (Chicago: University of Chicago Press, 1996).
4 Elijah Anderson, *The Cosmopolitan Canopy: Race and Civility in Everyday Life* (New York: W. W. Norton, 2011); Renato Rosaldo and William V. Flores, "Ideology, Conflict and Evolving Latino Communities: Cultural Citizenship in San Jose, California," in *Latino Cultural Citizenship: Claiming Identity, Space, and Rights*, ed. William V. Flores and Rina Benmayor (Boston: Beacon Press, 1997), 57; Gaye Theresa Johnson, *Spaces of Conflict, Sounds of Solidarity: Music, Race, and Spatial Entitlement in Los Angeles* (Berkeley: University of California Press, 2013).
5 Elaine Kim, preface to *Charlie Chan Is Dead: An Anthology of Contemporary Asian American Writing*, ed. Jessica Hagedorn (New York: Penguin Books, 1993); Sucheng Chan, *The Bitter-Sweet Soil: The Chinese in California Agriculture, 1860–1910* (Berkeley: University of California Press, 1986); Charles J. McClain, *In Search of*

Equality: The Chinese Struggle against Discrimination in Nineteenth-Century America (Berkeley: University of California Press, 1994); Jean Pfaelzer, *Driven Out: The Forgotten War against Chinese Americans* (Berkeley: University of California Press, 2008); Madeline Hsu, *Dreams of Gold, Dreaming of Home: Transnationalism and Migration between the United States and South China, 1882–1943* (Stanford, CA: Stanford University Press, 2000); Yuji Ichioka, *The Issei: The World of First Generation Japanese Immigrants, 1885–1924* (New York: Free Press, 1988); Eiichiro Azuma, *Between Two Empires: Race, History, and Transnationalism in Japanese America* (New York: Oxford University Press, 2005).

6 Ronald Takaki, *Pau Hana: Plantation Life and Labor in Hawaii, 1835–1920* (Honolulu: University of Hawai'i Press, 1983); Gary Y. Okihiro, *Cane Fires: The Anti-Japanese Movement in Hawaii, 1865–1945* (Philadelphia: Temple University Press, 1991); Moon-Kie Jung, *Reworking Race: The Making of Hawai'i's Interracial Labor Movement* (New York: Columbia University Press, 2006).

7 Joseph A. Reaves, *Taking in a Game: A History of Baseball in Asia* (Lincoln: University of Nebraska Press, 2002), 19–23, 29.

8 *San Francisco Chronicle*, November 25, 1887.

9 *Chicago Tribune*, June 28, 1908.

10 *San Francisco Call*, June 29, 1908.

11 Okihiro, *Cane Fires*, 16; Ronald Takaki, *Strangers from a Different Shore: A History of Asian Americans* (Boston: Little, Brown, 1989), 22–24.

12 Takaki, *Strangers*, 22–24.

13 Sucheng Chan, *Asian Americans: An Interpretive history* (Boston: Twayne, 1991), 26–27; Quoted in Yunte Huang, *Charlie Chan: The Untold Story of the Honorable Detective and His Rendezvous with American History* (New York: W. W. Norton, 2011), 20.

14 Takaki, *Strangers*, 132–179; Chan, *Asian Americans*, 26–27.

15 Chan, *Asian Americans*, 65; Erika Lee, *The Making of Asian America: A History* (New York: Simon & Schuster, 2015), 100–103.

16 Alexander Saxton, *The Indispensable Enemy: Labor and the Anti-Chinese Movement in California* (Berkeley: University of California Press, 1971); Madeline Y. Hsu, *The Good Immigrants: How the Yellow Peril Became the Model Minority* (Princeton, NJ: Princeton University Press, 2015); Lucy E. Salyer, *Laws as Harsh as Tigers: Chinese Immigrants and the Shaping of Immigration Law* (Chapel Hill: University of North Carolina Press, 1995); Andrew Gyorgy, *Closing the Gate: Race, Politics, and the Chinese Exclusion Act* (Chapel Hill: University of North Carolina Press, 1998); Erika Lee, *At America's Gates: Chinese Immigrants and American Exclusion, 1882–1943* (Chapel Hill: University of North Carolina Press, 2003); Lon Kurashige, *Two Faces of Exclusion: The Untold History of Anti-Asian Racism in the United States* (Chapel Hill: University of North Carolina Press, 2016).

17 Saxton, *Indispensable*; Hsu, *Good Immigrants*; Salyer, *Laws*; Gyorgy, *Closing*; Lee, *America's Gates*; Kurashige, *Two Faces*; Edlie L. Wong, *Racial Reconstruction: Black Inclusion, Chinese Exclusion and the Fictions of Citizenship* (New York: New York University Press, 2015).

18 Chan, *Asian Americans*, 66; Takaki, *Pau Hana*, 66.

19 Huang, *Charlie Chan*, 54–55; Chan, *Asian Americans*, 56–57.

20 Huang, *Charlie Chan*, 58–60.

21 Allen Guttmann, *Games and Empire: Modern Sports and Cultural Imperialism* (New York: Columbia University Press, 1994); Gerald Gems, *The Athletic Crusade: Sport and American Cultural Imperialism* (Lincoln: University of Nebraska Press,

2006); Robert Elias, *The Empire Strikes Out: How Baseball Sold U.S. Foreign Policy and Promoted the American Abroad* (New York: New Press, 2010).

22 Jonathan Kay Kamakawio'ole Osorio, *Dismembering Lāhui: A History of the Hawaiian Nation* (Honolulu: University of Hawai'i Press, 2002); Gary Y. Okihiro, *American History Unbound: Asians and Pacific Islanders* (Oakland: University of California Press, 2015), 101–107.

23 Osorio, *Dismembering*; Okihiro, *American History Unbound*; Noenoe K. Silva, *Aloha Betrayed: Native Hawaiian Resistance to American Colonialism* (Durham, NC: Duke University Press, 2004).

24 Osorio, *Dismembering*; Okihiro, *American History Unbound*; Noenoe K. Silva, *Aloha Betrayed.*

25 Okihiro, *American History Unbound*, 105; Osorio, *Dismembering*, 168.

26 Silva, *Aloha Betrayed*, 164–172.

27 Silva, *Aloha Betrayed*, 164–172; Okihiro, *American History Unbound*, 105–106.

28 Silva, *Aloha Betrayed*, 164–172; Okihiro, *American History Unbound*, 105–106.

29 Silva, *Aloha Betrayed*, 164–172; Okihiro, *American History Unbound*, 105–106.

30 *Hawaiian Gazette*, March 1, 1898.

31 Franks, *Barnstorming*, 27–31; Chris Pung, email correspondence with the author, August 24, 2012.

32 *New York Tribune*, February 25, 1906.

33 *Nippu Jiii*, May 28, 1936.

34 *Hawaiian Gazette*, November 22, 1907; January 14, 1908; *Pacific Commercial Advertiser*, March 26, 1908; January 21, 1909; January 30, 1911; *Honolulu Evening Bulletin*, February 10, 1910.

35 *Pacific Commercial Advertiser*, February 7, 1909; March 13, 1910.

36 *Pacific Commercial Advertiser*, August 9, 1903; November 24, 1905; *Honolulu Independent*, September 5, 1905; *Hawaiian Gazette*, January 7, 1908; *Honolulu Evening Bulletin*, April 6, 1908; *Hawaiian Star*, April 17, 1911.

37 *Hawaiian Star*, May 26, 1909; June 26, 1909.

38 *Hawaiian Star*, March 8, 1911; *Pacific Commercial Advertiser*, March 7, 1908; January 9, 1909; March 1, 1909; January 30, 1911.

39 *Pacific Commercial Advertiser*, May 22, 1910; Erika Lee, *America for Americans: A History of Xenophobia in the United States* (New York: Basic Books, 2019), 113–147.

40 Okihiro, *American History Unbound*, 86–87, 118, 125; Takaki, *Strangers*, 42–47.

41 Okihiro, *American History Unbound*, 86–87, 118, 125; .Takaki, *Strangers*, 142–155.

42 Franklin Odo and Kazubo Sinota, *A Pictorial History of the Japanese in Hawaii, 1885–1924* (Honolulu, HI: Bishop Museum Press, 1985), 78; Samuel Regalado, *Nikkei Baseball: Japanese American Players from Immigration and Internment to the Major Leagues* (Urbana: University of Illinois Press, 2013), 20–21; Allen Gutmann and Lee Thompson, *Japanese Sports: A History* (Honolulu: University of Hawai'i Press, 2001).

43 *Honolulu Star-Bulletin*, April 18, 1931; *Nippu Jiii*, May 28, 1936; Arnold Suehiro, *Honolulu Stadium: Where Hawai'i Played* (Honolulu, HI: Watermark Publishing, 1995), 33; Franks, *Asian Pacific Americans*, 46–48.

44 Silva, *Aloha Betrayed*; Gary Okihiro, *Island World: A History of Hawai'i and the United States* (Berkeley: University of California Press, 2008); Osorio, *Dismembering.*

45 Takaki, *Strangers*, 132–179; William Carlson Smith, *Americans in Process* (New York: Arno Press, 1970), 114.

46 Takaki, *Strangers*, 167–168; Okihiro, *Cane Fires*; Jung, *Reworking Race.*

47 *Pacific Commercial Advertiser*, September 24, 1906; November 5, 1906; *Honolulu Evening Bulletin*, September 24, 1906; March 28, 1908.
48 *Pacific Commercial Advertiser*, December 13, 1904; *Oakland Tribune*, October 17, 1907; *Newark News* quoted in *Reno Evening Gazette*, October 21, 1907.
49 *Pacific Commercial Advertiser*, July 13, 1911; July 28, 1911; Franks, *Asian Pacific Americans*, 35–55; Franks, *Barnstorming*, 27–64; Jung, *Reworking Race*, 10–55.

Chapter 2 The Travelers from Hawai'i

1 Franks, *Barnstorming*.
2 Franks, *Barnstorming*; Wong, *Racial Reconstruction*, 176–224; *Honolulu Evening Bulletin*, June 28, 1905; *Hawaiian Star*, August 11, 1905; *Hawaii Herald*, August 17, 1905.
3 Franks, *Barnstorming*.
4 Gems, *Sport*; Franks, *Asian Pacific Americans*, 15–22; *Honolulu Evening Bulletin*, June 17, 1911.
5 Franks, *Barnstorming*; Lee, *Making*, 122–136; Christopher Frayling, *The Yellow Peril: Dr. Fu Man Chu and the Rise of Chinaphobia* (London: Thames & Hudson, 2014).
6 John Kuo Wei Tchen, *New York before Chinatown: Orientalism and the Shaping of American Culture, 1776–1882* (Baltimore: Johns Hopkins University Press, 1999); Robert G. Lee, *Orientals: Asian Americans in Popular Culture* (Philadelphia: Temple University Press, 1999).
7 Tchen, *New York before Chinatown*; Robert G. Lee, *Orientals*; Lee, *Making*, 91; Gail Bederman, *Manliness and Civilization: A Cultural History of Gender and Race in the United States, 1880–1917* (Chicago: University of Chicago Press, 1996); Warren Goldstein, *Playing for Keeps: A History of Early Baseball* (Ithaca, NY: Cornell University Press, 1989).
8 Quoted in Mark Dyreson, *Making the American Team: Sport, Culture, and the Olympic Experience* (Urbana: University of Illinois Press, 1997), 54.
9 Franks, *Barnstorming*.
10 United States Census Bureau, Manuscript Census Schedules, City and County of Honolulu, 1910, Ancestry.com, accessed January 17, 2017; *Honolulu Star Bulletin*, October 21, 1912; Franks, *Barnstorming*, 137–138.
11 *Pacific Commercial Advertiser*, April 28, 1912; June 26, 1912; September 22, 1912; November 2, 1912; March 11, 1913; March 14, 1913; July 30, 1913; *Honolulu Star-Bulletin*, February 7, 1935; United States Census Bureau, Manuscript Census Schedules, Island of Maui, 1900, Ancestry.com, accessed April 13, 2009.
12 Franks, *Barnstorming*; United States Census Bureau, Manuscript Census Schedules, Hilo, 1900, 1910, Ancestry.com, accessed February 17, 2020; City and County of Honolulu, 1930, Ancestry.com, accessed June 7, 2008; Town of Wailua, 1900, Ancestry.com, accessed March 16, 2020; *Pacific Commercial Advertiser*, September 9, 1912; December 15, 1913; *Honolulu Evening Bulletin*, July 25, 1911, *Honolulu Star-Bulletin*, April 21, 1913; Buck Lai Tin and Loui Leong Hop, "Gleanings from an 'Old-Timer's' Scrapbook," *Honolulu Star-Bulletin*, February 12, 1935; *Honolulu Star-Bulletin*, February 21, 1935.
13 Franks, *Barnstorming*; United States Census Bureau, Manuscript Census Schedules, City and County of Honolulu, 1910, Ancestry.com, accessed March 8, 2010; *Honolulu Gazette*, May 4, 1909; *Pacific Commercial Advertiser*, April 12, 1912; May 5, 1912; March 3, 1913; December 31, 1918; *Maui News*, January 3, 1919.

14 Franks, *Barnstorming*; United States Census Bureau, Manuscript Census Schedules, City and County of Honolulu, 1900, Ancestry.com, accessed February 3, 2009; Town of Wailuku and Island of Maui, 1910, Ancestry.com, accessed July 14, 2009.
15 Franks, *Barnstorming*; *Honolulu Advertiser*, January 23, 1970; Honolulu City Directory, 1912, Ancestry.com, accessed June 14, 2017.
16 Franks, *Barnstorming*; Honolulu City Directory, 1935, Ancestry.com, accessed November 24, 2019; *Honolulu Advertiser*, February 20, 1933; April 18, 1951.
17 United States Census Bureau, Manuscript Census Schedules, City and County of Honolulu, 1900, Ancestry.com, accessed November 25, 2019; United States Census Bureau, Manuscript Census Schedules, City and County of Honolulu, 1910, Ancestry.com, accessed November 25, 2019; United States Census Bureau, Manuscript Census Schedules, City and County of Honolulu, 1930, Ancestry.com, accessed November 25; United States Census Bureau, Manuscript Census Schedules, City and County of Philadelphia, 1920, Ancestry.com, accessed May 30, 2007; Honolulu City Directory, 1915, Ancestry.com, accessed November 9, 2019.
18 *Pacific Commercial Advertiser*, March 10, 1897; June 10, 1904; December 8, 1904; October 24, 1909; February 21, 1910; September 17, 1912; *Honolulu Star*, November 12, 1901.
19 Peter T. Young, "President William McKinley High School," https://imagesofoldhawaii.com/president-william-mckinley-high-school/, November 26, 2019; *Pacific Commercial Advertiser*, November 4, 1911; February 16, 1912; March 15, 1912.
20 Sandra Kimberly Hall, *Memories of Duke: The Legend Comes to Life* (Honolulu, HI: Bess Press, 1996), 4; David Davis, *Waterman: The Life and Times of Duke Kahanamoku* (Lincoln: University of Nebraska Press, 2015), 29–42; *Hawaiian Star*, January 22, 1912; *Pacific Commercial Advertiser*, January 22, 1912; *Honolulu Star-Bulletin*, February 19, 1912; *Hawaiian Gazette*, February 23, 1912; *Day Book*, April 13, 1912.
21 Franks, *Barnstorming*, 64–156; Him Mark Lai, *Becoming Chinese Americans: A History of Communities and Institutions* (Walnut Creek, CA: Altamira Press, 2004), 278; United States Census Bureau, Manuscript Census Schedules, City and County of Honolulu, 1910, Ancestry.com, accessed July 13, 2007; *Honolulu Evening Bulletin*, December 7, 1908.
22 Franks, *Barnstorming*.
23 Franks, *Barnstorming*; *Honolulu Gazette*, May 15, 1896; *Pacific Commercial Advertiser*, July 25, 1900; March 30, 1906; *Honolulu Advertiser*, July 3, 1940; September 30, 1940; Bill Pacheco, "Stars of Yesteryear," *Honolulu Advertiser*, April 28, 1946; *Honolulu Star*, July 19, 1909; *Honolulu Star-Bulletin*, July 27, 1932; Buck Lai Tin, "'Gleanings from an Old Timer's' Scrapbook as told to Loui Leong Hop," *Honolulu Star-Bulletin*, February 14, 1935.
24 Chris Pung, email correspondence with the author, July 21, 2012; United States Census Bureau, Manuscript Census Schedules, City and County of Honolulu, 1910, Ancestry.com, accessed March 14, 2020; Honolulu, Hawaii, Passenger and Crew Lists, 1900–1959 for Wing Ming Pung, Ancestry.com, accessed March 14, 2020; Honolulu City Directory, 1907, Ancestry.com, accessed March 14, 2020; *Pacific Commercial Advertiser*, March 28, 1920; Thomas Kaulukukui, "The Development of Competitive Athletics in the Schools of Hawaii" (master's thesis, University of Hawai'i, 1941), 24.
25 *San Francisco Call*, October 9, 1906; Herbert G. Lowery, "That Hawaiian Trip," *Sporting Life*, February 15, 1908; *Washington Post*, December 27, 1906; February 3,

1908; *Atlanta Constitution*, March 19, 1908; *Honolulu Star-Bulletin*, February 11, 1927; *Pacific Commercial Advertiser*, November 30, 1912.

26 United States Census Bureau, Manuscript Census Schedules, City and County of Honolulu, 1910, Ancestry.com, accessed June 7, 2009; Steve Fugita, "Frederick Kinzaburo Makina," in *Distinguished Asian Americans*, ed. Hyung-chan Kim (Westport, CT: Greenwood Publishing Company, 1992); Takaki, *Pau Hana*, 155; Yukiko Kimura, *Issei: Japanese Immigrants in Hawaii* (Honolulu: University of Hawai'i Press, 1988), 90, 93; Buck Lai Tin, "Gleanings," *Honolulu Star-Bulletin*, February 2, 1935; *Honolulu Advertiser*, July 25, 1941.

27 Franks, *Barnstorming*.

28 Warren Sussman, *Culture as History: The Transformation of American Society in the Twentieth Century* (New York: Pantheon Books, 1984); William R. Leach, *Land of Desire: Merchants, Power, and the Rise of a New American Culture* (New York: Vintage, 1994); T. J. Jackson Lears, *Fables of Abundance: A Cultural History of Advertising in America* (New York: Basic Books, 1995); Mark Dyreson, "The Emergence of Consumer Culture and the Transformation of Physical Culture: American Sport in the 1920s," *Journal of Sport History* 16, no. 3 (Winter 1989): 261–281.

29 Dyreson, "The Emergence"; Steven Riess, *Touching Base: Professional Baseball and American Culture in the Progressive Era* (Westport, CT: Greenwood Press, 1980); Michael Oriard, *Reading Football: How the Popular Press Created an American Spectacle* (Chapel Hill: University of North Carolina Press, 1998); Peter Levine, *A.G. Spalding and the Rise of American Sport* (New York: Oxford University Press, 1985).

30 Deborah A. Shattuck, *Bloomer Girls: Women Baseball Pioneers* (Urbana: University of Illinois Press, 2017); *San Francisco Chronicle*, March 14, 1914; Franks, *Barnstorming*, 83–84; Robert K. Fitts, *Issei Baseball: The Story of the First Japanese American Ballplayers* (Lincoln: University of Nebraska Press, 2020), 74–90.

31 Franks, *Barnstorming*.

32 Edward Said, *Orientalism* (New York: Vintage, 1979); Renato Rosaldo, *Culture and Truth: The Remaking of Social Truth* (Boston: Beacon Press, 1989), 68–69; T. J. Jackson Lears, *No Place of Grace: Antimodernism and the Transformation of American Culture, 1880–1920* (Chicago: University of Chicago Press, 1994).

33 Tchen, *New York*; Joy S. Kasson, *Buffalo Bill's Wild West: Celebrity, Memory, and Popular History* (New York: Hill and Wang, 2015).

34 Said, *Orientalism*, 11.

35 Gems, *The Athletic Crusade*; Franks, *Barnstorming*.

36 Lears, *Grace*; Rosaldo, *Culture*, 68–69.

37 Elizabeth Buck, *Paradise Remade: Politics of Culture and History in Hawai'i* (Philadelphia: Temple University Press, 1993); Okihiro, *Island World*; Adria L. Imada, *Aloha America: Hula Circuits through the U.S. Empire* (Durham, NC: Duke University Press, 2012).

38 Franks, *Barnstorming*; Okihiro, *Island World*, 196–201; Kasson, *Buffalo Bill's*.

39 Susan Brownell, ed., *The 1904 Anthropology Days and Olympic Games: Sport, Race, and American Imperialism* (Lincoln: University of Nebraska, 2008); Robert Rydell, *All the World's a Fair: Visions of Empire at America's International Expositions, 1876–1916* (Chicago: University of Chicago Press, 1987); Linda Peavy and Ursula Smith, *Full Court Press: Girls from Ft. Shaw Indian School, Basketball Champions* (Norman: University of Oklahoma Press, 2008).

40 Sally Jenkins, *The Real All-Americans: The Team That Changed a Game, a People, and a Nation* (New York: Broadway Books, 2008); Bederman, *Manliness*.

41 Bederman, *Manliness.*
42 Franks, *Barnstorming.*
43 Harold Seymour and Dorothy Seymour Mills, *Baseball: The People's Game* (New York: Oxford University Press, 1990); Franks, *Barnstorming*; Neil Lanctot, *Fair Dealing and Clean Playing: The Hilldale Club and the Development of Black Professional Baseball* (Syracuse, NY: Syracuse University Press, 2007); Neil Lanctot, *Negro League Baseball: The Rise and Ruin of a Black Institution* (Philadelphia: University of Pennsylvania Press, 2011); Thomas Barthel, *Baseball's Peerless Pros: The Brooklyn Bushwicks of Dexter Park* (Haworth, NJ: St. Johann Press, 2008).
44 Harold Seymour, *Baseball: The Early Years* (New York: Oxford University Press, 1960); Levine, *A.G. Spalding*; Benjamin Rader, *Baseball: A History of America's Game* (Urbana: University of Illinois Press, 2018); Jules Tygiel, *Past Time* (New York: Oxford University Press, 2000).
45 Seymour, *Baseball: The Early Years*; Levine, *A.G. Spalding*; Benjamin Rader, *Baseball*; Jules Tygiel, *Past Time*; David W. Zang, *Fleetwood Walker's Divided Heart: The Life of Baseball's First Black Major Leaguer* (Lincoln: University of Nebraska Press, 1995); Jeffrey Powers-Buck, *The American Indian Integration of Baseball* (Lincoln: University of Nebraska Press, 2004); Adrian Burgos, *Playing America's Game: Baseball, Latinos, and the Color Line* (Berkeley: University of California Press, 2007); Joel S. Franks, *Whose Baseball? The National Pastime and Cultural Diversity in California, 1859–1941* (Lanham, MD: Scarecrow Press, 2001).
46 Franks, *Asian Pacific Americans*, 127–131, 158–160.
47 Rebecca T. Alpert, *Out of Left Field: Jews and Black Baseball* (New York: Oxford University Press, 2011).
48 Barthel, *Peerless Semipros*, 6–7.
49 Franks, *Whose Baseball?*, 167–199; Riess, *Touching Base*; Christopher Lasch, *Haven in a Heartless World: The Family Besieged* (New York: W. W. Norton, 1977).
50 Franks, *Barnstorming.*
51 Franks, *Barnstorming*; Franks, *Whose Baseball?*, 199–221.

Chapter 3 The Travelers Take the Field

1 Franks, *Barnstorming*, 27–64.
2 Franks, *Barnstorming*, 27–64; *Hawaiian Star*, April 4, 1912; April 12, 1912; *Pacific Commercial Advertiser*, November 30, 1912; *Honolulu Star-Bulletin*, April 10, 1917.
3 Franks, Barnstorming, 27–64; *Pacific Commercial Advertiser*, February 16, 1912.
4 *Hawaiian Star*, June 9, 1911; March 19, 1912; April 2, 1912; *Honolulu Evening Bulletin*, April 1, 1912.
5 Franks, *Barnstorming*, 27–64.
6 *Hawaiian Star*, April 24, 1912; May 9, 1912; June 6, 1912; June 13, 1912.
7 Barthel, *Baseball's Peerless Pros*, 3–5; Alpert, *Left Field*, 11–13.
8 Lanctot, *Negro League Baseball*, 9, 25.
9 *New London Day*, June 21, 1912.
10 *Hawaiian Star*, September 28, 1912.
11 Franks, *Barnstorming*, 130–131.
12 Franks, *Barnstorming*, 130–131; *Honolulu Evening Bulletin*, April 24, 1912.
13 S. H. Hoe, "America Invaded by Oriental Foes," *Baseball Magazine*, March 1914, 68.
14 Franks, *Barnstorming*; Lanctot, *Fair Dealing*; Barthel, *Baseball's Peerless Pros.*
15 *Honolulu Evening Bulletin*, April 24, 1912; *Honolulu Star-Bulletin*, August 25, 1928; Hsu, *Good Immigrants.*

16 *Sporting Life*, March 16, 1912.
17 *Sporting Life*, March 16, 1912; April 27, 1912; *Oakland Tribune*, March 28, 1912; *Pacific Commercial Advertiser*, April 10, 1912.
18 *Pacific Commercial Advertiser*, April 24, 1912; *Day Book*, April 24, 1912; *Chicago Tribune*, April 15, 1912.
19 *Cincinnati Times-Star* cited in *Pacific Commercial Advertiser*, May 17, 1912.
20 *New York Tribune*, May 22, 1912; *New York Sun* cited in *Pacific Commercial Advertiser*, June 8, 1912.
21 *New York Sun* cited in *Pacific Commercial Advertiser*, June 8, 1912.
22 *New York Sun* cited in *Advertiser*, June 8, 1912
23 *New York Sun* cited in *Advertiser*, June 8, 1912.
24 *Brooklyn Daily Eagle*, May 27, 1912; Buck Lai Tin, "Gleanings," *Honolulu Star-Bulletin*, February 14, 1935.
25 *Buffalo Commercial*, June 8, 1912; *Buffalo Courier*, June 3, 1912; *Schenectady Gazette*, June 18, 1912; *Binghamton News*, July 26, 1912; *Flint Journal*, September 16, 1912.
26 *Honolulu Star-Bulletin*, September 10, 1912; *Sporting Life*, August 24, 1912.
27 *Cleveland Plain Dealer*, August 19, 1912; *Chicago Tribune*, September 23, 1912.
28 *Hawaiian Gazette*, June 11, 1912; *Pacific Commercial Advertiser*, August 29, 1912.
29 *Honolulu Star-Bulletin*, September 12, 1912.
30 Franks, *Barnstorming*, 64–94.
31 *University Missourian*, April 22, 1913.
32 *Wichita Daily Eagle*, April 13, 1913; *Hawaiian Gazette*, June 27, 1913.
33 *Wilmington Daily Journal*, July 24, 1913; *Honolulu Star-Bulletin*, July 30, 1913.
34 *Honolulu Star-Bulletin*, January 30, 1935.
35 Franks, *Barnstorming*, 64–94; *Pacific Commercial Advertiser*, August 6, 1913; September 15, 1913.
36 *Honolulu Star-Bulletin*, May 23, 1913; July 6, 1913; July 12, 1913; October 6, 1913; Franks, *Barnstorming*, 64–94.
37 Franks, *Barnstorming*, 94–100; *Honolulu Advertiser*, March 31, 1946.
38 Franks, *Barnstorming*, 94–123; *Pacific Commercial Advertiser*, January 29, 1914; February 12, 1914; *Honolulu Star-Bulletin*, January 31, 1914.
39 Franks, *Barnstorming*, 99–100; Erika Lee and Judy Yung, *Angel Island: Immigrant Gateway to America* (New York: Oxford University Press, 2012); *Oakland Tribune*, March 12, 1914.
40 *Washington Herald*, April 19, 1914; *Waterloo Times-Tribune*, April 16, 1914; *Kokomo Tribune* cited in *Honolulu Star-Bulletin*, May 28, 1914.
41 *Pacific Commercial Advertiser*, April 24, 1914; *Honolulu Star-Bulletin*, May 28, 1914.
42 *Trenton Times*, June 15, 1914; *Honolulu Star-Bulletin*, July 18, 1914.
43 *Philadelphia Inquirer*, July 23, 1914; *Honolulu Star-Bulletin*, July 30, 1914; *Indianapolis Star*, September 13, 1914; *Brooklyn Daily Standard Times*, May 26, 1915.
44 *Brooklyn Daily Eagle*, August 24, 1914; *Honolulu Star-Bulletin*, October 19, 1914; December 18, 1914; *Brooklyn Daily Union*, January 22, 1915.
45 *Pacific Commercial Advertiser*, February 11, 1915; March 3, 1915; March 18, 1915; March 23, 1915.
46 Franks, *Barnstorming*, 129–130; *San Jose Mercury*, March 11, 1915; *Salt Lake Telegram*, March 15, 1915.
47 Lehigh University Yearbook, 1915, Ancestry.com, accessed April 28, 2011; *Sporting Life*, May 22, 1915; May 29, 1915.
48 *Cincinnati Enquirer* cited in the *Lincoln Star*, May 17, 1915.
49 *Carbondale Leader*, July 21, 1915.
50 *Carbondale Leader*, July 21, 1915.

51 *Carbondale Leader*, July 21, 1915.
52 *Carbondale Leader*, July 21, 1915.
53 *Carbondale Leader*, July 21, 1915; Gary Y. Okihiro, *Island World*: A History of Hawai'i and the United States, (Berkeley: University of California Press, 2008; Gary Y. Okihiro, *The Boundless Sea: The Self and History* (Oakland: University of California Press, 2019); Rosalind R. Chou and Joe R. Feagin, *The Model Minority Myth: Asian Americans Facing Racism* (New York: Routledge, 2016).
54 *Brooklyn Daily Standard*, July 10, 1915; *Brooklyn Daily Eagle*, September 1, 1915.
55 *Decatur Review*, July 29, 1912; *Brooklyn Daily Times*, May 26, 1915; *Honolulu Star-Bulletin*, September 9, 1915; Lanctot, *Fair Dealing*, 39–42.
56 *New York Age*, September 9, 1915; September 16, 1915; September 30, 1915.
57 Jorge S. Figueredo, *Cuban Baseball: A Statistical History, 1878–1961* (Jefferson, NC: McFarland, 2003), 116; *Honolulu Star-Bulletin*, November 2, 1915.
58 *Honolulu Star-Bulletin*, November 4, 1915; November 11, 1915.
59 *Pacific Commercial Advertiser*, April 6, 1914; April 20, 1914; June 27, 1914.
60 *Honolulu Star-Bulletin*, February 1, 1915; April 7, 1915; Luck Yee Lau, "A Baseball Trip to the Far East," *Ka Palapala Hawaii*, May 1916, 15.
61 *Honolulu Star-Bulletin*, April 5, 1915; April 7, 1915; May 7, 1915; *Pacific Commercial Advertiser*, July 20, 1915.
62 *Honolulu Star-Bulletin*, April 15, 1915; June 6, 1915; June 23, 1915.
63 *Boston Journal*, December 29, 1915; *Honolulu Advertiser*, November 3, 1951; Franks, *Barnstorming*, 156–175.
64 *Brownsville Daily Bulletin*, March 29, 1916; *Dallas Morning News*, April 2, 1916; Franks, *Barnstorming*, 163; *Honolulu Advertiser*, August 8, 1940.
65 *New York Telegram* cited in *Pittsburgh Press*, September 24, 1916; *New York Age*, September 21, 1916.
66 *Austin American*, April 1, 1916; *St. Louis Post Dispatch*, May 7, 1916; *York Daily*, July 22, 1916; *Indianapolis News*, September 26, 1916; *Stillwater Orange and Black*, April 22, 1916; *Honolulu Advertiser*, November 3, 1951.
67 *Commerce Journal*, April 14, 1916; *Brooklyn Daily Eagle*, June 19, 1916; *Chicago Defender*, October 7, 1916; *Sporting Life*, November 4, 1916.
68 Franks, *Barnstorming*, 62.
69 Franks, *Barnstorming*, 64, 66–67, 117, 155; William McNeil, *Black Baseball out of Season: Play for Pay outside of the Negro Leagues* (Jefferson, NC: McFarland, 2007), 52–55; *Pacific Commercial Advertiser*, November 29, 1915; *New York Age*, January 6, 1916.
70 Franks, *Barnstorming*, 64, 66–67, 117, 155; William McNeil, *Black Baseball out of Season: Play for Pay outside of the Negro Leagues* (Jefferson, NC: McFarland, 2007), 52–55; *Pacific Commercial Advertiser*, November 29, 1915; *New York Age*, January 6, 1916.
71 Franks, *Barnstorming*, 156–175; *Nippu Jiii*, April 11, 1927.
72 *Honolulu Star-Bulletin*, January 8, 1916.
73 Franks, *Barnstorming*, 102–103.
74 *Honolulu Star-Bulletin*, August 25, 1928.
75 *Honolulu Star-Bulletin*, August 18, 1928; February 14, 1935; April 8, 1940; *Honolulu Advertiser*, April 19, 1946.
76 *Trenton Evening Times*, February 16, 1928; *Brooklyn Daily Eagle*, January 21, 1945.
77 William V. Flores and Rina Benmayor, eds., *Latino Cultural Citizenship: Claiming Identity, Space, and Rights* (Boston: Beacon Press, 1997); Ronald Takaki, *Iron Cages: Race and Culture in 19th Century America* (New York: Oxford University Press, 2000); Franks, *Barnstorming*.

Chapter 4 Crossings of Baseball's Racial Fault Lines, 1917–1918

1 Lee, *America for Americans*, 113–147.
2 *Honolulu Star-Bulletin*, June 22, 1914; *New York Times*, December 6, 1914.
3 Franks, *Barnstorming*, 118–127.
4 Irv Goldfarb, "Charles Comiskey," Society for American Baseball Research, http://sabr.org/bioproj/person/8fbc6b31, accessed April 2, 2014.
5 *Pacific Commercial Advertiser*, December 11, 1914; *Honolulu Star-Bulletin*, December 16, 1914; *Hawaiian Gazette*, December 22, 1914; *Sporting Life*, December 26, 1914.
6 *Baltimore Afro American*, December 12, 1914; *Washington Post*, December 3, 1914; *Albany Evening Journal*, December 17, 1914; *Sporting Life*, December 19, 1914.
7 *Sporting Life*, December 19, 1914; *Syracuse Daily Herald*, December 12, 1914; January 2, 1915; January 8, 1915; *Lima Daily News*, January 10, 1915; William Phelon, "A Gay Winter," *Baseball Magazine*, March 1915, 19.
8 Franks, *Barnstorming*, 118–127; *Honolulu Star-Bulletin*, January 5, 1915; January 6, 1915.
9 *Honolulu Star-Bulletin*, September 6, 1912; May 13, 1913; July 25, 1913; October 14, 1913; September 5, 1916; *Pacific Commercial Advertiser*, September 14, 1912; November 13, 1912; June 15, 1914; March 21, 1915; *Brooklyn Daily Standard*, January 22, 1915; *Brooklyn Daily Eagle*, January 26, 1915; *Binghamton Press*, February 9, 1915; *Stockton Evening Mail*, March 16, 1915; *Ashville Citizen-Times*, March 16, 1915; *Sporting Life*, April 10, 1915.
10 *Honolulu Star-Bulletin*, July 14, 1914.
11 United States Census Bureau, Manuscript Census Schedules, Borough of Queens, City of New York, 1900, Ancestry.com, *accessed* March 13, 2018; Sheryll Cashin, *Loving: Interracial Intimacy in America and Its Threat to White Supremacy* (Boston: Beacon Press, 2017), 10.
12 *Honolulu Star-Bulletin*, December 4, 1916; *Philadelphia Public Ledger*, December 19, 1916; *San Jose Mercury*, February 28, 1917.
13 *Oakland Tribune*, March 24, 1917; *Portland Oregonian*, January 31, 1917; *Portland Telegraph* cited in *Honolulu Star-Bulletin*, January 1, 1917.
14 *Seattle Star*, April 3, 1917; *Rochester Democrat and Chronicle*, April 10, 1917.
15 *Seattle Post-Intelligencer*, April 3, 1917; April 15, 1917; May 21, 1917; Dan Raley, "Milestones 'N' Moments," *Seattle Post-Intelligencer*, December 23, 1999; *Seattle Times*, May 6, 1917; *Seattle Star*, May 21, 1917.
16 *Portland Oregonian*, May 25, 1917; May 28, 1917; June 1, 1917; June 19, 1917; *Oregon Journal*, May 28, 1917; *Anaconda Standard*, June 21, 1917; July 5, 1917; July 8, 1917; July 9, 1917; *Sporting News*, July 5, 1917; *Seattle Times*, July 11, 1917; July 12, 1917; "Baseball Reference," https://www.baseball-reference.com/register/player.fcgi?id=ayau--001---, accessed February 7, 2011.
17 *Seattle Times*, July 23, 1917; *Honolulu Star-Bulletin*, May 2, 1917.
18 *Philadelphia Public Ledger*, October 26, 1916.
19 Franks, *Barnstorming*, 181–188; Ronald Takaki, *Strangers*; *Frederick Post* cited in *Gettysburg Times*, June 5, 1917; "Class D Blue Ridge League," http://www.blueridgeleague.org/intro.asp, accessed January 12, 2022.
20 *Chambersburg Public Opinion*, May 12, 1917; May 16, 1917; *Gettysburg Times*, May 18, 1917; June 28, 1917; *Philadelphia Inquirer*, May 18, 1917; June 10, 1917; *Hanover Evening Sun*, May 14, 1917; *Gettysburg Star and Sentinel*, June 22, 1917; *Honolulu Star-Bulletin*, July 10, 1917.
21 *Philadelphia Inquirer*, April 22, 1917; September 26, 1917; September 24, 1917.

22 *Philadelphia Inquirer*, May 23, 1917; *Honolulu Star-Bulletin*, June 13, 1917.
23 Liz Spikel, "Cornersptted: 1421 Arch Street, Once the Central YMCA," *Curbed Philadelphia*, December 4, 2012, accessed January 12, 2022; U.S. Draft Registration, World War I, www.Ancestry.com, accessed September 28, 2004.
24 Franks, *Barnstorming*, 196–223; Lanctot, *Fair Dealing*; *Philadelphia Inquirer*, April 8, 1917; August 19, 1917; *Chester Times*, April 17, 1917; *Trenton Evening Times*, August 23, 1917. I will refer to Lai Tin as Buck Lai from now on, although the press in Hawai'i called him Buck Lai Tin.
25 *Honolulu Star-Bulletin*, June 25, 1917; July 27, 1917.
26 *Philadelphia Inquirer*, August 5, 1917; August 26, 1917; September 16, 1917; *Chester Times*, September 24, 1917.
27 *Honolulu Star-Bulletin*, August 17, 1917; "Baseball Reference," https://www.baseball-reference.com/players/b/bakerfr01.shtml, accessed May 23, 2015.
28 *Chester Times*, October 8, 1917; October 15, 1917; October 22, 1917; *Trenton Evening Times*, October 15, 1917; October 22, 1917; *Philadelphia Inquirer*, October 14, 1917; October 21, 1917; *Honolulu Star-Bulletin*, November 7, 1917.
29 *Bridgeton Evening News*, August 14, 1917; August 21, 1917; *Philadelphia Inquirer*, October 7, 1917; Lanctot, *Fair Dealing*, 62; Barthel, *Baseball's Peerless Semipros*.
30 *Brooklyn Daily Eagle*, March 23, 1917; *Brooklyn Daily Standard Union*, March 22, 1917; March 26, 1917; April 19, 1917; U.S., World War I Draft Registration Cards, 1917–1918, for Frederic J Markham, Ancestry.com, accessed April 3, 2020.
31 *Brooklyn Daily Eagle*, April 23, 1917; June 11, 1917; July 23, 1917; August 6, 1917; August 27, 1917; *Brooklyn Citizen*, June 4, 1917; June 11, 1917; *New York Sun*, April 27, 1917; June 25, 1917; June 30, 1917; *Brooklyn Daily Times*, June 11, 1917; *Honolulu Star-Bulletin*, June 13, 1917.
32 Riley Allen, "Honolulu Boys Making Good in Mainland Baseball," *Honolulu Star-Bulletin*, October 13, 1917; *Honolulu Star-Bulletin*, October 20, 1917.
33 *Washington Post*, March 24, 1918.
34 *Brooklyn Daily Eagle*, March 18, 1918; *Sporting News*, March 28, 1918; *Lima Daily News*, March 28, 1918; *Buffalo Enquirer*, April 1, 1918; *Des Moines Daily News*, April 7, 1918.
35 Robert Maxwell, "Lai, Phils' Hawaiian Star Divides Honor with Moran on St. Patrick's Day Ride," *Philadelphia Public Ledger*, March 18, 1918.
36 Franks, *Barnstorming*, 198; *Philadelphia Inquirer*, March 25, 1918; March 26, 1918; March 31, 1918; April 3, 1918; April 7, 1918; April 11, 1918; *Sporting News*, April 4, 1918; *Honolulu Star-Bulletin*, April 10, 1918; *Macon Weekly Telegraph*, April 11, 1918.
37 *Sporting News*, May 23, 1918; *Honolulu Star-Bulletin*, June 4, 1918.
38 *Bridgeport Telegram*, May 27, 1918; May 29, 1918; June 3, 1918; *Honolulu Star-Bulletin*, February 12, 1918; August 10, 1918; *Brooklyn Times Union*, April 8, 1918; *Brooklyn Citizen*, May 20, 1918; June 24, 1918.
39 *Bridgeport Telegram*, May 28, 1918; June 1, 1918.
40 *Honolulu Star-Bulletin*, July 18, 1918; August 19, 1918.
41 *Bridgeport Telegram*, June 18, 1918; June 19, 1918; June 28, 1918.
42 *Bridgeport Telegram*, July 10, 1918; July 11, 1918; July 12, 1918; *Philadelphia Public Ledger*, July 19, 1918.
43 *Sporting News*, June 13, 1918; *Bridgeport Telegram*, June 4, 1918.
44 *Honolulu Star-Bulletin*, June 25, 1918; *Pacific Commercial Advertiser*, July 27, 1918.
45 *Bridgeport Telegram*, July 23, 1918.
46 *Bridgeport Telegram*, July 29, 1918; *Pittsburgh Press*, July 29, 1918.
47 *Stockton Independent*, July 25, 1928.

48 *Reading Times*, August 26, 1918; *Philadelphia Inquirer*, August 15, 1918; September 7, 1918; September 28, 1918; September 27, 1918; *Chester Times*, September 23, 1918; *Bridgeport Telegram*, July 26, 1918; July 27, 1918.

49 *Chicago Defender*, June 15, 1918; *Chester Times*, July 12, 1918.

50 *Brooklyn Daily Eagle*, December 4, 1918; February 2, 1917; *Philadelphia Inquirer*, August 28, 1917.

51 Okihiro, *Island World*, 184, 199; *Harrisburg Patriot*, July 23, 1917; *Hawaiian Gazette*, August 10, 1917; "The Notorious Meddler: A Homegrown Collection of Short Stories, Songs, Poems, and More," "The Edison Files: Ford Hawaiians," http://www.randyspecktacular.com/2012/07/the-edison-files-ford-hawaiians.html, accessed January 13, 2020.

52 *Philadelphia Inquirer*, July 8, 1917; July 29, 1917; August 5, 1917; *Honolulu Star-Bulletin*, June 21, 1917; July 24, 1917.

53 *Philadelphia Public Ledger*, September 19, 1917; October 18, 1917; October 26, 1917.

54 *Philadelphia Public Ledger*, December 21, 1917; April 9, 1918; *Baltimore Sun*, December 7, 1917; *Lebanon Daily News*, December 8, 1917; *Honolulu Star-Bulletin*, January 23, 1918.

55 U.S. Army Transport Service, Passenger Lists, 1910–1939, Ancestry.com, accessed July 27, 2017; *Pittsburgh Press*, August 6, 1918; *Honolulu Star-Bulletin*, October 5, 1918; *New Castle News*, December 6, 1918; *Kansas City Star*, December 17, 1918; "Doughboy Center," "The Big Show: The Meuse-Argonne Offensive," http://www.worldwar1.com/dbc/bigshow.htm, accessed July 28, 2017.

56 *Brooklyn Daily Eagle*, December 5, 1918; *Honolulu Star-Bulletin*, May 10, 1919; March 18, 1922; U.S. Army Transport Service, Passenger Lists, Ancestry.com, accessed March 17, 2019.

57 Sunny K. Hung, "Tribute for Apau Kau Is the Subject; Was Popular Boy," *Honolulu Advertiser*, March 18, 1922; *Honolulu Advertiser*, March 20, 1922; *Honolulu Star-Bulletin*, February 2, 1920; February 21, 1941.

58 U.S. Army Transport Service, Passenger Lists; *Brooklyn Daily Standard Union*, May 6, 1918; *New York Sun*, May 13, 1918; *Honolulu Star-Bulletin*, September 6, 1918; October 5, 1918; Hung, "Tribute."

59 *Syracuse Herald*, September 4, 1915; *Honolulu Star-Bulletin*, November 4, 1915; July 25, 1916; *The Bucknellian*, June 5, 1916; Lehigh University Yearbook, 1916, Ancestry.com, accessed August 9, 2017; *Philadelphia Public Ledger*, July 9, 1916; Walter F. Dunn, "Strawbridge-Clothier Nine Whitewashes Chinese," *Philadelphia Public Ledger*, July 15, 1916; February 16, 1917; *Philadelphia Inquirer*, January 28, 1917; August 27, 1917; *Allentown Morning Democrat*, June 18, 1917; August 6, 1917; *Lebanon Evening Report*, July 9, 1917.

60 *Honolulu Star-Bulletin*, October 5, 1918; Pennsylvania, WW1 Veterans Service and Compensation Files, 1917–1919, 1934–1948, for Alfred Yap, Ancestry.com, accessed August 10, 2017; Richard Slotkin, *Lost Battalions: The Great War and the Crisis of American Nationality* (New York: Henry Holt, 2013).

Chapter 5 Peripatetic Pros, 1919–1934

1 Lee, *America for Americans*, 113–147.

2 Lee, *America for Americans*, 183–196.

3 *Hartford Courant*, April 16, 1919; June 24, 1919; *Bridgeport Telegram*, April 14, 1919; May 19, 1919; Roger Ferri, "Ray Grimes Reason for Keeping Lai at Short Is Mystery to Locals," *Bridgeport Times*, May 19, 1919; *Bridgeport Times*, May 20, 1919; May 22, 1919; June 21, 1919; June 26, 1919; *Sporting News*, May 29, 1919.

4 *Hartford Courant*, April 16, 1919; April 17, 1919; May 22, 1919; May 23, 1919; June 1, 1919; May 24, 1919; May 26, 1919; June 28, 1919; *Hurley Iron County Miner*, July 11, 1919; *Bridgeport Telegram*, May 21, 1919; May 27, 1919.
5 *Vineland Evening Journal*, September 15, 1919; *Philadelphia Inquirer*, September 18, 1919; *Wilmington News*, September 13, 1919; *Chester Times*, April 22, 1953.
6 *Bridgeport Telegram*, April 30, 1920; May 5, 1920; May 6, 1920; May 7, 1920; May 12, 1920; June 9, 1920; June 21, 1920; June 23, 1920.
7 *Bridgeport Telegram*, August 9, 1920; August 14, 1920; August 18, 1920; August 19, 1920; September 13, 1920; *Sporting News*, December 16, 1920.
8 *Sporting News*, February 24, 1921; *Springfield Republican*, March 11, 1921; *Bridgeport Telegram*, April 13, 1921.
9 *Bridgeport Times*, April 5, 1921; August 30, 1921; September 19, 1921; *Bridgeport Telegram*, May 2, 1921; August 16, 1921; September 19, 1921; "Baseball Reference," https://www.baseball-reference.com/register/player.fcgi?id=lai---002wil, accessed May 21, 2009.
10 *Philadelphia Inquirer*, October 16, 1921.
11 *Bay City Times*, June 24, 1919; *Rochester Democrat*, July 23, 1919; *Bridgeton Evening News*, July 24, 1919; September 23, 1919; *Philadelphia Inquirer*, August 4, 1919; September 9, 1919.
12 United States Census Bureau, Manuscript Census Schedules, City of Penns Grove and County of Salem, New Jersey, 1920, Ancestry.com, accessed March 18, 2007; *Pittsburgh Daily Post*, May 18, 1920; *Philadelphia Inquirer*, June 10, 1920; *Bridgeport Times*, April 8, 1921; Buck Lai Tin, "Gleanings from an 'Old Timer's' Scrapbook as told to Loui Leong Hop," *Honolulu Star-Bulletin*, February 2, 1935.
13 *Honolulu Star-Bulletin*, January 31, 1920; Buck Lai, "Gleanings from an 'Old Timer's' Scrapbook as Told to Loui Leong Hop," *Honolulu Star-Bulletin*, February 21, 1935; *Philadelphia Inquirer*, July 18, 1920; September 2, 1920; *Camden Post-Telegram*, July 9, 1920; *Camden Daily Courier*, July 12, 1920; *Philadelphia Public Ledger*, July 28, 1920; *Pacific Commercial Advertiser*, September 29, 1920.
14 *Bridgeton Evening News*, May 9, 1919; *Philadelphia Inquirer*, August 11, 1919; September 9, 1919; June 21, 1920; August 23, 1920; October 2, 1921; July 5, 1922; September 20, 1922; *Wilmington News Journal*, September 23, 1919; August 24, 1920; *Reading Times*, September 6, 1920; *Brooklyn Standard Union*, September 4, 1921; *Bridgewater Courier News*, September 14, 1922; *Delaware County Times*, September 7, 1951; *Camden Morning Post*, May 10, 1923; *Shamokin News-Dispatch*, May 21, 1923.
15 *Philadelphia Inquirer*, September 18, 1919; April 4, 1920; May 23, 1920; June 19, 1921; *Allentown Morning News*, April 8, 1921; *Honolulu Star-Bulletin*, April 15, 1950; *Wilmington News Journal*, September 27, 1921; October 3, 1922.
16 *Wilmington News Journal*, July 22, 1922; August 5, 1922; August 16, 1922; "Baseball Reference," https://www.baseball-reference.com/register/team.cgi?id=bf75389d, accessed April 4, 2009.
17 *Allentown Morning Call*, September 7, 1923.
18 *Philadelphia Inquirer*, August 27, 1919; August 20, 1920; June 1, 1923; July 13, 1923; August 10, 1923; *Trenton Evening Times*, May 9, 1924; June 3, 1924; *Honolulu Star-Bulletin*, February 9, 1935.
19 *Lethbridge Herald*, May 13, 1922; *Bridgeport Telegram*, April 26, 1922; Mary Lai, email correspondence with the author, December 2, 2009.
20 Robert Peterson, *Cage to Jump Shots: Pro Basketball's Early Years* (Lincoln: University of Nebraska Press, 2002); Murry Nelson, *The Originals: New York Celtics Invent Basketball* (Bowling Green, OH: Bowling Green State University Popular Press, 1999).

21 *New York Evening World*, December 15, 1921; *Bridgeport Telegram*, December 20, 1921; *Wilmington Evening Journal*, December 23, 1921; Nelson, *The Originals*, 20–21.
22 Lanctot, *Fair Dealing*, 57.
23 Judy Johnson quoted in Lanctot, *Fair Dealing*, 64.
24 *Trenton Evening Times*, May 22, 1922; July 11, 1922; *Philadelphia Inquirer*, April 23, 1922; May 2, 1922; May 7, 1922; May 12, 1922; May 21, 1922; June 16, 1922; July 5, 1922; July 8, 1922; July 13, 1922; July 22, 1922; September 5, 1922; September 20, 1922; *Wilmington Morning News*, September 8, 1922; *Philadelphia Public Ledger*, June 10, 1922.
25 *Chester Times*, March 7, 1923; April 20, 1923; Matt Zabritka, "Ebert Retires: Finally Gets Time to Paste Clippings," *Delaware County Daily Times*, July 16, 1962.
26 *Chester Times*, July 5, 1923; July 13, 1923; July 28, 1923; July 13, 1923; August 22, 1923; August 25, 1923.
27 *Altoona Tribune*, September 24, 1923; *Honolulu Advertiser*, October 14, 1923; Christopher G. Bates and Steven A. Riess, "Industrial Sports," in *Sports in America from Colonial Times to the Twenty-First Century*, ed. Steven A. Riess (New York: Routledge, 2015), 479–482.
28 *Trenton Evening Times*, April 25, 1924; May 9, 1924; Harry Coady Lindop, "Trenton Wins Double Header," *Trenton Evening Times*, May 31, 1924; Lindop, "Buck Lai Hits Two Homers in Hectic Struggle with Hilldale," *Trenton Evening Times*, July 22, 1924; Lindop, "Ad Swigler's Homer in Tenth Gives Tigers Win over Cubans," *Trenton Evening Times*, August 23, 1924; Lindop, "Trenton Proves Superior to Morgans before Large Crowd," *Trenton Evening Times*, August 24, 1924; http://www.negroleaguebaseball.com/teams/Brooklyn_Royal_Giants.html, accessed June 8, 2015; "Brooklyn Royal Giants," "Blackpast," https://www.blackpast.org/african-american-history/brooklyn-royal-giants-1905-1942, accessed January 14, 2022.
29 *Honolulu Star-Bulletin*, September 27, 1924.
30 *Wilmington Morning News*, May 3, 1926; Lanctot, *Fair Dealing*, 71; *Philadelphia Inquirer*, April 25, 1926; *Camden Evening Courier*, April 26, 1926; May 6, 1926; May 10, 1926; May 17, 1926.
31 E. Z. Crane, "Lai Tin Still Knocking Them Off," *Honolulu Advertiser*, July 24, 1927; Abe Carotis, "George Sheflot to Go South with Athletics Next Year," *Camden Courier Post*, September 28, 1927.
32 *Brooklyn Citizen*, May 1, 1922; Wm J. Granger, "Willie Kelleher Is Once More Winner for the Bushwicks," *Brooklyn Citizen*, July 3, 1922; Wm J. Granger, "Bushwicks Too Good for the Miners and the Gloucester Fishermen," *Brooklyn Citizen*, July 20, 1922.
33 *Brooklyn Daily Eagle*, September 15, 1924; *Brooklyn Standard Union*, September 22, 1924.
34 *Brooklyn Citizen*, March 20, 1925; *Brooklyn Daily Eagle*, July 27, 1925; *Chicago Defender*, May 1, 1926; July 23, 1927.
35 *Chester Times*, November 3, 1927; *Honolulu Star-Bulletin*, November 10, 1927.
36 *New York Times*, January 10, 1928; *San Francisco Examiner*, January 26, 1928.
37 *Gettysburg Times*, January 14, 1928; *Hagerstown Daily Mail*, January 16, 1928; *Florence Morning News*, January 19, 1928; *Seattle Times*, January 26, 1928.
38 *Chester Times*, January 10, 1928.
39 Lank Leonard, "Buck Lai to Get Trial," *Trenton Evening Times*, February 16, 1928.
40 Leonard, "Buck Lai to Get Trial."

41 *Honolulu Advertiser*, January 25, 1928; February 5, 1928.

42 Shelley Sang-Hee Lee, *Claiming the Oriental Gateway: Prewar Seattle and Japanese America* (Philadelphia: Temple University Press, 2011); *Japanese American Courier*, February 11, 1928; *Hawaii Hochi*, February 29, 1928.

43 Roscoe McGowan, "Frank Frisch Salutes Camp Bound Giants," *New York Daily News*, March 1, 1928; Bill Ritt quoted in *New Castle News*, March 9, 1928.

44 *Philadelphia Inquirer*, April 1, 1928; Stan Baumgartner, "Chinaman Refused to Take Pink Slip," *Philadelphia Inquirer*, April 1, 1928.

45 *Honolulu Star-Bulletin*, May 13, 1928.

46 *Camden Morning-Post*, March 12, 1928; March 19, 1928.

47 *Trenton Evening Times*, April 11, 1928; May 7, 1928; *New York Times*, April 13, 1928; April 16, 1928; *Brooklyn Daily Times*, May 4, 1928; *Sporting News*, May 26, 1928; July 5, 1928; *Honolulu Star-Bulletin*, July 14, 1928; *Brooklyn Daily Eagle*, July 6, 1931.

48 *Brooklyn Standard Union*, April 22, 1929; *Brooklyn Daily Eagle*, June 23, 1930; July 24, 1930; *Brooklyn Daily Times*, June 17, 1929; *Pittsburgh Courier*, June 22, 1929; Jimmy Powers, "Bushwicks Win 5-4 in Dexter Night Tilt," *New York Daily News*, July 26, 1930.

49 Harold Parrott, "Jap Collegians Get Real Taste of Enthusiasm," *Brooklyn Daily Eagle*, June 1, 1931; *Brooklyn Daily Eagle*, June 8, 1931; July 6, 1931; August 22, 1931; September 7, 1931; *New York Times*, June 1, 1931; *Brooklyn Standard Union*, September 12, 1931; Franks, *Asian Pacific Americans*, 181; "Baseball Reference," http://www.baseball-reference.com/nlb/team.cgi?id=ba694099, accessed June 3, 2015.

50 *New York Times*, September 24, 1932; *Brooklyn Daily Eagle*, September 24, 1932; May 1, 1933; Jimmy Powers, "Giants Defeat Bushwicks, 5-2, before 20,000," *New York Daily News*, September 24, 1932; April 7, 1933; *Brooklyn Times Union*, September 26, 1932; Irwin N. Rosee, "Mike Meola, Last Year's Semi-pro Mound Great, Sets Big League Career as Goal in Life," *Brooklyn Times Union*, September 21, 1933; *Chicago Defender*, September 22, 1933.

51 *Brooklyn Times Union*, July 6, 1933; Irwin N. Rosee, "Lai One of Semi-pros Colorful Stars," *Brooklyn Times Union*, October 14, 1933; *Honolulu Star-Bulletin*, November 13, 1933.

52 *Brooklyn Daily Eagle*, April 30, 1934; August 20, 1934; August 26, 1934; September 20, 1934; William J. Granger, "Buck Lai's Triple, with the Bases Loaded, Gives the Bushwicks Even Break with the Black Yankees," *Brooklyn Citizen*, June 4, 1934; Bill McCulloch, "See P. Waner Clinching '34 Hitting Title," *Brooklyn Times Union*, July 21, 1934; *Brooklyn Times Union*, September 20, 1934.

53 Irwin N. Rosee, "Lai Relives Early Thrills on Trip Here," *Brooklyn Standard Union*, June 8, 1935.

54 *Allentown Morning Call*, May 13, 1928; *Philadelphia Inquirer*, June 13, 1929; August 29, 1930; September 6, 1931; May 1, 1932; *Chester Times*, August 17, 1929; *Wilmington News Journal*, April 15, 1930; *Altoona Mirror*, September 15, 1930; *Middletown Times Herald*, July 11, 1933; July 25, 1933; August 1, 1933; *Camden Post-Courier*, March 26, 1931.

55 Frank Weitekamp, "Just Below the Majors," *Brooklyn Daily Eagle*, September 4, 1934.

56 Paul A. Kramer, *The Blood of Government: Race, Empire, the United States & the Philippines* (Chapel Hill: University of North Carolina Press, 2006).

57 Kramer, *Blood of Government*; Joel S. Franks, *Crossing Sidelines, Crossing Cultures: Sport and Asian Pacific American Cultural Citizenship*, 2nd ed. (Lanham, MD:

University Press of America, 2009), 63; Gerald R. Gems, *Sport and the American Occupation of the Philippines* (Lanham, MD: Lexington Books, 2016).

58 Franks, *Crossing Cultures*, 64; Franks, *Asian Pacific Americans*, 52–54.

59 *Harrisburg Telegraph*, May 28, 1931; *Shamokin News-Dispatch*, June 4, 1931.

60 *Washington Evening Star*, December 30, 1931; *Harrisburg Telegraph*, January 27, 1932; *Gettysburg Times*, February 1, 1932.

61 *Wilmington Morning News*, February 18, 1932; *Yonkers Herald*, March 16, 1934.

62 *Honolulu Star-Bulletin*, December 12, 1931; Andrew Mitsukado, "Eastern Cage Team Wants to Play Here," *Honolulu Advertiser*, December 17, 1931; *Hawaii Hochi*, December 17, 1931.

63 *Camden Morning Post*, June 4, 1928; May 1, 1929; *Camden Post-Courier*, August 6, 1930; September 19, 1930; May 9, 1931; August 28, 1931; September 21, 1931; September 8, 1932; *Wilmington Every Evening*, April 9, 1931; Salem City Directory, 1930, Ancestry.com, accessed January 17, 2020.

64 Scott Simkus, *Outsider Baseball: The Weird World of Hardball on the Fringe, 1876–1950* (Chicago: Chicago Review Press, 2014), 159–161.

65 *Detroit Free Press*, October 23, 1923; *Honolulu Advertiser*, January 25, 1945.

Chapter 6 The Travelers Back Home

1 Okihiro, *American History Unbound*, 221–265; Lawrence Fuchs, *Hawaii Pono: A Social History* (New York: Harcourt, Brace, and World, 1961); Jung, *Reworking Race*; Sally Engle Merry, *Colonizing Hawai'i: The Cultural Power of Law* (Princeton, NJ: Princeton University Press, 2000); Sarah Miller-Davenport, *Gateway State: Hawai'i and the Cultural Transformation of American Empire* (Princeton, NJ: Princeton University Press, 2019); Jonathan Y. Okamura, *Raced to Death in 1920s Hawai'i: Injustice and Revenge in the Fukunaga Case* (Urbana: University of Illinois Press, 2019).

2 Okihiro, *American History Unbound*, 221–265; Lawrence Fuchs, *Hawaii Pono*; Jung, *Reworking Race*; Sally Engle Merry, *Colonizing Hawai'i*; Sarah Miller-Davenport, *Gateway State*; Jonathan Y. Okamura, *Raced to Death*.

3 Jung, *Reworking Race*, 95–96.

4 Jung, *Reworking Race*, 10–55; Yasutaro Soga, "Saturday Notes," *Nippu Jiii*, March 10, 1934.

5 Jung, *Reworking Race*, 110; *Voice of Labor*, November 9, 1936; *Honolulu Record*, August 5, 1948.

6 Okamura, *Raced to Death*.

7 David Stannard, *Honor Killing: Race, Rape, and Clarence Darrow's Last Spectacular Case* (New York: Penguin Books, 2006); John P. Rosa, *Local Story: The Massie-Kahahawai Case and the Culture of History* (Honolulu: University of Hawai'i Press, 2014).

8 David Stannard, *Honor Killing*; John P. Rosa, *Local Story: The Massie-Kahahawai Case and the Culture of History*.

9 David Stannard, *Honor Killing*; John P. Rosa, *Local Story: The Massie-Kahahawai Case and the Culture of History*.

10 Fuchs, *Hawaii Pono*, 408.

11 *Honolulu Star-Bulletin*, April 18, 1919; July 11, 1919; November 7, 1919; Bill Gee quoted in *Honolulu Advertiser*, June 17, 1984.

12 Frank Menke, "Honolulu Turns Out Semi-pro Baseball Nines En Sue, 46-Year Old Chinese, Is Ty Cobb of Islands," *Idaho Daily Statesmen*, August 20, 1922.

13 *Pacific Commercial Advertiser*, June 18, 1919; November 19, 1919.
14 Rudolph J. Smythe, "All Chinese Grab League Championship by 4-1 Score," *Honolulu Advertiser*, September 9, 1921; *Honolulu Star-Bulletin*, June 19, 1922; Sunny Hung, "Chinese Favored in Ball League," *Honolulu Star-Bulletin*, April 16, 1924; Loui Leong Hop, "The History of Chinese Sports," in *The Chinese of Hawaii*, ed. Chock Lun, L. F. Kwok, Dormant C. Chang, and Min Hin Li (Honolulu, HI: Overseas Penman Club, 1929), 29.
15 *Honolulu Star-Bulletin*, September 5, 1925; Harry Shiramazu, "Announce Selections of First and Second All-Time All-Hawaii Baseball Teams," *Nippu Jiii*, October 19, 1931, Franks, *Asian Pacific Americans*, 29–30.
16 *Honolulu Star Bulletin*, October 4, 1920; November 30, 1920; April 18, 1921; August 29, 1921; "Kokee" Harry, "Asahis Become Japanese Champions of the U.S. as they Defeat Fresno," *Nippu Jiii*, September 15, 1924.
17 *Honolulu Star-Bulletin*, January 15, 1927; June 20, 1927; July 20, 1931; January 9, 1932; *Nippu Jiii*, August 8, 1927; March 23, 1929; April 9, 1934; Percy Kozumi, "Andy's Not Thru," *Hawaii Hochi*, January 12, 1932; *Nippu Jiii*, April 10, 1937; November 9, 1938; *Maui Rekoda*, April 5, 1938; Franks, *Asian Pacific Americans*, 181.
18 *Hawaii Hochi*, October 3, 1930; *Jitsugyo no Hawai*, July 1, 1930; George Sakamaki, "Andy Yamashiro Stresses Loyalty to Hawaii in Race for Legislature," *Honolulu Star-Bulletin*, September 10, 1930; *Honolulu Advertiser*, November 11, 1930; Andrew Yamashiro Jr., telephone conversation with the author, April 11, 2009; Andrew Yamashiro Jr., interview with the author, San Jose, California, June 22, 2009; Hiromi Monobe, "From 'Vanishing Race' to Friendly Ally: Japanese American Perceptions of Native Hawaiians during the Interwar Years," *Japanese Journal of American Studies*, no. 23 (2012): 88–89.
19 *Nippu Jiii*, October 31, 1930; November 3, 1930.
20 *Honolulu Star-Bulletin*, October 15, 1930; November 5, 1930; *Hawaii Hochi*, October 25, 1930; Stannard, *Honor Killing*, 78.
21 Fuchs, *Hawaii Pono*, 123, 135, 180–181.
22 *Honolulu Advertiser*, June 22, 1932.
23 *Nippu Jiii*, June 27, 1932; July 2, 1932; *Shin Sekai*, June 24, 1932; *Nichibei Shinbun*, July 30, 1932.
24 *Honolulu Star-Bulletin*, November 1, 1932.
25 *Honolulu Star-Bulletin*, August 11, 1932.
26 *Nichibei Shinbun*, September 4, 1932.
27 *Nippu Jiii*, September 12, 1932; November 2, 1932.
28 *Honolulu Star-Bulletin*, April 9, 1932; *Hawaii Hochi*, April 7, 1933; Monobe, "'Vanishing Race,'" 90; Michael Slackman, "The Orange Race: George S. Patton Jr.'s Japanese-American Hostage Plan," *Biography*, 7, no. 1 (1984): 1–22; *Project MUSE*, doi:10.1353/bio.2010.0688, accessed January 17, 2022.
29 *Nippu Jiii*, May 26, 1931; March 7, 1934; *Honolulu Star-Bulletin*, April 28, 1932; Buck Lai Tin, "Gleanings from an 'Old Timer's' Scrapbook as Told to Loui Leong Hop," *Honolulu Star-Bulletin*, February 2, 1935; *Honolulu Advertiser*, June 30, 1934; November 5, 1934; November 5, 1934; *Jitsugyo-No-Hawaii*, October 1, 1934; *Hawaii Hochi*, October 31, 1934; *Japanese American Courier*, November 3, 1934; Monobe, "'Vanishing Race,'" 89.
30 *Nippu Jiii*, March 22, 1940; July 26, 1941; *Hawaii Hochi*, September 26, 1940; *Honolulu Advertiser*, July 24, 1941; Franks, *Crossing*, 52–53.
31 *Honolulu Star-Bulletin*, December 16, 1924; July 13, 1925; September 5, 1925; January 18, 1928; Chock Lun, "Several Workers of Chinese Parentage Win at

Election," *Honolulu Star-Bulletin*, November 11, 1932; *Nippu Jiii*, October 25, 1932; November 1, 1932; September 23, 1936.

32 *Honolulu Star-Bulletin*, September 5, 1925; Loui Leong Hop, "Five Mandarins Selected for Stellar Nine for Honolulu Baseball League," *Honolulu Star-Bulletin*, October 3, 1925; *Honolulu Star-Bulletin*, July 27, 1929; United States Census Bureau, Manuscript Census Schedules, City and County of Honolulu, 1930, Ancestry.com, accessed March 12, 2013.

33 *Honolulu Star-Bulletin*, April 21, 1919; February 19, 1930; *Hawaii Hochi*, April 4, 1930; May 28, 1930.

34 *Honolulu Star-Bulletin*, May 7, 1924; *Honolulu Advertiser*, May 15, 1926; *Newark Advocate*, January 25, 1927.

35 Honolulu City Directory, 1938–1939, Ancestry.com, accessed June 14, 2017; *Honolulu Advertiser*, June 13, 1938; October 3, 1938; September 9, 1944; December 23, 1970; *Nippu Jiii*, September 16, 1938; *Jisugyo no Hawai*, September 27, 1940; Betty Dunn, *Jackie Pung, Women's Golf Legend: The Thrills and Heartbreak of an LPGA Professional* (Lincoln, NE: iUniverse, 2005), 4.

36 *Pacific Commercial Advertiser*, June 21, 1920; *Honolulu Advertiser*, April 29, 1930; *Honolulu Star-Bulletin*, September 30, 1921; October 27, 1921; November 30, 1921; Loui Leong Hop, "Visitors Beginning to Show Class," *Honolulu Star-Bulletin*, March 6, 1922; *Honolulu Star-Bulletin*, July 30, 1928; August 1, 1928; Hop, "Asahis Favored to Win 1929 Loop Title," *Honolulu Star-Bulletin*, April 6, 1929; *Hawaii Hochi*, April 16, 1926.

37 *Honolulu Star-Bulletin*, March 6, 1922; September 30, 1930; January 11, 1932; December 12, 1932; December 13, 1933; *Honolulu Advertiser*, September 30, 1940; "Board of Industrial Schools, 1916–1939," https://ags.hawaii.gov/wp-content/uploads/2020/03/hsa_PSD5_BoardIndustrialSchools_fa.pdf, accessed January 17, 2022; Davianna Pomaika'i MacGregor, *Na Kua'aina: Living Hawaiian Culture* (Honolulu: University of Hawai'i Press, 2007), 239; United States Bureau of the Census, Manuscript Census Schedules, City and County of Honolulu, 1930, Ancestry.com, accessed March 17, 2009; "Hawaiian Homes Commission Act, 1920," https://dhhl.hawaii.gov/hhc/laws-and-rules/, accessed October 9, 2019; J. J. Kehaulani Kauanui, *Hawaiian Blood: Colonialism and the Politics of Sovereignty and Indigeneity* (Durham, NC: Duke University Press, 2008), 165–166.

38 *Honolulu Star-Bulletin*, June 14, 1940; October 7, 1940; *Honolulu Advertiser*, June 14, 1940.

39 *Honolulu Advertiser*, March 22, 1922; April 10, 1922; May 19, 1924; November 9, 1932; Chock Lin, "Another Akana Comes into Prominence in Territory," *Honolulu Star-Bulletin*, February 21, 1929; *Honolulu Star-Bulletin*, September 1, 1930; May 23, 1931; September 17, 1932; September 22, 1932; December 22, 1932.

40 *Honolulu Star-Bulletin*, May 13, 1918; December 13, 1921; February 7, 1934; *Pacific Commercial Advertiser*, September 23, 1918; May 24, 1920; Rudolph J. Smythe, "All Chinese Grab League Championship by 4-1 Score," *Honolulu Advertiser*, September 19, 1921; *Nippu Jiii*, September 15, 1926.

41 *Nippu Jiii*, June 11, 1923; April 6, 1927; May 21, 1927; Wallace Hirai, "Moriyama Denies Sale of Franchise," *Nippu Jiii*, November 29, 1933; Andrew Mitsukado, "Moriyama Denies the Rising Suns Withdrew from Loop," *Honolulu Advertiser*, December 30, 1933; *Honolulu Advertiser*, April 16, 1938; April 30, 1938.

42 *Honolulu Star-Bulletin*, August 15, 1928; *Maui News*, December 6, 1922; August 18, 1928; October 26, 1928; August 26, 1929; July 14, 1930; George Sakamaki, "Where East Meets West," *Honolulu Star-Bulletin*, June 12, 1931; *Honolulu Star-Bulletin*,

November 11, 1932; *Nippu Jiji*, August 10, 1928; August 20, 1928; July 20, 1931; *Japanese American*, September 1, 1928; December 15, 1932.

43 *Honolulu Star-Bulletin*, October 13, 1925; *Nippu Jiji*, October 15, 1925; August 10, 1933. Honolulu City Directory, 1938–1939, Ancestry.com, accessed June 14, 2017; *Honolulu Advertiser*, June 13, 1938; October 3, 1938; *Nippu Jiji*, September16, 1938; *Jisugyo no Hawai*, September 27, 1940.

44 *Nippu Jiji*, April 11, 1927. *Honolulu Star-Bulletin*, April 12, 1927; Loui Leong Hop, "The Veteran Is Plenty Good," *Honolulu Star-Bulletin*, March 12, 1934; Franks, *Barnstorming*, 116–117.

Chapter 7 Buck Lai's Journeys, 1935–1937

1 Loui Leong Hop, "Slated to Get Here Jan. 24 on the Manalo," *Honolulu Star-Bulletin*, January 5, 1935.

2 *Nippu Jiji*, January 7, 1935; *Hawaii Hochi*, January 7, 1935; January 23, 1935.

3 *Honolulu Star-Bulletin*, January 11, 1935; January 25, 1935; March 3, 1935; *Brooklyn Daily Eagle*, February 17, 1935; *Honolulu Advertiser*, January 21, 1935; Ship's Manifest S.S. Manolo, Ancestry.com, accessed February 11, 2005.

4 *Nippu Jiji*, January 25, 1935; *Honolulu Advertiser*, January 26, 1935; January 27, 1935; *Honolulu Star-Bulletin*, January 30, 1935.

5 *Honolulu Star-Bulletin*, January 31, 1935; February 9, 1935; Buck Lai Tin, "Gleanings from an 'Old Timer's' Scrapbook' as Told to Loui Leong Hop," *Honolulu Star-Bulletin*, February 13, 1935; *Honolulu Star-Bulletin*, February 25, 1935.

6 Wallace Hirai, "Buck Lai Tin Is Champ of Locals," *Nippu Jiji*, February 5, 1935; *Nippu Jiji*, February 13, 1935; Brian Niiya, "Yasutaro Soga," http://encyclopedia.densho.org/Yasutaro%20Soga/, *Densho Encyclopedia*, accessed October 1, 2018.

7 *Honolulu Advertiser*, March 7, 1935.

8 *Honolulu Advertiser*, March 3, 1935; March 5, 1935; *Hawaii Hochi*, March 26, 1935.

9 Wallace Hirai, "Buck Lai Tin Requests Support," *Nippu Jiji*, March 23, 1935; *Nippu Jiji*, March 27, 1935.

10 *Hawaii Hochi*, March 5, 1935.

11 *Hawaii Hochi*, March 26, 1935; March 30, 1935; April 18, 1935.

12 *Honolulu Advertiser*, March 24, 1935; March 30, 1935; March 31, 1935.

13 *Honolulu Advertiser*, April 1, 1935; Loui Leong Hop, "Hawaii Team to Be Picked from Two Squads," *Honolulu Star-Bulletin*, April 1, 1935; HMK, "Old Timers as Spry as Ever," *Honolulu Star-Bulletin*, April 1, 1935.

14 *Hawaii Hochi*, April 3, 1935; *Honolulu Advertiser*, April 3, 1935; April 7, 1935; April 15, 1935; April 20, 1935; April 28, 1935; Loui Leong Hop, "Regards Team as Stronger Than the 1912 Aggregation," *Honolulu Star-Bulletin*, April 6, 1935; Hop, "Shinegawa and Moniz to Join Lai's Outfit," *Honolulu Star-Bulletin*, April 12, 1935; United States Census Bureau, Manuscript Census Schedules, City and County of Honolulu, 1910, 1940, Ancestry.com, accessed March 9, 2019; Honolulu, Hawaii Passenger Crew List, 1900–1959, Ancestry.com, September 6, 2019.

15 James Murphy, "Buck Lai Bringing All-Star Nine from Hawaii in Semi-pro War," *Brooklyn Daily Eagle*, February 14, 1935; Lanctot, *Negro League Baseball*, 30, 48.

16 *San Jose Mercury*, April 24, 1935; Cecilia M. Tsu, *Garden of the World: Asian Immigrants and the Making of Agriculture in California's Santa Clara Valley* (New York: Oxford University Press, 2013); Ralph M. Pearce, *From Asahi to Zebras: Japanese American Baseball in San Jose, California* (San Jose, CA: Japanese American Museum, 2005); Joel S. Franks, "Off the Bench: Asian Americans and

Sport in the Santa Clara Valley during the Mid-twentieth Century," in *San Francisco Bay Area Sports: Golden Gate Athletics, Recreation, and Community*, ed. Rita Liberti and Maureen M. Smith (Fayetteville: University of Arkansas Press, 2017), 113–129.

17 *San Jose Mercury*, April 27, 1935; *Honolulu Star-Bulletin*, April 26, 1935; May 7, 1935; *New World Daily News*, April 28, 1935.

18 *Honolulu Star-Bulletin*, May 7, 1935; Amy Essington, *The Integration of the Pacific Coast League: Race and Baseball on the West Coast* (Lincoln: University of Nebraska Press, 2018).

19 *Stockton Independent*, April 28, 1935; *Honolulu Star-Bulletin*, May 7, 1935; May 9, 1935.

20 *Honolulu Star-Bulletin*, May 14, 1935; May 10, 1935; June 7, 1935.

21 *Honolulu Advertiser*, May 20, 1935; *Emporia Gazette*, May 20, 1935; Johnny Kerr, "All Hawaiis Find Kansas City Monarchs as Strong as Any Major Loop Club," *Honolulu Star-Bulletin*, June 5, 1935; *Hawaii Hochi*, May 30, 1935.

22 *Chicago Tribune*, June 1, 1935.

23 *New York Evening Post*, June 8, 1935; *Brooklyn Daily Eagle*, June 10, 1935; June 17, 1935; *Brooklyn Times Union*, June 17, 1935; *Chicago Defender*, June 22, 1935; *Honolulu Star-Bulletin*, June 14, 1935; Johnny Kerr, "Johnny Kerr Marvels at Buck Lai's Cup Collection," *Honolulu Star-Bulletin*, July 4, 1935.

24 Kerr, "Johnny Kerr Marvels"; *Chester Times*, June 19, 1935; June 21, 1935; June 22, 1935.

25 *Honolulu Advertiser*, June 14, 1935; *Honolulu Star-Bulletin*, June 20, 1935; *Hawaii Hochi*, June 22, 1935.

26 *Patterson News*, July 5, 1935; *Pottstown Mercury*, July 6, 1935; *Brooklyn Times Union*, July 8, 1935; *Schenectady Gazette*, July 22, 1935; *Syracuse Herald*, August 7, 1935; August 10, 1935; Johnny Kerr, "Close Games Are Lost by Hawaii All-Star Outfit," *Honolulu Star-Bulletin*, September 2, 1935.

27 Audubon High School Yearbook, 1935, Ancestry.com, accessed November 14, 2015; *Pacific Commercial Advertiser*, May 27, 1920; *Honolulu Advertiser*, April 26, 1926; *Camden Courier-Post*, November 14, 1934; Johnny Kerr, "Team Shakes the Hoodoo: Making a Hit," *Honolulu Star-Bulletin*, July 13, 1935.

28 *Chester Times*, August 26, 1935; August 27, 1935; *Honolulu Star-Bulletin*, September 3, 1935.

29 Honolulu, Hawaii Passenger Crew List, 1900–1959, Ancestry.com, accessed February 19, 2011; *Honolulu Advertiser*, July 3, 1935; *Honolulu Star-Bulletin*, September 9, 1935; *Sporting News*, November 28, 1935; *Chicago Tribune*, November 19, 1935.

30 *Honolulu Star-Bulletin*, October 3, 1935; *Hawaii Hochi*, October 3, 1935; *Honolulu Advertiser*, October 9, 1935; October 10, 1935.

31 *Honolulu Star-Bulletin*, January 31, 1936.

32 Honolulu, Hawaii Passenger Crew List, 1900–1959, Ancestry.com, accessed February 19, 2011; Loui Leong Hop, "Now on Way to Islands," *Honolulu Star-Bulletin*, February 22, 1936; *Honolulu Star-Bulletin*, March 3, 1936.

33 *Honolulu Star-Bulletin*, February 14, 1936; Loui Leong Hop, "Boys Trying Out with S.F.," *Honolulu Star-Bulletin*, February 15, 1936.

34 *Honolulu Star-Bulletin*, April 3, 1936; April 17, 1936; May 4, 1936; May 6, 1936.

35 *Honolulu Star-Bulletin*, March 13, 1936; *Hawaii Hochi*, March 10, 1936.

36 *Honolulu Star-Bulletin*, May 11, 1936; May 12, 1936; *Hawaii Hochi*, May 11, 1936; Honolulu, Hawaii Passenger Crew List, 1900–1959, Ancestry.com, accessed September 6, 2019.

37 *Fresno Bee*, May 14, 1936; May 16, 1936.

38 *Honolulu Advertiser*, January 11, 1936; James "Hank" Graham, "Graham Writes about Team's Trip to Olympia," *Honolulu Star-Bulletin*, May 30, 1936.
39 Graham, "Graham Writes."
40 *Helena Independent*, May 24, 1936.
41 *Helena Independent*, May 27, 1936; *Missoula Missoulian*, May 26, 1936.
42 *Chicago Tribune*, May 30, 1936; *Elyria Chronicle Telegram*, June 2, 1936; June 4, 1936; June 5, 1936.
43 *Brooklyn Daily Eagle*, June 22, 1936; June 24, 1936; June 29, 1936; *Brooklyn Citizen*, June 22, 1936; *Brooklyn Times-Union*, June 29, 1936; "Semi-Pro Teams of Brooklyn," http://www.covehurst.net/ddyte/brooklyn/bushwicks.html, accessed June 22, 2015.
44 *Chicago Tribune*, August 31, 1936; September 5, 1936; *Pampa Daily News*, September 21, 1936.
45 *Honolulu Star-Bulletin*, October 5, 1936; October 24, 1936; November 22, 1936.
46 *Big Spring Daily Herald*, April 5, 1937; Josh Davlin and Hank Utley, "Alabama Pitts," Society for American Baseball Research, https://sabr.org/bioproj/person/alabama-pitts/, accessed June 24, 2015; Alpert, *Out of Left Field*, 42–43.
47 *Lubbock Morning Star*, May 14, 1937; *Ada Evening News*, May 16, 1937; May 20, 1937.
48 *Lubbock Avalanche-Journal*, May 16, 1937; *Pampa Daily News*, May 18, 1937.
49 Adam Doster, "The Myth of Jackie Mitchell, The Girl Who Struck Out Ruth and Gehrig," http://www.thedailybeast.com/articles/2013/05/18/the-myth-of-jackie-mitchell-the-girl-who-struck-out-ruth-and-gehrig.html, *Daily Beast*, May 18, 2013, accessed February 25, 2015; *Greenville Record-Argus*, June 11, 1937; *Franklin News-Herald*, June 21, 1937; *Warren Times Mirror*, June 22, 1937; *Mansfield News-Journal*, September 1, 1937.
50 *Springfield Republican*, July 13, 1937; July 20, 1937.
51 *Sayre Evening Times*, August 4, 1937; *Warren Times Mirror*, August 6, 1937.
52 *Chicago Tribune*, August 25, 1937; *Hammond Times*, August 21, 1937; August 23, 1937; *Rochester Democrat and Chronicle*, August 27, 1937; August 31, 1937; *Akron Beacon Journal*, September 1, 1937.
53 *Honolulu Star-Bulletin*, December 11, 1937.
54 Franks, *Asian Pacific Americans*, 93–95.
55 Joel S. Franks, *Hawaiian Sports in the Twentieth Century* (Lewiston, ME: Edwin Mellen Press, 2002).

Chapter 8 Playing in the Twilight

1 Ellen Tamura, *Americanization, Acculturation, and Ethnic Identity: The Nisei Generation in Hawaii* (Urbana: University of Illinois Press, 1994); Takaki, *Strangers*, 132–176; Okihiro, *Cane Fires*; Okihiro, *Unbound*; Fuchs, *Hawaii Pono*; Joel S. Franks, *Asians and Pacific Islanders in American Football: Historical and Contemporary Experiences* (Lanham, MD: Lexington Books, 2018), 57–58.
2 Franks, *Asian Pacific Americans*, 35–56.
3 Takaki, *Strangers*, 406–411; Jung, *Reworking Race*, 106–160; Okihiro, *Unbound*, 406–407; Fuchs, *Hawaii Pono*; Tom Coffman, *The Island Edge: A Political History of Hawai'i* (Honolulu: University of Hawai'i Press, 2003); Gerald Horne, *Fighting for Paradise: Labor Unions, Racism, and Communists in the Making of Modern Hawaii* (Honolulu: University of Hawai'i Press, 2011).
4 Coffman, *Island Edge*; Takaki, *Strangers*, 401–403.
5 Coffman, *Island Edge*; Okihiro, *Unbound*, 406–415.

6 Okihiro, *Unbound*, 406–408; Miller-Davenport, *Gateway State*, 19–49.

7 Okihiro, *Unbound*, 406–408; Miller-Davenport, *Gateway State*, 19–49; Coffman, *Island Edge*; John Whitehead, *Completing the Union: Alaska, Hawai'i, and the Battle for Statehood* (Albuquerque: University of New Mexico Press, 2004); Dean Itsuji Saranillio, *Unsustainable Empire: Alternative Histories of Hawai'i Statehood* (Durham, NC: Duke University Press, 2018).

8 Okihiro, *Unbound*, 406–415; Haunani Kay-Trask, *From a Native Daughter: Colonialism and Sovereignty in Hawai'i* (Honolulu: Latitude 20 Books, 1999); Saranillio, *Unsustainable Empire*; Judy Rohrer, *Staking Claim: Settler Colonialism and Racialization in Hawai'i* (Tucson: University of Arizona Press, 2016); *Beyond Ethnicity: New Politics of Race in Hawai'i*, ed. Camilla Fojas, Rudy P. Guevarra Jr., and Nitasha Tamar Sharma (Honolulu: University of Hawai'i Press, 2018).

9 Franks, *Asian Pacific Americans*, 35–56.

10 Franks, *Asian Pacific Americans*, 35–56; Cindy I-Feng Cheng, *Citizens of Asian America: Democracy and Race during the Cold War* (New York: New York University Press, 2013); Ellen Wu, *Color of Success: Asia Americans and the Origins of the Model Minority* (Princeton, NJ: Princeton University Press, 2013).

11 *Honolulu Star-Bulletin*, July 1, 1948; December 4, 1948; Franks, *Hawaiian Sports*, 128–129.

12 Franks, *Asian Pacific Americans*, 35–55.

13 *Honolulu Advertiser*, March 27, 1942; July 29, 1942; *Hawaii Hochi*, August 1, 1942.

14 *Honolulu Advertiser*, June 7, 1942; December 28, 1950; *Honolulu Star-Bulletin*, January 15, 1949; November 4, 1949; *Honolulu Record*, March 16, 1950; Saranillio, *Unsustainable Empire*; Miller-Davenport, *Gateway State*, 31–32.

15 *Honolulu Star-Bulletin*, July 22, 1942; March 31, 1950; *Honolulu Record*, March 16, 1950; March 6, 1958; July 3, 1958; Davis, *Waterman*, 189; Outrigger Canoe Club, "Forecast," http://www.outriggercanoeclubsports.com/wp-content/uploads/2016/05/August-1948.pdf, August, 1948, accessed May 16, 2019.

16 Mamalahoa, "Royal Order of Kamehameha I," https://www.mamalahoa.org/kamehameha/ruling-chiefs-of-the-order/, accessed May 16, 2019; *Honolulu Star-Bulletin*, June 1, 1951; *Honolulu Advertiser*, September 12, 1954; April 19, 1961.

17 *Hawaii Herald*, June 4, 1945; *Honolulu Advertiser*, March 31, 1946; August 30, 1950; Charles E. Hogue, "Jimmy Moriyama, American," *Honolulu Advertiser*, August 31, 1950; *Honolulu Star-Bulletin*, December 23, 1970.

18 *Honolulu Advertiser*, May 29, 1944; April 10, 1948; *Hawaii Herald*, May 29, 1944; *Honolulu Star-Bulletin*, April 28, 1948; November 3, 1944; November 26, 1947; April 15, 1948; Horne, *Fighting*; Center for Labor Education & Research, University of Hawai'i-West O'ahu, "CLEAR Biographies of Labor History Figures," http://www.hawaii.edu/uhwo/clear/home/LaborBios.html, accessed May 14, 2019.

19 Fuchs, *Hawaii Pono*, 412–413; Horne, *Fighting*, 158–159, 271.

20 Horne, *Fighting*, 272.

21 *Honolulu Star-Bulletin*, April 15, 1950; July 14, 1950; November 5, 1962; Justin F. Paul, "The Power of Seniority: Senator Hugh Butler and Statehood for Hawaii," accessed April 30, 2019, http://evols.library.manoa.hawaii.edu/bitstream/10524/361/JL09156.pdf; Yap quoted in Horne, *Fighting*. 286.

22 *Honolulu Star-Bulletin*, August 12, 1950; January 23, 1951; July 8, 1952; September 18, 1971; *Honolulu Advertiser*, December 3, 1951; January 8, 1953; September 16, 1954; March 1, 1959; March 25, 1964.

23 Ronald Takaki, *A Double Victory: A Multicultural History of America in World War II* (Boston: Little Brown, 2000).

24 Takaki, *A Double Victory*.
25 Takaki, *A Double Victory*; *San Francisco Chronicle*, February 15, 1946.
26 Mary L. Dudziak, *Cold War Civil Rights: Race and the Image of American Democracy* (Princeton, NJ: Princeton University Press, 2001); Cheng, *Citizens*; Wu, *Color*.
27 Jules Tygiel, *The Great Experiment: Jackie Robinson and His Legacy* (New York: Oxford University Press, 1983); Charles K. Ross, *Outside the Lines: African Americans and the Integration of the National Football League* (New York: New York University Press, 1999); Franks, *Asian and Pacific Islanders in American Football*, 201–207; Franks, *Crossing*, 139–165; Chad Carlson, "Basketball's Forgotten Experiment: Don Barksdale and the Legacy of the United States Olympic Basketball Team," *International Journal of the History of Sport* 27 (2010), 1330–1359; José M. Alamillo, "Richard 'Pancho' González and the Print Media in Postwar Tennis America," *International Journal of the History of Sport* 26 (2009), 947–965.
28 Peggy Pascoe, *What Comes Naturally: Miscegenation Law and the Making of Race in America* (New York: Oxford University Press, 2010); Cashin, *Loving*; Mark Brilliant, *The Color of America Has Changed: How Racial Diversity Shaped Civil Rights Reform in California, 1941–1978* (New York: Oxford University Press, 2012); Ronald Takaki, *A Different Mirror: A History of Multicultural America* (Boston: Back Bay Books, 2008).
29 Dudziak, *Cold War*; Cheng, *Citizens*; Wu, *Color*.
30 Cheng, *Citizens*; Wu, *Color*; Madeline Hsu, *The Good Immigrants: How the Yellow Peril Became the Model Minority* (Princeton, NJ: Princeton University Press, 2015).
31 Wu, *Color*, 111–145; Cheng, *Citizens*, 93–94.
32 Wu, *Color*; Franks, *Crossing*, 144–145; Michael Omi and Howard Winant, *Racial Formation in the United States* (New York: Routledge, 2014).
33 Randy Roberts and James Olsen, *Winning Is the Only Thing: Sports in American since 1945* (Baltimore: Johns Hopkins University Press, 1989); Kathryn Jay, *More Than Just a Game: Sports in American Life since 1945* (New York: Columbia University Press, 2004); *New York Times*, March 7, 1939; March 4, 1941; December 11, 1956; *Brooklyn Daily Eagle*, April 2, 1939; June 3, 1941; June 10, 1941.
34 *Camden Morning Post*, May 1, 1937; September 2, 1938; July 15, 1941; July 22, 1941; *Chester Times*, August 5, 1939; *Pottsville Republican*, July 1, 1940; *Delaware County Herald Times*, October 28, 1969.
35 *Pensacola News Journal*, March 31, 1942; *Brooklyn Daily Eagle*, October 15, 1947.
36 *Brooklyn Daily Eagle*, December 14, 1949; August 23, 1950; *New York Times*, January 16, 1951; Roberts and Olson, *Winning*, 73–76; Milton Gross, "Basketball's Busiest Bee," *Sport*, March 1952, 40; Dennis Gildea, *Hoop Crazy: The Lives of Clair Bee and Chip Hilton* (Little Rock: University of Arkansas Press, 2013).
37 Abe Chanin, "LIU Expected to Withdraw Cancellation of University of Arizona Game," *Arizona Daily Star*, January 19, 1951; *Arizona Daily Star*, February 16, 1956; *Brooklyn Daily Eagle*, January 21, 1951; *New York Daily News*, January 30, 1951.
38 Roberts and Olsen, *Winning*, 74–75; *Washington Post*, February 9, 1952.
39 *Brooklyn Daily Eagle*, January 7, 1955; *Traverse City Record Eagle*, December 6, 1955; Howard Tuckner, "Lai Wants No Neon Lights in L.I.U. Basketball," *New York Times*, December 11, 1956; *Springfield Union*, February 19, 1961; *Bridgeport Post*, December 12, 1959.
40 *New York Times*, March 7, 1961; June 2, 1963; *Troy Times Record*, November 24, 1964.
41 *Brooklyn Daily Eagle*, March 29, 1949; Long Island University Yearbook, 1952, Ancestry.com, accessed October 19, 2018; *New York Daily News*, June 9, 1950; May 23, 1954; *Boston Daily*, May 12, 1958; *New York Times*, June 3, 1958; August 3, 1960.

42 *Long Island Star and Journal*, March 25, 1955; March 24, 1964.
43 *Minneapolis Star-Tribune*, April 26, 1968; *Bridgeport Telegram*, April 27, 1968; *Honolulu Star-Bulletin*, July 18, 1969; *Greenville Record-Argus*, June 14, 1973; *Philadelphia Inquirer*, October 17, 1973; *Trenton Evening Times*, November 6, 1973; *Lumberton Robesian*, November 7, 1976; *New York Daily News*, December 16, 1983.
44 *Brooklyn Daily Eagle*, June 19, 1950; January 7, 1955.
45 *Berkshire Evening Telegram*, August 2, 1952; *Sporting News*, November 11, 1953; *New York Times*, February 21, 1956; August 3, 1960; *Official Baseball Guide, 1956* (St. Louis, MO: Sporting News, 1956), 56; Jerald Podair, *City of Dreams: Dodger Stadium and the Birth of Modern Los Angeles* (Princeton, NJ: Princeton University Press, 2017); Mary Lai, telephone conversation with the author, San José, California, June 22, 2009.
46 Fresco Thompson, foreword to *Championship Baseball from Little League to Big League*, by William T. "Buck" Lai (New York: Prentice Hall, 1954); *Brooklyn Daily Eagle*, January 19, 1954; *New York Daily News*, February 11, 1954; *Wilmington News Journal*, March 5, 1954; *Cleveland Plain Dealer*, April 25, 1954; William T. Lai, *Winning Basketball: Individual Play and Team Strategy* (New York: Prentice Hall, 1955), 6, 210, 211.
47 *Louisville Courier-Journal*, May 30, 1959; *Binghamton Press and Sun Bulletin*, June 5, 1959.
48 *Brooklyn Daily Eagle*, May 19, 1950.
49 LIU Brooklyn Blackbirds, "Buck Lai—Hall of Fame—LIU Brooklyn," https://brooklyn.liuathletics.com/hof.aspx?hof=67&path=&kiosk=, accessed January 19, 2022; *New York Times*, October 9, 2003.
50 *Honolulu Star-Bulletin*, April 4, 1938; United States Census Bureau, Manuscript Census Schedules, Town of Audubon, County of Camden, 1940, Ancestry.com, accessed October 31, 2011; World War II Registration Cards, Ancestry.com, accessed September 5, 2008; *Uniontown Evening Standard*, February 21, 1942.
51 *Brooklyn Times Union*, April 3, 1938; *Brooklyn Daily Eagle*, May 14, 1938; Tom Ryan, "27 Years on Diamond Is Buck Lai's Record," *Camden Courier-Post*, May 27, 1938; *Camden Courier-Post*, July 27, 1938; August 16, 1938; August 18, 1938; September 2, 1938; *Lancaster News Era*, December 29, 1938; *Chester Times*, July 1, 1939; *Vineland Daily Journal*, February 14, 1939.
52 *Camden Courier-Post*, February 21, 1939; April 11, 1939; October 5, 1939.
53 *Camden Courier-Post*, August 17, 1940; June 10, 1941; September 26, 1941; *Brooklyn Daily Eagle*, July 24, 1941; August 7, 1941; August 8, 1941; *Delaware County Times*, September 25, 1941; *Bristol Daily Courier*, January 6, 1940.
54 *Sporting News*, January 18, 1945; *Brooklyn Daily Eagle*, January 21, 1945.
55 *Trenton Evening Times*, August 12, 1951; *Camden Courier-Post*, May 8, 1950; March 2, 1952; May 17, 1952; April 10, 1967; *Flatbush Times*, November 6, 1953; *Philadelphia Inquirer*, May 9, 1954; *Delaware County Daily Times*, March 8, 1961.
56 *Hartford Courant*, September 3, 1964; *Camden Courier-Post*, September 9, 1964.
57 *Honolulu Advertiser*, November 9, 1977; *New York Daily News*, November 6, 1977; *Honolulu Star-Bulletin*, March 22, 1978; Social Security Death Index, 1935–2014, Ancestry.com, accessed May 17, 2019; Mary Lai, telephone conversation with the author, March 7, 2008.
58 *Wilmington Journal-Evening*, February 26, 1940; *Camden Post-Courier*, April 12, 1940; Elm McCormick, "Salem Co. Towns Join in Hailing of Armistice Signed Twenty-Four Years Ago," *Camden Morning Post*, November 12, 1942; *Camden Morning Post*, May 19, 1943; *Millville Daily*, August 2, 1946; June 4, 1959;

Wilmington News-Journal, February 12, 1991; New Jersey State Census, 1915, Ancestry.com, accessed January 16, 2020; Pennsylvania Marriages, 1852–1968, Ancestry.com, accessed March 4, 2020.

Conclusion

1 Moon-Kie Jung, *Beneath the Surface of White Supremacy: Denaturalizing U.S. Racisms Past and Present* (Stanford, CA: Stanford University Press), 55–83.
2 Omi and Winant, *Racial Formation*; Rogers M. Smith, *Political Peoplehood: The Roles of Values, Interests, and Identities* (Chicago: University of Chicago Press, 2015).
3 Albert G. Spalding, *America's National Game* (Lincoln: University of Nebraska Press, 1992), 395; Peter Levine, *Ellis Island to Ebbets Field: Sport and the American Jewish Experience* (New York: Oxford University Press, 1992), 144; Josephine Lee, *Performing Asian America: Race and Ethnicity on the Contemporary Stage* (Philadelphia: Temple University Press, 1997).
4 Hsu, *Good Immigrants*.
5 Imada, *Aloha America*; Okihiro, *Island World*.
6 Cashin, *Loving*; Pascoe, *What Comes Naturally*; Gina Marchetti, *Romance and the Yellow Peril: Race, Sex, and Discursive Strategies in Hollywood Fiction* (Berkeley: University of California Press, 1993), 20–33; *Honolulu Advertiser*, April 18, 1951; October 21, 1955.
7 Anderson, *Cosmopolitan Canopy*.
8 Clair Jean Kim, "The Political Triangulation of Asian Americans," *Politics and Society* 27, no. 1 (1999): 105–138.
9 Bill Staples, Jr. *Kenichi Zenimura: Japanese American Baseball Pioneer* (Jefferson, NC: McFarland & Company, Inc., Publishers, 2011).
10 Robert E. Park, *Race and Culture* (New York: Glencoe Free Press, 1950).
11 Raymond Williams, *Resources of Hope: Culture, Democracy, and Socialism* (London: Verso, 1989), 3–14.

Index

About the Author

JOEL S. FRANKS taught Asian American and American studies at San José State University for over thirty years. He has written several books related to Asian American and Pacific Islander sports history. Among these are *Asian Pacific Americans and Baseball: A History*; *Crossing Sidelines, Crossing Cultures: Sport and Asian Pacific American Cultural Citizenship*; *The Barnstorming Hawaiian Travelers: A Multiethnic Baseball Team Tours the Mainland, 1912–1916*; *Asian American Basketball: A Century of Sport, Community, and Culture*; and *Asians and Pacific Islanders and American Football.*